BMA

Ceri's involvement with the All Blacks has allowed the team to grow greater understanding of how we can perform far better under pressure. This has let the team use their abilities to far greater effect and in doing so enhance the All Black legacy.
– **Steve Hansen, All Blacks Coach**

Human performance in Formula One is about more than two drivers – it's a team of up to 1000 people, all of them elite performers in their own areas. Working with Ceri has helped us shape our ethos, strengthen the resilience of our internal culture and unlock greater performance from the team. Our people are our sustainable source of competitive advantage; Ceri's straightforward, practical and humble approach has been an important building block for the success of our team.
– **Toto Wolff, Team Principal and CEO, Mercedes–AMG Petronas Motorsport**

Performing under pressure is the platform for a successful career. Ceri helped me clear my mind, focus on decisive matters and strengthen my vision for the team. His contributions to the team helped them analyse what we faced and target individual and collective performance. Thank you Ceri for your great contribution.
– **Arsène Wenger, Manager, Arsenal FC 1996–2018**

Ceri's approach is a unique blend of pr
cutting edge of the pressure continuu
intuitive – it is scientific, practical and res
me with a more disciplined, clinical ar
understanding and dealing with pressu
encountered; and enabled our leadership team to embrace pressure and operate in an increasingly complex political environment.
– **Brendan Boyle, Chief Executive, Ministry of Social Development 2011–2018**

Ceri changes lives! Ceri's unique ability to take a complex, highly personal and often challenging subject and make it alluring, memorable and actionable is a true gift. The leaders on our programmes have embraced the RED–BLUE 'secret' for thriving under pressure and are building more effective organisations, communities and home lives as a result.

– Roz McCay, Co-Founder Hiakai CEO programme, Facilitator, NZ Global Women Break Through Leaders programme

Everyone in business wants to be world-leading, but very few are. Ceri's *Perform Under Pressure* programme provides leaders with the framework and tools to shift an organisation's performance towards its vision of excellence. Ceri has helped me focus on making decisions that drive positive movement towards this.

– Bill Moran, Chair of Sport New Zealand and High Performance Sport NZ

Ceri provided us with the common language and a united approach needed to thrive in investment attraction, a very competitive, pressure-filled environment. He shifted the conversation of high performance behaviour from a sensitive topic to an energising and fun experience.

– Dylan Lawrence, General Manager – Investment, NZ Trade & Enterprise

I harassed Ceri for a few months until he gave in to working with me as an entrepreneur, and I'm glad he did because he changed my life. Ceri brought my attention to unconscious habits that were slowing me down and causing me to fold under pressure. Now I'm more aware of my emotional state, make clearer decisions, and my business is performing better too.

– Sam Ovens, Entrepreneur

Ceri took an impossibly complex change environment and broke it down to a simple, clear and easy-to-use framework, delivering thinking beyond what we have seen before. He has held me to account and is relentless in his quest for improvement of both himself and our business.

– Garry Lund, General Manager, People and Culture, Gough Group

Ceri treated our coaches and 60 amateur teenage rowers vying for national titles with the respect of international athletes. He showed us that pressure is relative and universal, and taught us fun ways to deal with it. Ceri's sense of humour and language ensured that his message was relatable – his RED/BLUE analogy is still embedded in our squad culture three years on!

– Mark Cotham, Director of Rowing, Rangi Ruru Girls' School, Christchurch

Ceri's clear approach provides tools which can be used by anybody who wants to perform to their very best under pressure. His framework was enlightening and resonated with surgeons, who also face pressure and expectations of high performance.

– Andrew Vincent, Orthopaedic Surgeon

Perform Under Pressure was the most impactful – and challenging – leadership programme we have participated in as an executive team. Ceri armed us with knowledge and tools that have been invaluable in understanding how we each deal with pressure and drive improved performance. The real 'aha!' moment came when we discovered that our performance gap was in how we were working together, allowing us to commit to closing the gap together.

– Neal Barclay, CEO, Meridian

A wise adviser, perceptive facilitator and enlightened educator. He has helped me and the teams I work with immensely.
– Gilbert Enoka, All Blacks Manager – Leadership

We were a young, ambitious and highly successful team already leading our industry, but Ceri's approach completely changed our own perception of 'what good looked like'. It was a revelation – we found it refreshing, enjoyable and were excited to take it further, compressing months of work into a matter of weeks to regularly achieve timelines that even our own team would call absurd and ridiculous. It stuck – ruthless speed became our new 'normal' and the business results (and awards) flowed.
– Mark Soper, General Manager, Powershop 2016–2019

Excellence in any field requires our psychology and physiology to be in harmony. Forensic psychiatrist Dr. Ceri Evans' RED–BLUE model provides a unique and accessible framework that supports clear thinking and adaptive behaviour under pressure. He builds on contemporary thinking in physiology to explain the neurobiological basis for a counterintuitive mental strategy: challenging ourselves to face the threat and find a solution.
– David Paterson, Professor of Physiology, Head of Department, University of Oxford

PERFORM UNDER PRESSURE

DR CERI EVANS
Change the way you feel, think and act under pressure

Thorsons

IMPORTANT INFORMATION

While this book is intended as a general information resource and all care has been taken in compiling the contents, it does not take account of individual circumstances and is not in any way a substitute for medical advice or treatment. It is essential that you always seek qualified medical advice if you suspect you have a health problem. The author and publisher cannot be held responsible for any claim or action that may arise from reliance on the information contained in this book.

Thorsons
An imprint of HarperCollins*Publishers*
1 London Bridge Street
London SE1 9GF

www.harpercollins.co.uk

First published in 2019 by HarperCollins*Publishers* (New Zealand) Ltd
This edition published in 2019 by Thorsons

1 3 5 7 9 10 8 6 4 2

Cover design by Darren Holt, HarperCollins Design Studio
Illustrations by Renzie Hanham
Typeset in Sabon LT Std by Kirby Jones
Author photo by Diederik van Heyningen, Lightworkx Photography

A catalogue record of this book is
available from the British Library

ISBN 978-0-00-831316-6

Printed and bound in Great Britain by
CPI Group (UK) Ltd, Croydon, CR0 4YY

MIX
Paper from
responsible sources
FSC
www.fsc.org
FSC™ C007454

This book is produced from independently certified FSC™ paper
to ensure responsible forest management.

For more information visit: www.harpercollins.co.uk/green

In memory of my father, Gwyn, and mother, Joy,
both pioneers in their own way.

Te waka taiuhu, monā I whakatau akē, ngā ngaru āwhā.
The prow of the waka will cut a decisive pathway
through the stormiest of ocean waves.

Contents

List of illustrations by Renzie Hanham

PERFORM UNDER PRESSURE

PERFORM
UNDER
PRESSURE

FOREWORD

Richie McCaw

In 2015 I played my final game of rugby with the All Blacks. It was our second consecutive Rugby World Cup final victory. No other team had achieved that. We felt a huge expectation but were able to deliver. As captain, I couldn't have wished for a better way to retire.

Roll back the clock to when I was captain in 2007 and it was a very different story. Despite being favourites we had, yet again, failed to win on rugby's biggest stage. We'd even left the tournament earlier than any previous All Blacks team. We hadn't dealt with the pressure and knew that something needed to change.

We looked around for answers and it became evident that Ceri was an obvious choice.

You've only got to speak to Ceri for a few minutes: he doesn't just tell you how it is, he takes you with him. The things he said and the way he said them struck a chord with me straight away. As well as being a doctor working in forensic psychiatry, he'd been a pro-footballer. He made things real.

Ceri explained what happens to the brain under pressure. He showed us examples of how people react differently under pressure and how they go 'into the RED'. It all made sense. He helped us understand that it's OK to feel pressure and showed us ways to manage ourselves differently. I learned it wasn't about pretending it doesn't happen, it was about how you deal with it. We started to use the RED–BLUE model and straight away I began to see it work.

Over time, we completely changed the way we dealt with pressure.

In the last 20 minutes of the 2011 final, when we really got tested, I realised how important that was. The match was touch and go and I felt myself going into the RED. It could have unfolded like in 2007, but I got back into the BLUE and thought, 'This is the moment I have pictured and prepared for.'

Not everything was perfect towards the end, but I felt calm. I could see what I needed to do, and I felt myself getting stronger. I wanted to be there.

The tools Ceri gave me had worked but after the weight of expectation in the four years leading up to the 2011 World Cup and the energy it took, the thought of repeating it all again felt too much.

Ceri helped change my perspective. He said, 'If you try to do it the same way again, you set yourself up to fail.' From that I knew I needed to look at things differently. He talked about being pioneers, becoming the first team to win back-to-back world cups. I got excited again. He helped change the mindset from 'What happens if we lose?' to 'What happens if we win?' Simple but powerful.

The things that are really worth chasing involve pressure and that's what makes them rewarding. I knew we needed to be tested under pressure to be taken to our limits. I began to crave those moments.

No matter what the challenge was, Ceri always had an idea or angle to help me anticipate, deal with it or improve. I was always intrigued to see what he had next. RED–BLUE was just the start.

Now I'm retired from rugby, the things I learned with Ceri are still relevant. I'm a husband, a father, a pilot and although these might not look the same as playing rugby, the lessons in this book relate to anything you do.

When the pressure is on, we all know it affects the way we behave. Anyone can feel under pressure from many different factors: dealing with stress, conflict at work, managing relationships. If you're curious about how to learn and do those things better, the tools in this book will help you develop the ability to step back, clear your head and deal with it all much more effectively.

From my time in rugby I remain most proud of how we went from a team that struggled to deal with pressure in the big moments to, by the end of my time playing, leading the way. The expectation became that, when it was tight at the end of a match, the All Blacks would get there. Whatever was thrown at us we had learned to find a way. Ceri was a huge part in that turnaround, helping shift our mindsets and raise our thresholds to deal with pressure.

Whatever it is you want to improve in your own life, this book will help you do it. I can't recommend it highly enough.

RM, 2019

INTRODUCTION

When I hear the phrase 'high performance', the word 'PRESSURE' automatically comes to mind. I don't think you can have one without the other.

But for many of us, 'high performance' feels out of reach – just getting through the day feels like a struggle. That's why I prefer to think in terms of **performance under pressure**.

I'm talking about *all* fields of performance here. Whether your arena is the stage, the classroom or the shop floor, or whether you're trying to lead an executive team, an operating theatre or your family, if you face a mental barrier that has, to this point, limited you from reaching your goals, this book is for you.

Whatever your performances look like, the aim of this book is to change the way you feel, think and act in high-pressure situations. But my bigger goal is to show you how you can reach your full potential through powerful responses to powerful moments. I want to help you go from ordinary to extraordinary.

The key lies in those moments of truth when we either shy away from a challenge or rise to the occasion. Because these moments carry more significance, they carry more pressure.

Most of us try to minimise the number of these moments in our lives, because they make us feel uncomfortable, and we're afraid we might fail. But some individuals, teams or organisations relish these moments and seek them out deliberately.

If you want to get better at what you do, pressure is unavoidable – but does it stop you in your tracks, or open a window into a new world of opportunity?

In this book you'll learn about the **RED–BLUE mind model**, which helps explain why pressure has such an impact on all of us. The **RED–BLUE tool** and related techniques for performance under pressure will provide you with practical help to think and feel clearly – and perform better – when you need it the most.

Why I Developed the RED–BLUE Mind Model

In my teenage years I was either kicking a ball or reading a book – usually about how our bodies and minds worked. The crossover between the sporting and mental worlds fascinated me. Everyone in sport seemed to know that the mind was critical to performing well – but no one really seemed to be able to explain in a practical way what was going on inside someone's head that caused them to perform poorly or well. In those days, the attitude towards psychology in sport was sceptical and often cynical. In team environments, 'seeing the shrink' was taken as a sign of mental weakness. Later, my work as a forensic psychiatrist in hospitals, prisons and the courts gave me new perspectives. Understanding the mind was one thing, but understanding how it worked at its limits, under stress, was what captivated me the most.

One relationship stands out as the turning point. I met Renzie Hanham – co-developer of the RED–BLUE mind model, and illustrator of this book – and things began to fall into place. Renzie is a highly accomplished martial arts instructor and gifted graphic artist. His perceptive insights, and ability to translate those insights into graphic format, showed me the way forward.

I remember the day when I asked him to produce a diagram that would map out the pathways to both effective *and* ineffective performance. I had an 'aha!' moment, and realised that the diagram should be colour-coded. The first RED–BLUE mind model was born.

The learning curve was steep: some of our early efforts were too complex and confusing, and others were too obvious and simplistic. (I figured it was about right when the criticism was evenly balanced between the two!)

But despite the false starts and cringe moments, two things rapidly became clear. First, people *got* the RED–BLUE mind model – quickly – and second, it really seemed to *help* them.

The implications of the model soon spread beyond the sports world. Countless individuals, teams and organisations were involved in 'stress-testing' the model not just on the pitch, but also in the classroom, on the stage, in the workplace, and in many other environments. Their insights have been invaluable. Every tool in this book has been used many times by many people who are serious about what they do and how they do it.

When people tell me they've used the model – with their children, with their partner, or for themselves – and seen a real shift in their performance, it feels hugely satisfying.

The RED–BLUE mind model draws on several different schools of thought, but in the end it has one intention: to help you gain emotional self-control to enable you to think clearly and act effectively when you need it most – when you're performing under pressure.

The RED–BLUE mind model has taken me down an immensely rewarding path. It's the central piece of a jigsaw in which many things I'm passionate about come together.

Here are **10 reasons** why I strongly believe in the RED–BLUE mind model:

1. **It works.** It wouldn't exist if people didn't feel it had significantly helped them. (Nor would this book!)

2. **I use it myself (*all* the time).** My best and worst moments – as a parent, footballer, clinical director or speaker – all relate back to my use (or *non*-use) of the model in my own life.

3. **It's for all of us.** I have seen the best in the world get mentally better – and worse – in different moments. I have also seen those in the mid-range, and those with everything against them, get mentally better – and worse – in different moments. Everyone is on the same RED–BLUE page.

4. **It's practical.** I've met experts who know more about the theory behind the brain than I ever will, but just like the rest of us, they're still held back in their performance when it comes to putting it into practice. No amount of theory can alter that.

5. **It changes lives.** It has encouraged people, time and again, to venture into more challenging areas, which have proved to be personally significant, and occasionally life-changing.

6. **It provides balance.** In every performance environment I've experienced there is an opportunity to be exceptional in the technical aspects of that field and the mental elements, but few are exceptional at both. Even in those fields seemingly ruled by technology, human elements still have their say – and often the final word.

7. **It's easy to use:** People quickly pick up on the main RED–BLUE ideas and make them work, because the model is intuitive.

8.   **It works for young and old.** I'm not an expert in child psychology, but (as you'll see) ten year olds have picked up the model and run with it; and I've seen people of advanced age change their philosophy even after a lifetime of unhelpful mental habits.

9.   **It's enjoyable.** It takes what for many is an unwelcoming area – performing under pressure – and turns it into a personally relevant road map.

10. **It surprises people.** It surprises – and even shocks – experienced performers when they suddenly realise that they have been trying to 'get better' most of their lives by trying to become *more* comfortable when they perform, guided by an unspoken assumption that this is the only or best way forward. The idea that significant opportunity exists in the space of becoming more effective when they are *uncomfortable* can come as a revelation.

The bottom line is that most people do not chase their potential or, if they do, they only get some of the way. We have all experienced that daunting sense of being overwhelmed when the world closes in on us. Even top performers falter and are undone in moments when the pressure gets to them. And one in five of us has serious procrastination issues! The world is full of untapped human potential.

If you restrict yourself to performing only in comfortable situations, your life will miss the fulfilment available to those who *don't* restrict themselves. But if you embrace them, those challenging, high-pressure moments can be especially powerful and rewarding.

Pressure – your friend or your foe? By the end of this book, I hope you'll look at that question in a different light.

Performance under pressure is a fact of life. But because it holds the key to unlocking your potential, pressure is priceless.

PART 1

RED AND *BLUE* – UNDERSTANDING PRESSURE

An abnormal reaction to an abnormal situation is normal behaviour.

Viktor Frankl, psychiatrist (1905–1997)

CHAPTER 1

THE NATURE OF PRESSURE

Pressure is confronting. It can smack us in the face. The sharp edge of reality has a way of cutting our fantasies to shreds.

Pressure is universal. No matter what our level of performance, we all fall victim to it in the same ways.

Pressure is real. What happens inside our heads and bodies – anxiety, tension, frustration, exasperation, foggy thinking, tunnel vision – is not imagined. And when it comes to the effects of pressure, there is no immunity.

Pressure is a mystery. The simple rules of the external world of cause and effect don't hold. The mental world is a non-linear, invisible, cryptic one, where our unconscious often lurks in the background with sinister intent. With success within their grasp – and therefore also the prospect of failure – some people suddenly collapse under pressure, and we don't really understand why. Because the mental world seems hard to comprehend, many people don't make an effort to do so. The very thing that is the most variable, and has the greatest impact, is the least pursued.

Pressure is captivating. Tight sporting contests, precarious business decisions and tense armed stand-offs seem very different situations, but they draw us in for the same reasons. We don't know how they will turn out, and the outcome matters. Predictability is boring and, especially when the stakes are high, unpredictability is thrilling.

Pressure is perilous. The knife-edge, risk–reward seesaw explains why many people do everything they can to avoid or escape from stressful situations.

But a minority of people do the opposite. They *walk towards* these moments of truth, seeking the things they also fear.

Pressure can be an incredibly sobering, painful or even crushing experience, from which we may struggle to recover, or a stirring, heartening one, which resets our life trajectory upwards.

Welcome to the world of pressure.

Two Kinds of Threat

At the heart of pressure is fear. But not all fear is equal.

Imagine someone is walking in the country, in a relatively reflective state, when a wild dog bursts into their path, locks eyes with them, snarls and runs directly at them.

How do they react? Their eyes fixate on the dog, their body becomes tense and their thinking shuts down, all in a split second. They are in a state of fear.

Now imagine a golfer leading his first big championship by one shot. (Please note that all examples in this book, unless otherwise stated, are fictional and any resemblance to real situations is purely coincidental.) At the final hole he is confronted with a difficult water hazard that has claimed his tee shot in the last two rounds.

How does he react? His eyes fixate on the water, his body becomes tense and his thinking shuts down, all in a split second. He is in a state of fear.

These two reactions look identical at face value. They are both internal fear reactions to external situations. But they're different in one key respect: the wild dog is a genuine external threat, while the golf hole is not. The golf shot holds the potential for judgment, but no direct physical threat (unless the golfer falls in the water).

The wild dog triggers a split-second reaction, directly provoked by an external stimulus: sharp teeth. But we can't say the same thing about the golf shot. The golfer's state of fear is triggered by what the external situation stirs up *inside* him. The threat is not an animal with teeth, but feelings that bite.

The tournament or crowd don't directly cause the fear. It's the change in situation that creates the threat: getting close to the end, on the cusp of winning. Which also means possibly losing, with instant audible and visible judgment from the crowd. This possible judgment stirs up deep-seated feelings from long-forgotten past performances, leading to anxiety and tension.

So, there are **two kinds of threat**: one that is triggered by real external danger, and one that is prompted by an internal emotional conflict.

Faced with the first kind of threat – the wild dog – just about everyone would have a similar reaction. But in the case of internal emotional threats, there's a lot of variation in how people react. Some people become fearful and some don't, with all grades in between.

What determines who becomes fearful and who doesn't? And when does this become a problem for performance?

To answer these questions, we'll need to learn more about the human brain …

CHAPTER 2

TWO MINDS – INTRODUCING *RED* AND *BLUE*

Our brain is the part of our body that has the greatest influence on our performance under pressure.

Even when a challenge is mainly *physical* – such as training for a marathon – pressure places demands on us *mentally* as we solve problems, make decisions, adjust timing, fight through the discomfort, and much more. Our *mental* response is what makes the difference.

Our brain is easily the most complex organ in our body – in fact, it's the most complex thing in the universe. The numbers people use in talking about the brain are so big, and at the same time so small, that they're hard to fathom.

The human brain contains roughly 100 billion neurons (nerve cells), which generate trillions of synapses (connections) with other neurons. At the other end of the scale, the average neuron is just one-tenth of a millimetre in size. A piece of brain tissue the size of a full-stop on this page could hold 10,000 synapses, allowing cells to pass information to each other as they branch out from the brain through the spinal cord and nerves to reach, and control, every corner of our body.

Whichever way we look at it, our nervous system is impressive, even though in terms of our knowledge of its complexity it remains a vast, unknown frontier.

This complexity is necessary for neuroscience, but not for us. Fortunately, we can easily simplify how the brain functions into just two interactive systems.

But first, to appreciate why the RED–BLUE mind model makes sense in performance situations, it will help if we understand some basic facts about how the brain is structured.

We can view the structure of the brain in terms of three parts, or levels.

The first level, located at the base of the brain – at the top of the spine – is the **brainstem**, which is responsible for our major physiological drives and functions and our basic survival responses. It is fully developed at birth. We share this part of the brain with reptiles and other mammals.

The second level, sitting at the heart of the brain, is the **limbic system**, which is responsible for processing information about our emotional and physical state, and emotional information about those around us. It develops after the brainstem, going through significant change in the first year of life. A set of nuclei (nerve centres) located around the limbic system, called the **basal ganglia**, are closely associated with our unconscious physical habits.

The third level is the **cerebral cortex** – the outer layers of the brain – made up of two halves: the **left** and **right hemispheres**, joined by a thick bundle of fibres called the *corpus callosum*. The cerebral cortex, which controls advanced mental processes such as language and reflection, is the last part of the brain to develop, and is still maturing in our mid-20s.

THE HUMAN BRAIN
External structure

Front view

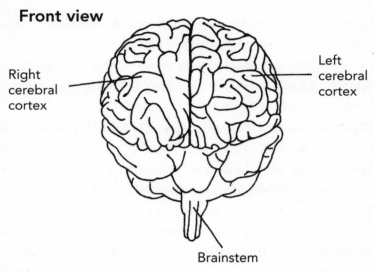

Right cerebral cortex

Left cerebral cortex

Brainstem

Side view

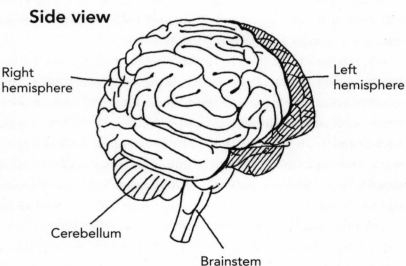

Right hemisphere

Left hemisphere

Cerebellum

Brainstem

From the outside, the brain is dominated by two large cerebral hemispheres.

Although nearly all mental tasks are based on a combination of left- and right-hemisphere activity, one will dominate, because they function very differently in terms of the types of information they process.

Right-hemisphere processes are automatic, fast, and largely unconscious. The right hemisphere works in the here and now, using non-verbal information such as images, and has the capacity to see the big picture, taking an instant snapshot of the situation.

Left-hemisphere processes are deliberate, slower, and conscious. The left hemisphere works by matching current reality with past experiences, using language and calculation to construct stories, explanations and timelines.

The three parts of the brain – and the two hemispheres – function within a **hierarchy,** with the brainstem at the bottom, the limbic system in the middle, and the cerebral cortex at the top. The later-developing cortex has the power to hold back or refine the more primitive reactions from the **sub-cortical structures** (the limbic system and the brainstem), giving *top-down* control.

The right hemisphere, which matures before the left hemisphere, is more concerned with our immediate safety and sense of where we are in the world, while the left hemisphere is more concerned with analysis and setting goals. Likewise, the **back** of the brain processes raw sensory data (like visual images), while the **front** of the brain is more concerned with refining these images through meaning and interpretation. Altogether, our brain develops in a *bottom-to-top, back-to-front* and *right-to-left* direction.

To keep things simple, we can see both our right hemisphere and our limbic system and brainstem as dealing primarily with **feeling,** and our left hemisphere as dealing mainly with **thinking.**

The feeling system is primed for **survival** – including our essential physical processes and the fight–flight reaction. It runs

THE HUMAN BRAIN
Internal structure – Side view

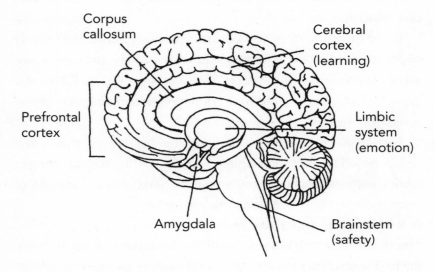

Corpus callosum

Cerebral cortex (learning)

Prefrontal cortex

Limbic system (emotion)

Amygdala

Brainstem (safety)

On the inside, the human brain is organised into three main functional areas: the brainstem at the base; the limbic system in the middle; and the cerebral hemispheres at the top.

on raw, unprocessed data: when a large dog suddenly appears in front of us, all we need to see and sense is that it's angry and growling, not its name, species or favourite park. The defining feature of this survival system is speed. Because it's linked to emotions such as fear, it has been described as 'the hot system'. I call this system **RED**.

The thinking system is primed for **potential**. Once we're safe from the dog, we can think about how to avoid crossing its path in future – maybe we need to buy an even bigger dog ourselves! This system allows us to solve problems, set goals, learn and adapt. Because it's linked more to thinking and rational analysis, it has been described as 'the cool system'. I call this system **BLUE**.

RED

The RED system is strongly connected to our body through powerful nerves, to maintain the overall functioning of our body and main organs within certain, comfortable limits, and to allow us either to run away or to defend ourselves when the situation demands.

There are two RED brain abilities that are particularly relevant to performance under pressure:

1. Emotional regulation
2. Fight–flight–freeze

1. Emotional regulation

The RED system runs essential physiological processes like sleep, hunger, thirst, sex drive and our heart and lung function. We don't want to think much in most of those situations, so the RED system runs our **internal world** automatically and unconsciously by monitoring sensory information from our main organs. And we can't switch it off – it never sleeps, even when *we* do.

Our RED brain is also constantly monitoring emotional information from our **external world.** It processes multiple information channels simultaneously to keep pace with cues in our social and emotional environment. The RED system regulates (controls) our emotions, and since our emotional self-control directs our behaviour at all times, the RED system sits at the forefront of how we experience the world around us.

Our RED brain specialises in processing social and emotional information in a non-linear, holistic way. To give us vital split-second reactions, it runs on broad images, impressions and feelings, delivering an unending stream of moment-to-moment, gut-based judgments about our constantly changing world.

The trade-off is that a lot of detail is lost or not processed, resulting in an approximate system that provides rapid judgments at the expense of accuracy. Information is combined to provide an overall synthesis of a situation, rather than being broken down into smaller categories.

To understand this, let's look more closely at the role of the limbic system in regulating our emotions.

The limbic system adjusts our emotional state in two main ways: by regulating our level of arousal, and by controlling whether this feels good or bad. It's like an extremely powerful internal thermostat, turning our energy level and emotional temperature up and down in an instant.

Nothing is more important to our day-to-day functioning than emotional regulation because it helps keep our body functioning within certain comfortable parameters, where we operate most efficiently. This maintenance of our physical and mental state within a relatively comfortable mid-range or zone is called **homeostasis**, an essential process for all living organisms. (We will see that understanding – and overcoming – this powerful force to stay comfortable can unlock our performance under pressure.)

2. Fight-flight-freeze

Life would be straightforward if we were able to function in comfortable conditions all the time. But we know that in our evolutionary past, we faced deadly threats and had to be constantly on our guard. Think of it in terms of a predator and its prey: the prey either has to react aggressively to deter the predator, or has to get away from the situation in a hurry. We saw this same response earlier in the person confronted by the ferocious dog.

Our RED system has evolved not just to keep us within a comfortable physiological window when conditions are safe and allow it, but also to keep us alive when we face significant threat. It does this through the fight, flight and freeze reactions, which are our **stress** reactions. Within a split second, our brain and body are ready either to flee from the threat, or to fight it off.

Our two **amygdalae**, considered the most primitive parts of the limbic system, act as our threat detectors. They're constantly on high alert and exquisitely sensitive: they can be triggered simply by picking up on the dilation of another person's pupils, a sign of potential hyper-vigilance or fear. They can respond unconsciously within 30 milliseconds, much faster than the 250 to 500 milliseconds it takes us to consciously focus attention with our BLUE brain. This is why we can find ourselves reacting to something without knowing why; then our conscious BLUE mind will catch up and recognise the threat that our RED system saw a quarter to half a second beforehand. In life-threatening situations, our amygdalae allow us to act first and think later.

If we can't overcome or get away from our opponent, we feel trapped, and a more primitive reaction can kick in: **freeze**. This reaction has a slightly different biological pathway from the fight–flight mechanism, and it works in the opposite way: it *shuts us down* physically. It's a last-ditch response to danger, when horror kicks in. In the animal world, this is where caught prey plays dead, hoping the predator will lose interest and enable it to escape. In the human world, we look blank and stare. Freeze starts out with a spike of arousal, but then transforms into a profoundly low-arousal state.

Psychologically, we disconnect from our body. If we can't get out of there *physically*, we certainly don't want to be present *mentally*. We go numb as endorphins are released to protect us from physical and mental pain. The technical term for this is **dissociation**, a mechanism that has fascinated psychologists for over 200 years.

Sometimes dissociation even involves a loss of muscle tone, leading us to fold or collapse – a bit like when a team of defeated players fall to the ground at the final whistle, when just moments before they were desperately trying to turn things around.

The autonomic nervous system

A well-organised RED limbic system will ensure that we are emotionally stable, flexible and resilient. It will allow us to fine-tune our physical and mental state when we are safe, react quickly to defend ourselves when we are under threat, and settle efficiently once the threat has gone.

It makes these adjustments using the **autonomic nervous system (ANS)**, which, as the name suggests, functions automatically. It's a RED system based on feeling, so we don't have to think to turn it on.

The autonomic system has two main branches: the **sympathetic** branch and the **parasympathetic** branch. We now know that there are in fact *two* parasympathetic branches, both related to the large **vagus nerves**, which run from our brainstem at the base of our skull upward to our facial area, and downward to organs in our chest and abdomen. The two parasympathetic pathways are called the **ventral vagal** and **dorsal vagal** pathways. (Ventral means 'front' and dorsal means 'back', reflecting their relative positions within the nerve.)

The bottom line is that to properly understand how our fight, flight and freeze reactions work – and therefore what's happening when we perform under pressure – we need to consider how *three* autonomic branches interact.

The **sympathetic branch** runs down the middle part of our spinal cord, to connect with our heart and lungs via spinal nerves. It responds to threat by preparing us for movement and action: the **fight-or-flight** response. To do this, it releases adrenaline, which increases our heart and breathing rates, and shifts blood flow away from our extremities to our limbs. Our vision fixates on the immediate threat. When our sympathetic system is stimulated, we feel agitated and tense.

The **dorsal vagal pathway**, found in reptiles as well as mammals, connects the brainstem with nerves in the abdomen. Like the sympathetic branch, it responds to extreme danger. But the dorsal vagal pathway is triggered when escape via fight or flight is not possible, so that we feel trapped, which leads to the **freeze** response. When this pathway is activated, we go into a state of mental and physical shutdown. Mentally, we stop feeling, our thoughts become fuzzy, and we feel alone. Physically, we lose energy, feel fatigued and become numb. If fight–flight is a *mobility* reaction, freeze is an *immobility* reaction.

The ventral vagal pathway, also called the **social engagement system** because it is activated when we feel safe enough to communicate with others, connects (along with some associated nerves) the brainstem to the neck, face, eyes and ears as well as the heart and lungs. It puts the 'brakes' on our sympathetic system activation to calm us and allow more flexible responses (except in an emergency, when it releases the brakes). Because it allows us to engage and explore rather than defend and retreat – and to compare it to the defensive fight–flight and freeze reactions – we can think of it as our **face and find** response: it allows us to **face** challenging situations, and **find** a way to overcome the challenge even when the way forward isn't immediately obvious, which sets us mentally *free*.

The three pathways work in a predictable order. When we are at our best and feel safe and connected so that the social engagement system is operating, we can connect with others, think flexibly, see different options and follow through with plans, and are generally organised and on top of things. The moment we sense threat, the sympathetic branch of the ANS kicks in and prepares us to defend ourselves through flight or flight. And if neither the social engagement nor the fight–flight mechanism helps and we feel trapped, the dorsal vagal pathway activates the freeze reaction, driving us into a primitive shutdown state.

If our limbic system, working through the ANS, is both stable and flexible, we will be able to maintain a healthy physical and mental state, and also deal with stressful situations.

A poorly organised limbic system, lacking a good balance between the three pathways, leaves us prone to extended periods or abrupt spikes of over- or under-arousal. When this happens, it means our RED brain is overactive and our top-down, BLUE control is inadequate.

Putting it all together

So it seems the RED system is honed to get us out of tricky or demanding situations – quickly – and return us to a more even, balanced state. It provides a short-term fix to escape or resolve challenging moments. But what do these RED mind mechanisms, fine-tuned over millennia to keep us safe and sound, mean when it comes to performing under pressure?

What has been the biggest scare you've ever experienced? At that time, RED was dominant. It is primed for unthinking action and would have kicked into action immediately. But in other situations in which we face a daunting task but not immediate physical danger, our RED system can be less helpful, becoming activated by social threat and disrupting our ability to think clearly.

In some aspects, the RED system provides precisely what we need for performance. But in others, it seems to create more problems than solutions. Instead of a world of performance, it can take us into a world of interference.

Which is why, to counteract RED, we need BLUE.

BLUE

The BLUE world is one of logic and reason. As we've seen, this system is responsible for higher mental functions such as prioritising, planning, abstract thinking, decision-making, goal-setting and problem-solving. These more advanced intellectual functions are linked to the frontal lobes, which sit behind the forehead.

There are three BLUE brain abilities that are particularly relevant to performance under pressure:

1. Logic, language and numbers
2. Metacognition
3. Working memory

1. Logic, language and numbers

The BLUE system processes information that has already been handled by the RED system. That means that it is a secondary system to the RED, always dependent on the information it is given, but it also means it can provide a feedback loop and revise the RED information. And because it has the capacity to form words it enables us to communicate all this through language. The RED system uses images, but the BLUE system is able to put names and labels to things, and to number them.

BLUE brain processes are conscious, slow and rule-bound, in contrast to RED processes, which are fast and unconscious. Our BLUE mind processes information in a linear way, one piece after another. Timelines and sequencing are its specialities. This means that the BLUE mind is often explaining and making sense of events that have already unfolded.

The BLUE mind is constantly interpreting our environment, breaking it down into a basic architecture of structures, categories and sequences to enable logical analysis. These attributes help with reflection, interpretation, planning and goal-setting. It allows us to understand the environment in an objective way and therefore try to anticipate and predict what happens next, based on stored information.

It is not suited to new situations or operating under stress, and is more at home with using a narrow focus to detect patterns, so it can create a narrative about the past or the future.

2. Metacognition: Thinking about thinking

Our BLUE mind enables us to *think* about how we think and feel, an extraordinary ability shared only with some primates in the animal kingdom. This process of stepping back and reflecting on our own and other people's mental states is called **metacognition,** and it is this ability that allows us to adjust our emotional reactions. If we can't reflect and review, how can we ever learn?

Metacognition occurs when our RED brain processes information from our body and environment through the limbic system, then passes it over to our BLUE brain for a second look. The RED and BLUE systems meet at the **right orbitofrontal cortex,** which is located in BLUE territory (as we've heard), behind the right eye socket. This is the key way-station, where the information is handed over for further review by the BLUE brain, particularly the **left pre-frontal cortex.** It assesses and adapts our perception of the current situation, considers how this matches with our goals and objectives, and makes conscious adjustments, before the information is returned to the right orbitofrontal cortex, which arrives at the final RED–BLUE combination.

Metacognition is critical for maintaining control over our mental responses, and for learning to perform under pressure. (It sits at the heart of the **RED–BLUE tool,** which we'll meet later in the book.)

3. Working memory: Our mental laptop screen

Picture the mind as working like a laptop.

A laptop has a lot of files stored away in its hard-drive memory, where we can't see them. We've forgotten most of the files, but they're still there somewhere. Our mind is the same, with a huge number of files stored away in our unconscious mind, beyond our awareness.

The working surface of our laptop is the screen, which sits at the interface between the inside and outside worlds. We draw up information from memory storage (our inside world) and we also draw in information from the internet, or by inputting new data (our outside world).

Although it occupies the crucial interface position, the screen has a big limitation: we can only work on a small number of files or channels at a time, otherwise we quickly become overloaded and lose track of things.

Our brain works the same way. The mental equivalent of our laptop screen is called our **working memory**, a vital mental function located in prime BLUE-mind real estate in our **prefrontal cortex**, the part of the frontal lobes that sits just above our eye sockets.

Though our long-term memory has enormous storage capacity, the capacity of our working memory is tiny. A famous psychology experiment in the 1950s showed that we can only hold between five and nine items in our working memory at any one time. (This is one reason why telephone numbers are usually seven or eight digits long, and why we break them up into chunks.) This experiment was later revisited because it was based on simple, learned sequences of items like numbers. When pieces of real-life information were used, the capacity dropped to just four or five.

But in some ways the human mind *doesn't* work like a computer. On our laptop, our files are emotionally neutral and stored in a binary system of 0s and 1s, which allows the exact same file to be reopened every time. But in our mind they're stored according to emotions, which constantly adjust the file contents, so that files are continually modified over time.

When it comes to operating under pressure, our working memory capacity can plummet. Normally we call up files (memories) when we want them, but when we're under pressure, any memory that's emotionally similar to the ones we have open can make its way to the surface. Worse still, thanks to our RED brain, any memories that contain threat – and therefore emotion – take precedence. Our working memory loses capacity quickly, so that we can only focus on one thing at a time, and have trouble accessing even basic information. We become self-conscious, just as worried about *how we look* as what we're doing. And the content of our working memory changes from minute to minute, so we keep losing what we were working on.

In the end our screen may overload and freeze, and we need a moment to shut down and reboot before we can see things clearly again.

As the screen sitting at the interface between our internal and external worlds, our working memory sits at the heart of our mental performance under pressure. It acts like Brain HQ, because it's where we gather information from our immediate environment, match it against information and patterns that we call up from our memory banks, manipulate the information a bit, then make a decision and act.

When our screen is clear and at full power, it drives us forward. But when our RED mind interferes, our crucial BLUE capacity is compromised.

Through metacognition, the BLUE pre-frontal cortex has a huge role in keeping RED activation in check. RED overdrive, which leads to shrinking or disintegration of our BLUE mental screen, and loss of braking power on our RED system, is a double whammy for performance under pressure. Our BLUE logical analysis, metacognition and working memory can all be severely affected – and quickly.

Zac is a competitive gamer in the middle of a tense duel. He doesn't want to lose and face the social media backlash he suffered last time around.

He's playing right at his limit when he receives a text message from his girlfriend, asking why he hasn't turned up to meet her as promised. He completely forgot in the midst of his online battle, and now he's facing an argument.

He loses concentration, and his opponent strikes and gains the advantage, which makes Zac angry and even more distracted. Things go from bad to worse. He gets tunnel vision and starts missing background details. He becomes erratic, swinging between being too hesitant and being too impulsive. He can't think straight, and his mind keeps jumping to how he's going to explain things to his girlfriend. He feels like he is playing against two opponents – the one online and himself!

Performing effectively under pressure is about keeping our BLUE mental screen clear even during significant RED mind activity.

RED and BLUE

Like it or not, our RED and BLUE minds have an intimate reciprocal relationship. It is, in a sense, like a lifelong marriage.

How we manage that marital relationship will go a long way to determining how far we travel towards our potential. When RED and BLUE are working harmoniously together, we are in a position to do more with our life. When they are at odds, our performance suffers.

For effective performance under pressure, we need RED and BLUE to be operating in the right proportions to suit the situation.

In life-threatening moments, RED beats BLUE because survival beats potential. When we're in genuine danger it's time for emergency action, not reflection. The RED fight–flight mechanism goes into overdrive and more or less shuts down BLUE functioning.

In the reverse direction, the BLUE system can dampen down the RED response, but can't switch it off. Survival never entirely goes out of fashion!

So the RED–BLUE dynamic is that RED operates in the here and now and can at any moment severely disrupt BLUE with emotions; while BLUE constantly works away to keep the emotional RED reactions and impulses in check, probing the past and scanning the future. At our best, our RED and BLUE minds will complement each other as they work in tandem.

RED and BLUE are both important to performance under pressure, but both are able to undermine it too. The key lies in our ability to adjust the balance, because that will govern how we pay attention in any given moment. Our ability to balance the two will go a long way in influencing which mental pathway we go down when we are uncomfortable.

How Our Early Years Set the Pattern

The way our brain develops in the first two years of life will have a large say in whether we can hold our nerve in high-pressure situations as adults.

Attachment theory is based on the idea that strong emotional and physical attachment to at least one parent or caregiver is essential for early development. This psychological model can help us understand the impact our early years have on our ability to regulate our emotions later in life.

A strong emotional connection between infant and parent allows the infant to retreat to the parent when they are fearful (**attachment**), but to continue to explore the world if the parent is reassuring and seems unconcerned about the situation (**exploration**). The key is that the infant reacts to signals that reveal the parent's mental state.

The interesting thing is that this attachment behaviour is learned without words. It's a constant process that happens before we can talk, and even before we can move independently. Our parent intuitively matches our emotional state, providing signals through tone, touch and look, with the eyes being the critical connection point.

On the biological front, our brain goes through a massive growth spurt over the first year of life, to more than double in size to weigh over a kilogram. Our brainstem and limbic system are already maturing, with the amygdala – our superbly sensitive threat detectors – fully functional at birth. Our sympathetic nervous system develops in our first year, to give us the energy to engage and explore visually. If bonding goes well, this first year has a very positive impact on the infant, and most interactions are soothing and joyful.

In the second year of life the parasympathetic branch of our ANS matures and connects with our right orbitofrontal cortex. This happens as we're becoming more mobile and therefore more in need of frequent interventions from our parent to set limits that keep us safe. The signals increasingly come from a slight distance, and largely through face and eye contact.

This is a big change in tone. We've become used to mainly positive parental reactions, but now we're faced with a real mixture of encouragement to explore, and signals to hold back.

When we see our parent's concerned reaction, our anxiety spikes, but our parasympathetic nervous system down-regulates our stress levels and careful matching from our parent restores the connection. When there is a good connection, our parent is said to be **attuned** to us.

By 18 months, we've been exposed to many, many interactions. The right orbitofrontal cortex is providing the final adjustment of the output from our limbic system, regulating our arousal level and emotions up or down.

By the end of the second year, we've built up an ability to cope with some fear and stress, and to quickly return to exploring when the situation is safe enough. If it's not safe, we're able to quickly seek contact with the parent and come back under emotional control so we can re-energise (a process known as **refuelling**). We learn to tolerate fear without becoming overwhelmed or lost, and to settle quickly if we do become distressed. This is called a **secure attachment**.

However, an unhelpful pattern can be set up if the parent is unresponsive, or too responsive, or if their behaviour is inconsistent and the infant is never sure what to expect.

If the parent is *too* quick to soothe, the infant isn't exposed to any fear and doesn't learn any tolerance of stress and discomfort. Over time, the infant will develop a tendency to become agitated, restless and *over*-aroused.

On the other hand, if the infant is looking for reassurance and it is delayed, or not provided, the infant's distress increases. If the distress continues to rise, the infant can reach its threshold and suddenly shut down, becoming quiet and still. It learns that help and reassurance should not be expected, so it starts to isolate itself and become lethargic (under-aroused).

Both of these patterns – and a situation where there's *no* clear pattern – are called **insecure attachments,** where the infant's ability to regulate their emotions is impaired. (A word of caution:

no parent can be attentive all of the time, and this is not a platform for judging the quality of our parents – or anyone else's.)

The quality of the parent–child interaction is more important than the circumstances in which a child grows up. People can be emotionally resilient despite a difficult early family life, while emotional fragility can sometimes emerge from what appears to be a solid family environment.

Memory

The signals we receive from our parent and our reactions to them are absorbed into our memory and act as powerful automatic templates or 'scripts' for our responses to later events. By the time we're 18 months old, encoded memory scripts are ingrained in our limbic system and automatically guide how we manage our arousal in new situations.

During our critical first two years, a huge number of nerve cells are produced, which are pruned back to reflect our dominant reactions, good or bad. Our RED reactions become hard-wired. We form memories of automatic procedures that are either healthy and flexible, or rigid and unhelpful.

Our memories can be divided into two main types:

1. **Explicit memories,** which encode *facts and events*
2. **Implicit memories,** which encode procedures for *how to do things*

An **explicit memory** records what happened and when, and labels it as either pleasant or unpleasant. To form an explicit memory, we have to consciously focus our attention, which requires our BLUE mind. But explicit memories are not true records of what happened, because they are also encoded with emotion from our RED mind, which makes them more vivid. In addition, they are influenced by the way we are paying attention at the time. We can generally recall a memory more easily when we're in the same emotional state we were in when the memory was formed.

Implicit memories are unconscious records that show us how to do something, such as writing. As we've seen, these are formed from birth through repeated experiences. We don't consciously have the experience of 'remembering': when we are writing, we just do it. Our implicit memories run automatically.

The early scripts that capture how we think, feel and act in response to cues from our environment are examples of powerful implicit memories. We have no sense of recall when they are triggered; we just 'find' ourselves functioning in a certain way that feels entirely *natural*, whether it is helpful for us or not.

But certain implicit memories formed during childhood can modify this early emotional template, and can have a particularly powerful effect on our performance under pressure.

Shame and trauma

Emotionally overwhelming events are stored in the brain as **traumatic memories**. Because they are processed in extreme conditions, our memory only records fragments of the event. It seems that during the recording, our RED brain emotion disrupts BLUE brain attention.

Sometimes people do not mentally process the scene and only the body-based experience is recorded as an implicit memory, which is why people can re-experience the same feelings as in the original event, even without a visual memory.

But it's important to make a distinction between **big-T trauma** – reserved for major events like natural disasters and violent incidents, commonly associated with helplessness and loss of control – and **little-t trauma**, referring to lesser events that are not life-threatening but still carry some emotional impact.

In big-T trauma situations, some people can develop highly distressing memories that come into their mind out of the blue.

Some powerful memories called flashbacks actually take us back into the moment as if we were re-experiencing the trauma; the sense that it happened in the past is lost. People suffering from post-trauma syndromes have symptoms of high arousal (feeling jumpy and on edge, experiencing flashbacks) or low arousal (detachment, numbness), or both, often swinging erratically between the two.

Most of us have a lot of little-t and perhaps a few large-T traumas encoded in our memory systems. And some of our first little-t traumatic memories date from the attachment process during our early years.

When we become mobile and our parent starts setting limits, we're suddenly confronted by the sight of their face showing disapproval of our behaviour, and our urge is to feel **shame**. It's an abrupt, painful reaction that leads to silence, avoidance of eye contact, and feelings of isolation. These emotions can be seen in the face of a child before they learn to talk.

How we manage shame in early life plays a major role in how we learn to regulate our emotions. These moments are absorbed as implicit memories and become automatic procedures when similar moments are encountered later. If moments of shame are managed well, we'll be able to maintain emotional control while experiencing moderate levels of discomfort. But if the attachment traumas become consistent, we'll feel like we can't tolerate and cope with the strength of the feeling and develop a strong tendency towards becoming anxious and agitated (over-arousal), or washed out and flat (under-arousal) when we become uncomfortable.

None of us can recall our earliest traumatic experiences. But most of us can remember moments of shame or embarrassment from our schooldays – whether we tripped on the stage at school, fluffed our lines in the school play, failed an exam or missed an open goal.

Our RED system doesn't forget these moments, because they're moments of social threat. The RED brain is brilliant at storing these moments away as implicit memories, even if we can't recall the moments explicitly, so it can warn us if similar situations reappear. When that happens, our RED memory of the event – apparently asleep for years but in reality only resting with one eye open – springs to life. It reminds us, in an instant, of the social threat, and our RED survival system is reactivated. It doesn't matter that these days we don't consciously recall the original threat; the RED system makes us feel it anyway.

This explains why we can find ourselves in a performance situation, thinking (with our BLUE mind) that we have it under control, but feeling anxious without really knowing why. Our subconscious mind is recognising some aspect of the current situation that is symbolic of the old event, and the old feelings come up. Some subtle aspect of the situation – a tone of voice, certain words, even a smell – triggers our deeply stored RED memories, and the reactions that follow. Instead of growing large and facing the moment down, we find ourselves shrinking and hesitating under pressure.

Remember the golfer facing the final hole in Chapter 1? He experiences fear not because of a physical threat, but because of the potential judgment of the crowd. He's undoubtedly faced other situations involving judgment throughout his life. Some of those experiences will have been associated with strong emotions like anger, guilt and grief.

The golfer won't, and can't, recall all those situations right now, but he still gets an instant negative emotional hit. The golfer has an unconscious emotional blueprint, which has gradually formed throughout his life, and is now triggered during any situations involving judgment.

In RED–BLUE mind-model terms, uncomfortable feelings like fear occur when our RED mind dominates our BLUE mind. Our ability to face and handle these uncomfortable states provides the template for our performance under pressure.

Although you may not have thought about it this way before, your performances started at birth. When you did something – anything – you performed, and that elicited a reaction, good or bad, from your parents or caregivers. This happened with your first milestones. Then at school. It happened with your friends. At work. On the stage or on the sports field.

Our lives have developed into a sequence of performances, and nuanced emotional interactions with those who watched us. Our responses to this have been encoded as a collection of performance memories. Over time we have developed a highly individual, and strong, mental blueprint relating to performance. It has been built on the numerous occasions in which we felt we have been exposed to judgment, and it is this subconscious blueprint that is activated when we encounter new performance or judgment situations.

Significant physical injuries suffered in the past, or psychological blows such as major losses or humiliations, can all affect our current performance. But the greater the emotional regulation we have, the more we'll be able to cope with the trials and tribulations of harsh, distressing or even traumatic performance experiences.

What little-t performance trauma can you recall from your childhood or adolescence? What was your emotional reaction at the time? Can you see a link between this and how you react to similar situations now? Do you become too 'hyper' and lose your ability to think and feel clearly? Do you become distant or shut down? Or can you cope, recover and recharge yourself to continue with your performance?

Changing our brain

The great news is that however our RED system reacts under pressure, we can increase our BLUE control over those reactions, thanks to a property of our brain called **plasticity**.

As much as our mental blueprint is laid down during our childhood, one of the major discoveries of modern science has been that our brain continues to adapt and adjust itself at the microscopic level throughout our life. Remarkably, if part of the brain is damaged, then other nerve cells, especially the adjacent ones, can sometimes help out to compensate for the loss.

Much like the memories in our brain, the patterns encoded in our nerve-cell networks when we were young still influence how we feel and act in current situations. Like a pathway through a forest, the more we use the same nerve-cell pathway, the clearer and easier it becomes. We find ourselves following the path without really thinking why we are doing it; it just feels natural. Which it is: it is now *in our nature* to react a certain way in difficult moments.

The opposite is also true. If we *stop* using a particular pathway, it will become overgrown and not so easy to go down. In a high-pressure situation, every time we resist the urge to escape the discomfort by following a certain path, that nerve-cell escape path is weakened – and the uncomfortable path is strengthened. What we consciously experience is that the urge to escape that moment is reduced and we can tolerate a little more discomfort.

The pathways in our brain are constantly being strengthened and weakened. We *strengthen* the impulse to escape every time we reward it by moving away from discomfort – and we *weaken* it every time we tolerate the urge to move away.

Our performance habits are not random. If we want to change our performance under pressure, then we need to change the biology that drives it.

The RED–BLUE tool is all about being **comfortable being uncomfortable**. Under pressure, do we give up or rise up? As someone wise once said: 'Pain is inevitable. Suffering is optional.'

THE HUMAN BRAIN
Structure & function

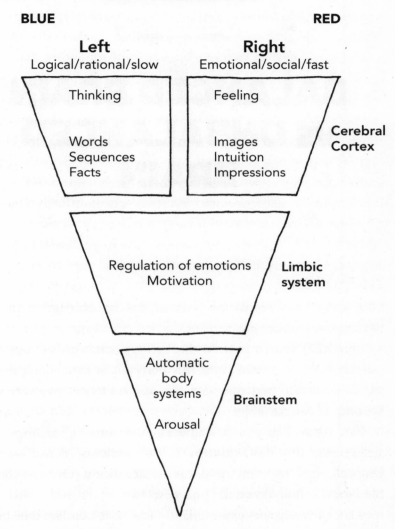

BLUE   **RED**

Left   **Right**
Logical/rational/slow   Emotional/social/fast

Thinking	Feeling
Words	Images	**Cerebral Cortex**
Sequences	Intuition
Facts	Impressions

Regulation of emotions
Motivation   **Limbic system**

Automatic
body
systems   **Brainstem**

Arousal

The brainstem and limbic system connect primarily with the right hemisphere to provide emotional regulation, operating through images, feelings and direct experience (RED). The left hemisphere operates through language, logic and reflection (BLUE).

CHAPTER 3

BALANCED BRAIN vs UNBALANCED BRAIN

Our emotional regulation system sits at the heart of our performance under pressure.

Our RED system evolved through repeated connections with our primary caregivers, and this determines how much feeling we can tolerate and how flexible our responses are when we become uncomfortable.

Far from being a wishy-washy system of feelings and sensations, the RED system is the primary driver of our psychological reaction in pressure situations. Our emotional blueprint – laid down in our first two years and constantly revised through life experience – has a lot to do with how we respond to pressure, and whether we become prone to unhelpful behaviours. When our emotional regulation is poor and RED dominates, our attention becomes divided or diluted and our focus is dragged away from the present moment. We lose emotional flexibility and the ability to think clearly and our behaviours default to basic survival instincts, out of keeping with the situation.

In my experience the most commonly identified pattern is for performance under pressure to cause *over*-arousal – too much RED – rather than *under*-arousal. But one trap is to assume that *under*-arousal comes from too little emotion, when in fact it often comes from too much anxiety and tension and a partial freeze reaction. Going 'flat' can look relaxed, but is actually very different – and is sure to lead to poor performance.

Trying to ignore or suppress our RED mind is a weak strategy, because it has evolved to never be snubbed or shut down. In fact, trying to overlook it actually powers up our RED response until it gets our attention. If need be, it will take over and make its presence felt.

But whatever template we have now does *not* fully determine how we respond to pressure. Our BLUE system is designed to exert some control over the feelings and impulses that emerge when we are emotionally uncomfortable. Our BLUE mind can kick in to provide balance and control of our RED system, and we can get the two systems back in sync.

Our BLUE system controls RED emotion first of all by naming it – remember our left hemisphere has the power of language – and simply naming a vague, hard-to-describe physical experience has a very settling effect. Our BLUE system can then reappraise the situation by focusing on the negative experience and modifying its meaning. Left-brain naming and meaning-change dampen down the RED emotional intensity.

It's important to remember that the RED system is not inherently good or bad, any more than emotions are good or bad. Our feelings are a normal and essential part of life. Without them we would never experience the joy of close connections or the thrill of chasing goals and achieving them. The RED emotional system is what gives us drive and energy; it gets us going. It's just when RED goes into overdrive and we lose control that we meet problems.

It would be a serious mistake to label RED as bad and BLUE as good. Both systems are very useful for their intended purposes. Too much RED may be more common, but being too BLUE can be just as harmful to performance. It can cause us to lose emotional connection, becoming detached, aloof and even cold. Team spirit would be impossible within a completely BLUE world.

This book is fundamentally about finding our RED–BLUE balance, not about casting RED as a villain and BLUE as the hero of the piece.

My aim is to help you perform effectively when you're out of sorts and stressed, not when it's plain sailing. As we've learned, under pressure we will experience discomfort, so we need to learn to be **comfortable being uncomfortable** – not just *coping* with discomfort, but *thriving* within it.

How well we perform depends on the quality of our attention. And our control of attention is driven by the interaction between our RED and BLUE mind systems.

Whether RED and BLUE are in sync or out of sync will have a large say in whether we can perform under pressure. If we are badly prepared, pressure can take us down. If we are well prepared, pressure can lift us up to new heights.

In this chapter, I'll look at the most common *ineffective* patterns of feeling, thinking and acting under pressure, and contrast them with the most common *effective* patterns of feeling, thinking and behaving under pressure. Understanding these patterns provides us with a better chance of detecting when we are going *off track*, and more idea of how to get back *on track* once it happens.

Threat vs Challenge

Threat

> Tony is running late for an important meeting at work with his boss. He has tension in his neck and shoulders, his heart and thoughts are racing, and he feels a little sick. There's no direct physical threat here. He knows that in the same situation, most of his colleagues would not be bothered at all. If he does arrive late his boss probably won't even comment. But still he feels anxious.

Now that we've met the RED–BLUE mind model, we can understand what Tony is going through. Somewhere in his past, being late has led to some painful feelings. Perhaps it was being late on the first day of school. Maybe it was a combination of several occasions when he was late or cut it fine for sports practice and got yelled at by the coach, which caused him some embarrassment. These painful experiences have been long since buried among Tony's unconscious memories. But today, as he sees he's running late, a fusion of those painful memories and the feelings linked to them is once again automatically triggered by his RED system, which is primed to react to threats (whether real or imagined). No specific memory comes to mind, but the familiar feeling does. And so Tony's anxiety system kicks in, and he ends up tense and anxious.

Turning up on time is a **performance moment**. No gold medals are at stake here, but being punctual is personally significant to Tony, while for others it's not particularly important.

It goes to show that even apparently mundane, everyday events can carry a hidden performance agenda. And so when we enter an arena where the stakes are *genuinely* high, it should come as no surprise that our emotional reaction can skyrocket.

Think about this reaction as an unconscious, two-stage process. The first step is that old, painful feelings get automatically stirred up. The second step is that the feelings trigger an anxiety reaction to block those feelings from surfacing. These steps happen so fast that we usually only notice the second one – the anxiety reaction – which makes it seem like that happened first. But some people pick up a spike of emotion – perhaps a hot feeling surging up through their core – before the anxiety reaction comes in over the top to shut the emotion down.

Anxiety can make us feel tense or go flat if we hit our threshold, which can disrupt our thinking and senses. It can also cause a host of other physical sensations through our fight, flight or freeze reaction. But they're different from the primary feelings of anger, guilt or grief. Anxiety is a *secondary reaction*.

The combined effect of the primary painful feelings and secondary anxiety is that we experience discomfort. This discomfort doesn't appear out of nowhere. It comes about because of a process inside of us. And it isn't random – it's very predictable. We will get anxious in the same types of situation, again and again, when others do not.

Tony's experience shows us that the common phrase 'performance anxiety' oversimplifies what actually happens inside our body. The external performance – being on time or not – activates Tony's unconscious blueprint of feelings, which then trigger his anxiety.

The middle step is key. Though it usually happens so fast that we are not aware of it, it's most definitely there, because otherwise, why would people react so differently to the same external situation?

As we've seen, external fear arising from real physical danger is hard-wired within us and is an automatic survival mechanism, driven by our biology. In brain terms, we react long before we can consciously think it through. And internally driven fear, or anxiety, is generated by our personal psychology. It's not a genuine survival moment in the physical sense, although it *is* in the psychological sense: the anxiety is generated by doubt about our ability to *mentally* survive the occasion.

Although most performance situations don't literally involve threat to our physical survival, it might threaten our psychological existence if we mentally live and die with our image and reputation. If we subconsciously frame these moments in survival terms, we will trigger survival responses.

The bottom line is that performance situations stir up deeply ingrained emotions held in our body, and anxiety in the form of tension can instantly lock things down, making us uncomfortable and affecting our ability to think clearly under pressure.

Performing under pressure usually means performing when we are uncomfortable.

Challenge: Going beyond threat

If our RED mind is primed for survival, our BLUE mind is primed for potential.

Safety comes first. If we are not safe, our RED mind is activated and dominates our thinking and behaviour. But once we are safe and the RED mind is calm enough, other opportunities open up. (It doesn't have to be *completely* calm, just within the window of discomfort where you can still operate.)

The BLUE mind is well suited to looking at our immediate environment, solving problems and adapting. When we're not forced to pay attention to getting out of a situation we don't want to be in, our mental effort can be focused on creating a situation that we *do* want. In modern language, we call this **goal-setting**.

With its emphasis on language and logical analysis, our BLUE mind sees possibilities, nuances and opportunities by matching the current situation against prior experience. That's how it evolved – as a creative, forward-thinking, adaptive mechanism. If the RED mind is the security at the door, the BLUE mind is the creative headquarters tucked safely inside, where plans are hatched and problems are solved.

When we engage our BLUE mind in pressure situations, a fundamental shift in mindset can occur: **threat** is replaced by **challenge**. Instead of trying to flee and bring the situation to an end as quickly as possible, our BLUE mind draws us *towards* the obstacle that's in our way, using all mental resources at its disposal to adapt, adjust and improvise so we can overcome the challenge.

In a survival situation, there is a simple threat focus on outcomes such as living and dying, or winning and losing. With a challenge focus, our attention is drawn to the process of finding a way through. Judgment is replaced by movement. Instead of 'Will I survive?', the question becomes 'How far can I go?'

If we regard the situation as a challenge, we'll focus not on the outcome but on our capacity to deal with the demanding and difficult moments. Rather than a burden to bear, we'll see the discomfort as stimulating.

Of course, with this challenge mindset, we will regularly fall short. But the key is in the *method*, not the *outcome*. What matters is our state of mind when we perform under pressure, not whether we succeed or fail. We don't lose heart when we don't meet the challenge, because we appreciate that the learning we've just experienced is precious. Moments of failure arguably create more opportunities to get better than moments of success. The critical step is to embrace the pressure situation in the first place.

No one can meet every challenge. If we do, then we've set the bar too low and the challenges we've set don't really deserve the name.

To reach our full potential, we have to keep pushing ourselves to our limit and beyond. We have to put ourselves in a position to deal with more and more demanding tasks. It's about full commitment to the moment.

This is more difficult than it sounds. The discomfort makes most people flinch, so they never fully test themselves.

The word test comes from the Latin *testum*, meaning an earthen vessel. The idea was that the vessel was used to examine the quality of a substance placed within it – like a test tube. Some material was put inside it and subjected to different conditions, like heat.

Our performance arena is the equivalent of a test tube. Our mind is the material inside it. And the condition we're being subjected to is pressure.

Our personal properties are being deliberately examined under pressure. When we face the heat, what qualities do we display? How do we function as we approach our limit? Do we retain our resilience, or melt and lose our mental structure?

When we start approaching test situations with relish, our tolerance of discomfort increases. Don't worry, you don't have to actually *enjoy* the discomfort – you just have to appreciate what it achieves. Discomfort is not a punishment, it's a testing moment we've earned, and an invitation to step up to the next level.

The big mental shift in performance under pressure comes when we can feel fear but accept deep inside that we will mentally survive the moment. Once the mental threat in a situation is contained, it loses its power to overwhelm us emotionally and shut us down, allowing us to re-energise and face the challenge.

A challenge mindset means feeling the discomfort, but facing down the challenge without flinching.

Alex, a freestyle skier competing at a big championship event, is about to start her second run after her first one ended in a fall. A second poor run would see years of hard work end in misery.

In that moment, Alex is scared. Not of falling, or of missing out on a medal, but of the shame she'll feel when she sees her coach, parents and teammates afterwards. She feels empty inside. She's facing psychological devastation. It's a RED alert moment.

But she has prepared for this possibility. At precisely the instant when everyone else gives up on her and sees what she might *lose*, she sees an extraordinary opportunity and what she might *gain*: a comeback story for the ages.

She breathes in deeply and imagines energy filling her core, and as she breathes out, she pictures fire spreading heat and energy throughout her body. She stands tall and feels herself growing in power as others cower down. Nothing could be better in her mind: this is no longer a championship event to compete in, it is her championship moment to own. No longer empty, hollow and cold, Alex can feel the fire burning inside. Her confidence restored, she attacks the run.

Our mirror neurons – specialised nerve cells that allow us to pick up on how other people are feeling – allow us to feel the fear in others. And when we see people feel the fear but take on the challenge anyway, we are inspired. It is a signature moment for performance under pressure.

If we mentally flinch or fold, our performance will be compromised, but if we know we can survive this moment, we can take it on with relish. And much better to take it on with courage than to dither and stall. The true meaning of courage is to act with heart when you are scared.

We are not defined by pressure moments unless we let them define us. Move through and past the psychological threat to see the wonderful opportunity presented to us to go as far as we can. Instead of becoming mentally subdued, numb and frozen, we will come alive. It will be life-changing.

Reflect on your mindset when you hit discomfort. What's your habitual response? Are you stimulated by the challenge of these moments, or does the threat loom larger? Do you walk towards them or walk away?

The discomfort of pressure: threat or challenge?

Overthinking vs Connecting

Overthinking

When I ask athletes to describe their worst 10 minutes in sport, one word always causes moans of recognition: **overthinking**.

It's a strange word. Can we think too much, really? And are there particular thoughts that we can think too much about?

The athlete usually goes on to explain that they were trying their level best to right a wrong, or raise their game, but their best intentions backfired. The harder they tried, the worse things got. It even felt like there was pressure building up inside their head. They had too many thoughts, too fast, and it held them back.

Under pressure, elite sportspeople do not want to think too much or too fast, because it causes problems for their performance. A busy mind gets in the way of clarity. And that is universally seen as a bad thing.

Imagine yourself in a high-pressure moment. Your confidence is taking a battering. The casual remedy is just to think positively, which assumes that we can just replace our negative thoughts with positive ones. But that is simply throwing fuel onto the RED fire.

Your BLUE mind is telling you: 'I can!' It's not a particularly strong voice, perhaps even a bit squeaky. Because while it's speaking there's a far stronger, deeper, RED voice booming out the opposite message: 'I can't!'

It's like having two independent minds going in opposite directions and arguing about which one is best. BLUE versus RED. And the RED message feels authentic, while the BLUE voice sounds hollow and unconvincing. (Remember, only our BLUE mind can use words; your RED mind speaks in the language of feelings and sensations. There are no words, but it certainly sends its message.)

In these situations, RED usually beats BLUE. The RED system will not lie down and be ignored – after all, it's in charge of our survival. The survival parts of our brain appeared on the scene first and got prime position in our nervous system – right on the centre line, or close to it. The RED system cannot be switched off, and the harder the BLUE mind tries to suppress it, the louder the RED voice becomes. Every time we think something positive, a stronger negative thought or feeling comes bouncing back.

Mental chatter overloads our BLUE head, taking the top-down brakes off so that our RED head drives our behaviour more or less unchecked. RED is only interested in the here and now, so with the loss of our BLUE ability to read the play, our sense of direction and our awareness of possible consequences, we become prone to acting too fast, or too slow. That's why we see even experienced performers become impulsive or hesitant in big moments.

RED vs BLUE STATE

RED	BLUE
THREAT / AWAY	**CHALLENGE / TOWARDS**

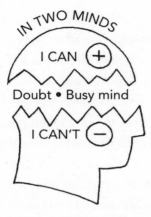

Hesitant / Impulsive

Decisive action

When we are 'in the RED', we can lose emotional control,
overthink and get diverted. When we are 'in the BLUE', we
can hold our nerve, maintain our focus and stay on task.

Connecting

When I ask athletes to describe their *best* 10 minutes in sport,
the one response that stands out is that they felt **connected**.

Instead of the overthinking that is the hallmark of their
worst moments, their sense of connection with their immediate
environment meant that they weren't thinking much at all.
Everything seemed so obvious and easy. They perceived, and
they acted. They sensed, and they moved. They saw, and they
did. The usual middle piece of thinking seemed to disappear.
They were 'in the zone'.

This intensely positive experience of connection is an example of complete absorption with our immediate environment. It's when our connection with the external environment is so complete that we can effortlessly pick out small details that are overlooked by others, and act upon them decisively. It feels simple to get the timing right; in fact, time seems to slow down, allowing us to easily anticipate events and respond to them.

This is only possible when there's no sense of disconnection. The most common disconnect occurs when we start to think not about how we are performing the task but how we are *looking* while we do it. We can only be completely on task when we lose our self-consciousness. The key is to commit all our attention to the external world, rather than splitting it between the external environment and a struggle within our internal world.

Instead of being distracted by doubt, we need to **trust** our ability to handle what is in front of us. This self-trust forms the RED backbone to support our BLUE focused attention. Banishing doubt and worry avoids overthinking – that busy mind that arises from an internal debate about what we're doing.

But what about our discomfort, which we've seen is a key feature of pressure? We have to move through it. We can't magically avoid or escape it, but we *can* choose not to focus on it. It just isn't the main issue. We can make the discomfort an internal focus, leading to overthinking, with suffering in the foreground. Or we can simply notice the discomfort and let it subside into the background, while our focus returns to the immediate task. With this external focus on *doing*, our mind becomes still.

When our external environment is more captivating than our internal concerns, RED and BLUE can be in sync, which makes us feel single-minded as we go about our business.

In some cases this sense of connection is so complete – and the self-consciousness so absent – that the barriers between the individual and the environment seem to disappear, and performers say they feel completely at one with their setting.

Some activities are so dangerous – doing BASE jumps, surfing huge waves or free-climbing vicious rock faces – that they demand full attention to the external world. Any major internal diversion risks serious accident or tragedy. During these activities, extreme athletes need to be completely in the zone.

The zone isn't something that we can simply think our way into, but we can certainly think our way out of it. If we're completely absorbed by our environment and responding intuitively, then thinking is the last thing we should be doing.

Most athletes can recall one or two times when they were in that perfect zone. But most of us don't perform in a situation where we need to focus so completely on the external world, or in dangerous physical environments where our physiological state is heightened, or else! Is the zone – that perfect sense of connection – even a reasonable target? If the zone makes things seem effortless, then making an effort to get there feels like the wrong thing to do.

Perfection – aiming for the zone – can be a trap. Instead, let's return to the simple idea of trying to connect with our external world and removing our focus from our internal world. Let's put more emphasis on the process of how to get where we want to go, and less on how we feel about where we are at the moment. Let's regard being in the zone as something we may, or may not, achieve.

Being in the zone – physically and mentally – is an **outcome**. The **process** we use to get there is to control our attention. We set our external target, lock on to it and maintain our focus of attention, with full acceptance of our internal world. If we become diverted by internal discomfort, we just notice it then return to the task at hand.

When it comes to dealing with turning overthinking into connecting, **acceptance** beats **resistance**. Being deliberate about our external focus and allowing the discomfort to subside kick-starts our BLUE mind and allows us to find our RED–BLUE balance and get moving smoothly. And occasionally, very good things can happen.

Cast your mind back to the best 10 minutes of your best performance. How did you get into that state of mind? Was there anything deliberate you did other than focus intently on the task in front of you? Or did it just come out of the blue?

Yes, that's right. It did indeed just come out of the BLUE.

Split Attention vs Dual Focus

Split attention

'Pay attention!'

Growing up, how many times did we hear that from parents, teachers, coaches and others?! The reason why we heard it so often is that it's great advice! It cuts right to the heart of performance under pressure, because the prime issue is our control of attention.

But as sound as it is, this advice is so familiar that it washes over us. We hear it all the time and so we stop hearing it. How ironic that the single best piece of advice we can receive for performing under pressure – 'Pay attention!' – doesn't get our attention!

All those adults saw what was going wrong inside our head: we had lost our focus. We needed to learn how to deliberately pay attention to what we were doing, to hold it there despite potential diversions, and to shift it to a new focus when needed.

It sounds so straightforward because these are everyday mental processes that we take for granted. Surely something so basic and commonplace cannot be so important for performance?

It's not only important, it is core to performing under pressure. In most demanding situations this most fundamental mental ability of all – how well we pay attention – has the largest influence on the outcome. If we don't get that part right we are definitely going to struggle.

The emphasis on attention is important because it is arguably our greatest limitation. Our capacity to pay attention seems very big but it is, in fact, very small.

Remember that under pressure, the rules change, and the capacity of our working memory plummets. When the task in front of us is demanding, we can really only focus on one thing at a time. For conscious, demanding tasks, multitasking is a myth. No problem to talk on our phone while shopping at the supermarket: two easy, almost automatic tasks. But even then, mistakes can occur – we accidentally pick up the wrong item, we miss things that were on our list. Now add some pressure – a screaming child, time pressure to get to an urgent appointment – and the errors flood in. At the brain level, RED has disrupted BLUE and our once-clear mental screen has shrunk down and clouded over.

When we take on a demanding task but our attention is split, we go downhill fast. Doing two tricky things at a time – such as playing the piano while reciting verse – makes our performance deteriorate not just a bit, but dramatically. The fall-off is more a cliff than a gentle slope. I often tell athletes that when their attention is divided, they are half the player.

The magical question to ask ourselves when reviewing our performance under pressure is: 'What were we paying attention to in that moment?' Paying attention in performance situations is our most powerful – but vulnerable – mental tool, and so understanding what disrupts it is a revealing starting point. One of the most common attention traps is the **negative content loop**: a self-defeating, circular pattern of thinking and feeling. Instead of focusing fully on the task in front of us, we find our attention diverted towards potential or past negative outcomes, such as losing, making a mistake, or missing a deadline. We see threat in the situation, our negative perception of the threat sparks an emotional response, and our emotions lead to unhelpful behaviours. Those behaviours reinforce our negative perception, starting the loop off again, causing a self-reinforcing, downward spiral.

Remember Tony? He's running late for another important meeting; this time he's due to present an important pitch to senior colleagues. In his mind he can already imagine the looks of judgment as he walks in late. He's angry with himself for miscalculating how long it would take to get ready, and at the same time he's worried about the potential fallout for his pitch. He feels anxious and tense, his thoughts are racing and he can't concentrate. Despite a late night rehearsing, his mind is suddenly foggy about his presentation and he feels himself starting to freeze. That alarming realisation only reinforces his negative self-judgment, and the negative content loop is set up.

Initially Tony had a positive picture in his head about how the situation would ideally work out. But the threat within the situation – his lateness and the negative attitude it will spark – has changed his perception. What he wanted and what he is likely to get are now at odds with each other. His fantasy and the reality clash, creating an internal conflict.

It's almost as if he has one mind trying to do its best to prepare for his performance, and another mind that's much more concerned about how he'll be judged. He's caught in two minds.

Instead of focusing on his presentation, he finds his attention stuck on exactly the outcomes he didn't want. Sure, some of his attention still seems to be carrying him along, so that it's not as if he's completely stopped functioning. But a good chunk of his attention is now caught up in the negative spiral. He's drowning in a flood of pessimistic thoughts and uncomfortable feelings, and is fast losing focus and effectiveness.

And it all seems to feed into the loop and strengthen it, so Tony finds it more and more difficult to get back on task. The loop becomes a downward spiral: the deeper he goes, the harder it is to climb out.

The reason why a negative content loop is so damaging for our focus is that it takes us out of the current moment. It diverts our attention from the present into the past (a mistake or missed opportunity) or the future (negative outcomes and the criticism and judgment that will result). Our mental horsepower is cut in half right when we need it most.

This looping into the past or future also gets our mind and body out of sync. Our body can only exist in the here and now, but when we are trapped in a negative content loop our thoughts are fixated on the past or future and drag us there mentally. This mind–body split takes its toll on how we think, feel and act.

One classic negative loop is the **'poor me' loop**. Something goes wrong in our environment. We start to feel sorry for ourselves, seeing ourselves as the victim of circumstance. Life is unfair; we don't deserve this. This swirl of feelings and thoughts makes us uptight, frustrated, angry. We get stuck on the injustice, feeling more and more self-righteous. And the situation just keeps compounding itself.

In a nutshell, we're sulking. This kind of behaviour is meant to be restricted to children, but adults can turn it into an art form. Sulking involves both passive and aggressive elements: we withdraw and go silent, but make sure that everyone knows we are far from happy! We're moody and resentful, and our sullen, brief replies, when we give them, are intended to annoy others.

Many of us demonstrate this behaviour. A lot.

From the performance point of view, sulking is a very unhelpful mental state to adopt. It leads to a lack of action and movement. Not only that, but the sulker also deliberately affects those around them. Because they feel like they are being punished, they punish others back.

Some people really know how to hold grudges. They are so adept at sulking that they can remain in that state not just for minutes or hours, but days, weeks, months, even years on end.

Next time you're watching a sporting event, follow the competitors' eyes. When an unfortunate incident occurs, they often look downwards, which can show they're stuck in a 'poor me' loop, turning their attention inward. Or they may look upwards, questioning whatever higher power they deem responsible for the injustice. The origins of this type of 'poor me' behaviour lie in the attachment behaviour we looked at earlier. When the parent is well attuned to their child's distress, they can provide comfort through non-judgmental facial contact and a soothing voice, but when the relationship is unpredictable or unresponsive, the child will come to associate their discomfort with a lack of eye contact. Later in life, when the same individual faces disappointment and discomfort the same pattern will emerge. The 'poor me' loop, and other negative content loops, are a deadly attention trap for performance. This kind of mental state doesn't matter that much if we're just going about our everyday tasks. But when we're in a more demanding situation, it can become our sworn enemy. It sucks away treasured attention that we could be using to extract maximum information from our environment, solve problems or overcome obstacles.

Think about our golfer from earlier, feeling anxious as he takes the final shot in his first big championship. He might be focusing on where he wants the ball to go, but because his RED mind has taken over, part of his attention is also diverted to the water trap and where he *doesn't* want the ball to land. He starts to worry about the water trap and a negative content loop is triggered. Out of nowhere, some self-defeating self-talk – 'I'm going to miss the shot ... I'm going to lose the championship!' – and negative feelings – shame, frustration – seem to burst onto the scene.

His mind now contains images of two 'targets': the one he wants to hit and the one he doesn't. And because he's trying to perform while he's split in two by doubt, his shot inevitably falls somewhere in the middle.

> Cast your mind back to a recent performance moment when you lost mental focus. What diverted your attention in that moment? Did you get trapped in a negative content loop and partially fixated on what you didn't want to happen? It was as if part of you was doing everything it could to defeat you in that moment.
>
> You were caught in two minds.

Dual focus

For a head chef in a reputable restaurant, which is more important: having a laser-like focus on the food, or keeping an eye on her team, the supply chain, the wait staff, the table service and a long list of other factors? Narrow focus on food, or broad focus on the general restaurant situation?

The answer is that *both* are necessary. The head chef cannot afford to take her eye off the overall situation, *and* she most definitely cannot let substandard food pass. Both the **overview** and the **specific detail** are required. One without the other would be a recipe for disaster.

Our actions should always take place within the big picture of what we are trying to achieve, which requires attention to context. At the same time, we need a narrow focus on the specific task we're engaged in, which requires attention to detail.

While the RED mind can process many things unconsciously at the same time, the BLUE mind is linear, allowing us to concentrate on only one thing at a time. The head chef is intuitively aware of both the wider situation and specific tasks through her RED mind, but still consciously focuses on each in turn. It seems simple, but it works.

A **dual focus** requires a tight, constant feedback loop between the overview and the specific task, with each informing the other. At any one time, our dominant focus will be on either one. The key is to move back and forth between the two, rather than **splitting attention** between them.

Here's a puzzle: dual focus and split attention both imply that our attention has to be in two places at once. So why does dual focus *feed* performance, while *split* attention *starves* it?

Let's use an example to paint a picture of the differences.

Leo has just dropped a simple catch and gifted the opposition the upper hand in the closing stages of an important match. In the minute or so that follows, his mind goes back and replays the memory of his fumble and the moans of the watching crowd over and over. At the same time, he's constantly looking at the clock and seeing the final seconds of the game tick by, and his mind keeps flashing forward to the devastation of his teammates in the dressing room after the game finishes. His attention is split between the present, past and future. His RED mind becomes hyperactive and he loses the capacity to think clearly. Mentally pulled in different directions, he becomes stuck – a deer in the headlights, frozen to the spot.

Now, imagine Leo is able to use dual focus to keep his focus in the present moment. He glances at the scoreboard and sees that he has two minutes left. He has the overview.

He then focuses on the immediate task, which is to help get the ball back in a coordinated team effort. The team have practised two-minute scenarios many times in training to prepare for this type of situation. He has the specifics.

He goes into dual focus – moving flexibly back and forth between the situational overview and his specific tasks – as the end of the game unfolds. There is a vague feeling of discomfort at the back of his mind that seems to be calling out, but he just accepts it and focuses his attention on communicating with his teammates. It's time to hold his nerve, find his move and nail any opportunity to emerge, while maintaining a good RED–BLUE balance. In the final two minutes, Leo sets up teammates in good attacking positions three times. Although his team fall just short, afterwards Leo's coach praises his ability to rebound from his disappointment and remain focused and engaged in the game.

Split attention divides attention in time and place; the different parts interfere with each other, and they all seem to occur simultaneously. Dual focus keeps the connection in the present moment.

Dual focus also trumps split attention because of the type of information being processed. When our attention is split, the diversion is inevitably about the negative meaning of a situation.

Problems become jumbled up with solutions. When we have dual focus, we're tightly focused on the process of completing our task (detail) while constantly reading shifts in our environment (overview). It's about looking ahead without disconnecting from the moment.

I find that many people assume they already routinely use this two-level control of attention without any significant interference, when in reality they habitually fall into attention traps that lead them to think too much or too little.

Some fall for one-level attention, becoming preoccupied with either the overview or the detail, but not both. Having a single focus is simplistic: we will either miss shifts in the wider context and react slowly, or miss crucial detail in the specific task we're working on.

Others add a third element to the dual focus and let themselves be diverted by a negative loop. Having a triple focus is too complex when it involves a RED mist that interferes with BLUE clarity.

Yet experts across countless fields have the capacity to switch their attention between perspective (the overview) and precision (the detail) when the heat is on. Skilful control of attention – avoiding negative content loops and maintaining their dual focus – is what separates them from the rest.

The lead violinist in an orchestra doesn't just look at the music (detail) but also focuses much of the time on remaining in sync with the conductor and setting the rhythm for the whole orchestra (overview). This is so important that the second violinist turns the pages for their more senior colleague.

For flight crews, losing focus on the overview (called **situational awareness**) can and does lead to tragedies. Dual focus isn't a desirable add-on, it's a sharp-edged performance essential. It's vital for flight crews to execute tasks accurately but it's also vital for them to remain alert to changes in their environment.

It's common for surgeons to face complications within an operation, or timing issues requiring careful rearrangement of their surgical list. Experienced surgeons have told me that as their decision-making abilities have developed in these areas, so has their execution. They make fewer errors when they make better decisions. If we are constantly updating our overview and continuously adjusting the specifics of the task we're doing, we are in a good place.

Dual focus is nothing more than an ordinary, everyday mental process – paying attention – but maintaining this focus under an extraordinary set of circumstances is another matter again. High performers do not have different mental apparatus when it comes to paying attention. Everyone can check the overview and focus on the task, in ordinary circumstances. Whether you're a surgeon, teacher, taxi driver or graphic artist, the trick is not letting your focus fall away into split attention when the pressure is on.

Under pressure, do you tend to get diverted into the RED and halve your mental efficiency, or do you do double time into the BLUE and accelerate with undivided attention?

Which are you more skilled at: the situational **overview** or the task **detail**? Would other people who know you well say that, under pressure, you are both **aware** and **accurate**?

Going APE vs Deciding to ACT

APE

Under pressure we all fail in predictable ways.

We've looked at how the same emergency reactions seen in animals – **fight, flight** or **freeze** – are triggered in modern-day performance situations, although usually more by social threats than physical danger. To help us translate them from the animal kingdom to our world of performance, let's modernise the behaviours by renaming them.

Rather than fight, think **aggressive**. Under pressure, people raise their voices, threaten, bully, confront, insult, reject and exclude.

Rather than flight, think **escape**. Under pressure, people remove themselves from the fray by being late or not turning up, taking sick leave, resigning, or getting sent off the sports field.

And rather than freeze, think **passive**. People who can't get out of a situation may not go completely immobile, but they go quiet and look down when volunteers are requested, always letting others go first and staying a step behind, just generally going through the motions.

For my money, the **passive** reaction is the invisible killer of performance. People can hide in plain sight by being present and operating at a minimum standard, doing just enough to avoid drawing attention to themselves as not contributing. It's a silent epidemic that can completely undermine a team dynamic.

Many team-sport athletes know this type of player: the one who is on the field but never really gets their hands dirty, and always seems to be one step off the pace. Large organisations are often full of people who say the right things but whose actions lack impact.

Sometimes the passive state can be misread as being relaxed: a basic but common error in the sports world. Unless we are an animal playing dead and hoping to escape, it is a poor performance state.

These three styles of behaviour, **aggressive**, **passive** and **escape** – **APE** – are the three most unhelpful reactions we have under pressure. They all arise from RED, high-arousal reactions; even the **passive** reaction, involving low arousal, follows an initial high-arousal spike. The APE acronym reminds us that we share these responses with most members of the animal kingdom – and they are most definitely within us all.

In our early years, we all develop a personal pattern that means one of these three becomes our default reaction to extreme pressure. Or it might be a combination of two, or all three. Passive–aggressive behaviour is a classic example.

Recognising our personal defensive behaviour style and how it hurts our performance will show us what traps to avoid in the future. If we take this step, we are already in a stronger position to perform under pressure.

> What APE pattern do you default to when you fall apart under pressure – A, P, E, or a deadly combination?

ACT

Under pressure we all succeed in predictable ways.

> Peter is a foreman leading an expensive new house build that is just three weeks out from the date when the owners expect to move in. His team is facing pressure on several fronts. The architect has identified a large area of plastering that will need to be redone. One of Peter's senior builders has had an accident onsite, which has triggered a health and safety investigation and left Peter short-handed. Plus, Peter's usual subcontracting electrician isn't available because of a family bereavement, and the replacement is not fitting in well with his team. On top of that, there's been an extended spell of poor weather.
>
> It would be very easy for Peter to fall into APE behaviours that block progress instead of moving his team forward. The pathway ahead, though, is clear.
>
> First, he needs to stay **aware** of his internal reactions, to limit any APE behaviours. It won't help for him to go deep RED right now!

Second, he needs to be *clear* about the proper process for the health and safety investigation, the repair timeline for the plasterers, and his expectations of the replacement electrician.

Third, he must stay on top of his crew and make sure that each *task* is finished calmly and efficiently, so that they get the house built on time.

This **aware–clear–task** sequence – or **ACT** – stands in contrast to the RED-fuelled APE reactions, which are characterised by *lack* of self-awareness, *lack* of clarity, and *off*-task behaviours. No matter how big the moment of pressure, we are well served by an ACT approach because it leads to specific actions that create movement.

ACT needs our BLUE mind to fire strongly. Because the BLUE mind is linear, it loves short sequences, so the three ACT steps are a good fit. (As we'll discover, the **RED–BLUE tool** is based on the very same sequence.)

To be **aware** requires us to step back and reflect, which is a core BLUE-brain activity. Once we have a good idea of our external situation and our personal reaction to it, we can ensure we're **clear** about what needs to be done first, and how to do it. Plenty of people start doing things without being **aware** and **clear,** and so the impact of their actions is diluted. There's a lot to be gained from a deliberate process of considering alternatives and consequences before deciding to act.

Once we've made our decision, we can carry out our **task** accurately. If we are aware and clear, there is no doubt or vagueness to divert us, and our actions will have impact.

BLUE-based ACT responses are based on a desire to function better *in* challenging situations, while RED-driven APE reactions are based on getting *out* of threatening situations.

When we are in the zone, we will already be in an ACT state of mind. But for the majority of our lives we need a simple set of steps to follow under pressure. The great thing is that by not concentrating on getting into the zone and just following the process, we are more likely to end up in the zone anyway.

The ACT sequence is intended for repeated use because most performances involve a series of separate challenges. **Aware** provides our personal overview of the situation. **Clear** gives us a strategy to put into action. And **task** gets us going.

Instead of reacting to pressure defensively with APE behaviours, we can use the ACT sequence to face the pressure, and find a way to adapt and move forward.

It wouldn't make sense to bury ourselves in the **task** without constantly reviewing our context and strategy. Every time we check on the context, we can adjust our strategy. Every time we adapt our strategy, we can adjust our actions. And every time we act, the context changes slightly, so we can circle back to the top. A key mental building block for performance under pressure is flexibility.

Choose a recent moment when you had to step up under pressure, and did. Can you recognise a moment when you put a stop to your APE behaviour, and got a grip on your reaction to the context (aware), formed a strategy (clear) and went to work with conviction (task)? If so, you've already intuitively discovered the ACT structure and applied it successfully.

ESC-APE vs IMP-ACT

ESC-APE

Some moments are just too big for us.

Sometimes, under pressure, we hit our threshold, and it's then that our damaging APE behaviours emerge.

Most pressure arises from our fear of possible judgment. And the key elements of judgment are **expectations, scrutiny** and **consequences** (**ESC**).

Before we perform, people are **expecting** us to reach a certain standard. *During* our performance, we are **scrutinised**, often publicly. And *afterwards*, the quality and outcome of our performance will have **consequences**.

Sometimes we will be affected by one element more than the others, but generally they work together as a tight, inescapable sequence. As the level of expectations, scrutiny and consequences rises, so does the pressure. And it works in the opposite direction: if expectations, scrutiny or consequences are reduced or taken away, pressure evaporates.

More expectations and scrutiny always mean bigger and wider-ranging consequences. These consequences extend beyond success and failure to include material outcomes such as salary increases and promotion. And these material outcomes are rocketed upwards by media reactions and – perhaps the ultimate judgment – the impact on our reputation. The higher the level we are operating at, the more we have to lose through consequences.

Not all moments are equal. Every elite performer has had moments that carried greater significance, when they failed to cope.

Most people, when they go to work or undertake an activity, are not looking for ESC. In fact, most people try to avoid judgment as much as possible. The less ESC there is, the more comfortable they are. This returns us to the idea that operating when we are uncomfortable is at the heart of performance under pressure.

The external origins of pressure – **ESC** – plus the most unhelpful behaviours under pressure – **APE** – create the **ESC-APE** model. There are some moments that carry too much pressure for us to bear because of the level of ESC, and this level of discomfort causes us to go APE. Rather than thinking clearly, we act impulsively out of emotional tension. We avoid the discomfort through **aggressive** or **passive** behaviours, or by **escaping** from the situation altogether.

Try applying the ESC-APE model to your personal performance history. If you're honest, looking back, which behaviours are you least proud of? Which behaviours have damaged your reputation the most? Can you recognise how expectations, scrutiny and consequences created pressure that affected your behaviour? Perhaps you stepped out onto a bigger 'performance stage' than normal, with a larger audience watching to see whether you could cope. But instead of performing at your best, you got loud, boisterous, and belligerent; or you cried off and said you were unwell when you really could have turned up; or you performed, but you were quiet and restrained and just never got going.

IMP-ACT

Newton's first law states that an object will remain in its current state of motion unless an external force acts on it to change its momentum. We humans are the same: we only move because of pressure. It's all about inertia, a resistance to change.

Most people need *external* pressure to move them. But there's a smaller group driven by pressure from *within* – and they're the ones who inevitably go further.

If *externally* driven people respond to pressure, it's because they're moved by expectations, scrutiny and consequences (ESC) from their employers and others. But what if we're *internally* driven?

Instead of someone else's expectations, we're driven by our own **intention**. Instead of being affected by someone else's scrutiny, we have a clear sense of where we are right now, in this **moment**. And instead of someone else's consequences, we are focused on our current **priority**. The mental recipe for internally driven people is **intention, moment, priority**, or **IMP**.

Start with the context: think of a current situation that's challenging you. First, in that situation, what is your **intention**? Look into the future and decide what outcome you want and the way you want to operate. How it will look and feel to close observers? Second, what is the reality in this **moment**? What is currently working well and what isn't? There's probably a gap between your intent and your current reality. Third, what is your **priority** for closing this gap and making progress towards the desired outcome? Be specific: what will your first step be?

If we are internally driven, we are far less affected by external pressure, because the drive from within is stronger. We are not immune to it, but it is less disturbing.

Performers who are externally driven also tend to identify *external* factors that are limiting their ability. This is more comfortable because it makes it not their fault. Internally driven performers tend to look at internal obstacles and see their primary opponent as themselves.

Being internally driven also *feels* different. Instead of feeling the weight of expectation coming down on us from the outside, we feel power flowing up from within. External pressure breaks us down, makes us shrink, and burdens us; internal drive builds us up, makes us grow, and energises us.

IMP sets us up to be far more resilient mentally in the face of external pressure. When we need external ESC pressure to move, we are vulnerable to RED aggressive, passive, escape (APE) reactions. The two go hand in hand, forming the unhelpful ESC-APE pathway that leads us to disengage under pressure. In contrast, the internal IMP factors tend to drive the BLUE aware, clear, task (ACT) responses, forming the constructive IMP-ACT structure, which keeps us engaged under pressure.

Instead of feeling or deciding that the moment is too big for us, which causes us to ESC-APE, we stand our ground and have IMP-ACT. Moderate performers are *pushed* along by others and tend to escape when the pressure comes on, while elite performers are *pulled* forward by their own ambitions.

But the acronyms ESC-APE and IMP-ACT represent more than words, because when we follow them, they lead to different biological responses. ESC-APE behaviours follow threat, setting off our RED mind. IMP-ACT is linked to challenge, which strongly activates our BLUE mind, especially our left pre-frontal cortex, a part of the brain stimulated by goal-setting and new learning.

Sophie and her teenage daughter Emily are exploring the capital city of a foreign country. Sophie, an experienced traveller, deliberately takes a back seat when it's time to head home from a day visiting various landmarks so that Emily has to work out how to get them there.

It's getting late and they are tired, so Sophie suggests to Emily that she can lead the way back to their hotel despite the different language (**expectation**), that Sophie will be watching her as she works out the way on public transport (**scrutiny**), and that they can't rest or stop for food until they get home (**consequences**).

It would be easy for Emily to go RED – become **aggressive** or **passive**, or **escape** (in a taxi) as quickly as possible. But she checks herself and decides to go down the BLUE IMP-ACT pathway.

First, she reminds herself of her **intention**, which is to demonstrate that she can be trusted to travel independently.

Second, she focuses on the **moment,** and sees that she has no idea where they are or the quickest route home, and has only a smattering of the local vocabulary to get them out of the situation. Third, she works out her **priority**, which she quickly sees is to get to the nearest underground metro station and find a transport map to work out a good route home.

Following these three steps allows Emily to move towards BLUE behaviours, remaining **aware** of her emotional tone, **clear** about what she needs to do, and ready to get on with her **task**. She takes the IMP-ACT pathway and comes across as composed, clear and collaborative.

In the same high-pressure moment, we have two alternatives: to ESC-APE the tension, or to have IMP-ACT *despite* the tension. That first step – refusing to step over the RED line into ESC-APE territory – is critical. Sometimes there is no coming back.

When we stand near the RED ESC-APE line we are at an emotional crossroads. If we decide to be drawn over the line, we need to be clear that *we* have allowed that to happen, not *blame* others and justify it with *excuses* – the ESC-APE artist's signatures.

If we make it *our* decision to step over it or not, rather than relinquishing the decision to the forces of pressure, we will be stronger mentally. We might not immediately get on top of the situation, but stepping over the line into BLUE IMP-ACT territory is a good start, because it ends our internal debate about whether to give in to the pressure. We have enough on our plate in this moment. It's not a time to overthink the situation, it's a time to take emotional control.

Riaz, a surgeon, is moving smoothly through an operation, but the cosmetic result at the end does not look neat. He feels disappointed, angry and tense as he imagines explaining it to the patient later, and in that moment he notices a junior assistant laughing with the anaesthetist. He feels on the verge of an aggressive outburst, but sees the RED ESC-APE line in his mind, takes back the control, and decides to have IMP-ACT. He takes a deep breath and closes up the final wound again with extra care.

Ari, a 17-year-old, is on an outdoor leadership course, and although he is very comfortable with the physical activities, he is having difficulty overcoming his social anxiety. The course leader asks for volunteers to lead the next task. Ari wants to raise his arm, but tension holds him back. He feels himself going passive, but sees the RED ESC-APE line in his mind and realises he is allowing himself to be dragged over it yet again. In that moment, he chooses to have IMP-ACT. He thrusts his arm up into the air and takes a step forward.

Refuse to mentally buckle. Instead, choose to have IMP-ACT.

When you look at your personal performance history, would you say you are more externally (ESC-APE) or internally (IMP-ACT) driven?

Are you reliant on your coach's stirring words before the game, or your chief executive's rousing speeches? Or do you become even more energised when things are not going to plan, drawn in by the challenge rather than discouraged by the obstacle?

Make sure your energy comes mostly from within, and draws you forward into the challenge.

Overload and Overwhelm vs Overview and Overcome

Overload and overwhelm

Right in the middle of the ESC-APE process, we can have an experience so destructive that without it, I would not be writing this book: **overwhelm**.

The state of overwhelm feels like a force overpowering us, a load so heavy we think we can't cope with the weight.

The heaviness comes from the burden of the external ESC pressure – the **expectations**, the **scrutiny** and the **consequences** of judgment. When those three aspects are rolled into one dense load, the situation becomes too much for us to bear. Our thinking, our feelings, in fact our whole perception becomes **overloaded**. And that mental overload pitches us into a state of **overwhelm**.

We all have a particular load that we can tolerate. It is not set in stone, and fluctuates with time. But the mental formula is always the same: when our current limit is reached, we become overloaded, then overwhelmed.

As well as overpowering us mentally, it feels like the external world of pressure is having a physical impact on us. Our posture changes, shrinking us down. We start to stoop, tense our jaw, hunch our shoulders, and bend at the knee, bracing ourselves against the invisible weight. Our breathing becomes shallow, our voice weak. We are a picture of tension, as if we're *really* carrying a heavy load on our shoulders.

At its most severe, overwhelm can be traumatic. We feel swamped, drowned, flooded, or even buried.

Overwhelm is an extremely difficult state of mind to exit. Feeling engulfed means that we have to mentally climb out of the gulf, the hole we've fallen into.

The pressure forces our attention onto the physical feelings inside us. The weight above us dominates our mind and body, trapping us inside the situation, so that the burden is all we can see. Our mental world shrinks down to focus exclusively on the immediate source of pressure, and this has ramifications – serious ones. It wouldn't matter so much if we weren't involved in a high-pressure moment – but we are, and that is the issue.

Imagine there's a mental arm wrestle going on inside us between RED and BLUE. The pressure reduces BLUE's power. We try to hold on, but BLUE suddenly caves in. Now, RED impulses can be released without the BLUE handbrake. As BLUE self-control is lost, we mentally give up and give way.

The part of our mind that provides situational awareness and controls our impulses – the BLUE part – is overpowered by our RED urges and impulses. Our personal brand of **aggressive**, **passive** and **escaping** behaviours is released, none of which actually helps us to deal with the constant, smothering pressure. We lose problem-solving capacity and devote all our mental energy to a dire internal battle for survival.

This helps explain why we can suddenly display unexpected behaviours under pressure. It means these 'unexpected' APE behaviours are, in fact, entirely predictable. We wouldn't expect our APE behaviours to show up every day, but in the world of pressure, the rules are different.

We cannot overestimate the potential psychological cost of this experience. It can leave emotional scars that may resurface later when that feeling of overload starts to kick in. Our RED system is on the lookout for these moments because they are so threatening.

Fortunately, though, overwhelm is not a permanent state. When the pressure subsides and we can get some physical or mental distance, life outside the cauldron of pressure re-emerges and the heavy feeling slowly subsides. As the physical part of the overwhelm experience reduces, our mental flexibility also returns.

Go back to those big ESC-APE moments you identified in the last section. If you can bear to, step back into one of those moments. Go back inside your body and mind to remember how they felt at the time – just as far as you want to. Mild discomfort is fine, no more than that.

Look at these moments again through the lens of the overload–overwhelm experience. Remember you can step out of the situation at any point. But if you can, notice how right at the centre of the overwhelm experience there was a specific moment when you started to lose perspective and felt suffocated. Overwhelm is a full mind–body experience, not a detached mental process.

Becoming familiar with the state of overwhelm is a wonderful building block for performance under pressure, because it builds humility. No one is immune.

If we learn to respect overwhelm, we will have taken another important step forward in our pursuit of performance under pressure.

Overview and overcome

When we feel trapped under pressure and struggling, changing the way that we mentally picture the situation can prevent us from being a mental captive and give us a mental release.

Visualise Laura, a paramedic, arriving at the scene of an accident in which a truck has collided with a car. She's confronted by a scenario that goes beyond anything she's seen in her career so far. There are multiple young victims, there are fatalities, and there are complicated additional risks because of fuel leakage and power-line damage. The sheer tragedy and complexity are overloading her RED and BLUE minds. She feels herself slow down and go quiet and numb. The situation seems bigger than she is, she's surrounded by problems with no way out, and it feels like a weight is coming down on top of her. In that moment, her mind is dominated by overwhelm and she's a psychological prisoner.

She pictures herself underneath the pressure, which is much bigger than she is. She can't see past it to the outside world, so it keeps her trapped inside the situation.

Then she makes a decision to mentally step back *outside* the situation, seeing herself looking down on it from above. Now she's *outside* the pressure, it's seems as though she's bigger and the pressure has shrunk.

She immediately feels the tension release and the weight lift. She quickly comes to her senses and starts hearing and seeing things she didn't notice before. She's able to survey the scene more objectively and grasp the bigger picture. She can see her surrounding environment – the leaking fuel, the power lines, the victims, the gathering crowd, other emergency services on their way to assist. She can see the technical details that she has to attend to first to make the situation safe, and then a way to attend to the multiple victims. Mentally, she's on the move again.

The critical thing is to take a decisive **step back** in our mind. This gives us the mental and emotional breathing space that we need to regain some perspective and free ourselves up for action. Rather than the situation mastering *us*, *we* now become the master of the situation.

When we're *inside* the threatening pressure situation and our RED system is in overdrive, it reduces access to our memories of how we've handled similar situations in the past. It works in the here and now, putting us in direct contact with the pressure. A flood of stimuli overloads and overwhelms our senses, triggering a massive physical rush that tips us over into a momentary freeze.

As we mentally step back or out, we force our BLUE system into service, calling on our left-brain abilities of reflection, goal-setting and logical analysis. Activating our BLUE mind helps dampen some of our RED overdrive, and allows our BLUE working memory capacity to increase and our mental screen to clear. We can start looking at the situation from different angles, regain the **overview** and **overcome** the challenge.

This mental manoeuvre – stepping back outside the situation – is deceptively simple but powerful, because it takes an abstract concept like pressure and gives it a location in physical space. We can either stay *inside* or *underneath* the situation, or move *outside* it or *on top* of it looking down.

The remedy to **overload** is the **overview** – stepping back or out to see the bigger picture and removing the mental load. Once we have the overview, we can see our options and make decisions that will allow us to **overcome** the situation, instead of heading in a downward spiral to overwhelm. As the **overload–overwhelm** partners in crime are replaced by the **overview–overcome** performance companions, the threat changes to a captivating challenge.

Think of a recent situation when you felt mentally trapped but recovered to perform well. Recollect the picture you had in your mind at the time. Did you feel you were inside or underneath the pressure, or were you outside or looking down? And did you notice a change in your mental picture that coincided with a shift in your performance?

You'll never be able to avoid pressure, but you can always change the way you picture your relationship with it.

Under pressure, do you tend to get stuck underneath or inside the situation, or do you get moving mentally so you can get moving in the real world?

Fixation vs Flexibility

Fixation: Worry and regret

'Stop worrying!'

If we're prone to worry, this kind of advice is not only unhelpful, it's also infuriating. It flippantly implies we can just switch off the worry loop, cold. Which is not how it works. And that's the problem: worrying is the last thing we want, but we just can't seem to stop it. Being told not to worry is like telling the tide to stop coming in. We don't need other people to point out that worrying is futile, because we know that as well as anyone. But try as we might to focus on the now, our mind remains stuck on possible trouble *ahead of* us. Our attention is sucked into the *future.*

Regret is in the same category. We've all done things we don't look back on with fondness. We might feel remorseful. And we might have a sense of loss connected with this regret, perhaps even bitterness and grief. We can't change what has happened, and we understand regret is often a pointless activity, but try as we might to focus on the now, our mind remains stuck on the trouble *behind* us. Our attention is sucked into the *past.*

Regret and worry are negative content loops that get us nowhere, dragging our precious attention out of the present moment. They are unwanted thoughts that seem to force their way into our mind, and take away valuable mental grunt that we could have put to good use to actually solve the problem. We become distracted, preoccupied and troubled. A worry or regret loop in the middle of a performance is especially troubling if we need to be alert and react quickly.

So why don't we just stop them?

First of all, it's worth saying that some worrying can be *helpful*, because it keeps us on our toes. Many people worry even though they know that things usually work out in the end.

But worrying becomes an issue when we can't let things go, and they start to cause us distress and interfere with our performance.

The crux of the problem is being unable to accept a particular outcome – losing, making a mistake, failing an exam – which **fixates** our attention. Our RED mind is doing its job well, because it won't let us ignore the threat. It's trying to look after us. But under pressure, becoming too fixated on an outcome is a big problem.

If we can't face the various outcomes of what we are about to do (**worry**) or have already done (**regret**), we set ourselves up for divided attention through a negative content loop, taking our focus out of the moment. Our RED mind, primed to see threat, will home in on our unwanted outcome and highlight this for us. It might make itself known as a negative voice telling us to watch out for the obstacle, or as a dark premonition – but it will send its message one way or another.

> Kim is in the final stage of a big match. His team is behind and making mistakes. The clock and the scoreboard are drawing his attention away from the game and onto the outcome. He rushes at the very time when he needs composure, and he has less attention on the present moment at the very time when he needs more. His attention becomes *fixated* on the final score, he starts to worry, he loses his rhythm, and his team loses the game.

Things rarely go smoothly in high-pressure situations. Worry and regret are traps, **fixating** our mind on disturbing thoughts. No one else is forcing us to think this way.

Think back to the biggest regrets or worries in your own performance history – moments when you had a very clear idea about how you wanted things to turn out, but they did not go to plan. Can you see the conflict between the ideal and the real, the fantasy and the reality? And did that gap energise you and pick you up, or burden you and bring you down?

In those moments, to what extent did you fall for the regret and worry traps?

Flexibility: Learn, don't judge

The remedy for the regret and worry loops is to be interested in results, but not tied to them.

The secret lies in the mental clash between what's ideal and what's real. *Regret* is the gap between what we *wanted* to happen and what *actually* happened. *Worry* is the gap between what we *want* to happen and what will *probably* happen. In both cases, an ideal outcome in our mind conflicts with reality – and we struggle to accept it.

How can we avoid this internal conflict? It can only occur if we are mentally attached to the image of an ideal outcome in the first place. That's not to say that it isn't useful to have an idea of what ideal performance looks like, because it is. It's more about the level of attachment we have to that idea when it doesn't eventuate. If we can't face anything short of the ideal, then we are sentencing ourselves to constant worry and regret.

The solution is to stop *avoiding* the painful feelings linked to loss and disappointment, and *walk towards* them instead. Avoiding reality stops us from learning and getting better, and will only bring us more pain sooner or later.

If we *face* the painful outcome, our RED mind won't have a threat to get fired up about in the first place. And that means removing the judgment.

The place to start is with ourselves, because if we are vulnerable to judgment from others, the chances are we are even harder on ourselves. It's easy to underestimate how much disapproval, criticism and scolding we put ourselves through.

Remember our golfer from earlier, hoping to win his first big golf tournament? The commentators can't help but talk about how this is a defining moment for the golfer, but let's examine that line of thought. Is he *really* going to be a different person as a result of whether or not a small, round, white ball falls into a hole in the grass?

If we closely identify *who* we are with *how successful* we are, then the more the outcome is at risk, the more our identity is at risk too. Instead of being someone who happens to win or lose, we become a winner or a loser. Our core self is now under constant threat.

Most athletes see what I mean immediately when I explain this to them – but they usually acknowledge that they set themselves up in much the same way, defining the outcome of a sports event as important to their identity. 'If I do this, it means I am *this*; if I don't do it, it means I am *that*.' They might even see it as essential to their success, because without the drive to win, they would lose their drive to perform. *Not* to focus on winning would mean to be *indifferent* to winning – an attitude that has no place in their mindset.

But *indifference* is not the alternative to winning or losing. To free ourselves of this kind of **fixation** on the outcome, we need to adopt a mindset of mental **flexibility** in the moment. Our focus should be on *learning* from our performance instead of judging it. No matter what the outcome, every action provides valuable information. Curiosity replaces judgment. We are mentally free, because we've faced the situation and tried to find a way, rather than becoming defensive through fighting, fleeing or freezing.

Of course, being flexible about the outcome doesn't mean that we don't care about what happens. We should still aim to perform in a committed, effective way. It's just that we should also aim to reflect on our performance later so that we can learn and improve.

If the golfer's RED mind alerts him to negative outcomes and he becomes **fixated** on them, he's buying into the judgment trap, which could set off a negative content loop. At that point he's no longer performing, he's thinking. Much better for him to get back into his performance, then reflect on the process afterwards to improve his understanding of what went wrong in that moment. Judging prevents learning – he won't be in a good position to understand the situation *objectively* if he's *subjectively* judging it.

Confusing the time to perform with the time to learn is not a good formula for performance. We need to commit totally to perform in the moment, then learn from it afterwards. Judgment fires up our RED mind, but learning activates our BLUE mind.

Once we've completed our performance, we can ask ourselves questions about what interfered with it. No one else has to hear these questions, but they help us keep learning and avoiding the judgment trap. Top performers ask top questions. (We'll look at this in Chapter 12.)

If we feel we have nothing more to learn, we lose our inquisitiveness and become closed-minded. Zen philosophy speaks of 'beginner's mind', in which we focus on learning and assume that others will know things we don't, which leads to humility. In contrast, in the expert's mind there is a focus on demonstrating expertise and already having all the answers, which leads to a defensive ego. The beginner's mind is curious and interested, and therefore sees new possibilities; the expert's mind is judgmental, resistant and closed, and therefore sees few alternative possibilities.

The open mind is seen as more advanced than the closed mind because it requires more mental strength and security not to feel a need to demonstrate our knowledge to others. With less need to impress, we are more open to learn.

> Under pressure, do you tend to show a beginner's or an expert's mindset?

Hot-Headed vs Cold-Blooded

RED hot-headedness

Think of our level of RED arousal in terms of emotional temperature.

I use the word RED to describe a mental state in which our emotional temperature is too high or too low and out of balance with BLUE. RED is also the colour most associated with physical heat in many cultures. And when we experience a RED emotional state we will actually feel *physically* hot. Our language preserves this insight in everyday phrases: 'hot under the collar', 'hot and bothered', 'hot air'.

So where does this sensation come from? The world of pressure is a world of judgment, and judgment hurts emotionally. The natural reaction to physical or emotional pain is anger, usually described as a hot feeling starting low down in our legs or pelvic region, and rising like a flash up through our core to our head and arms. The feeling of anger has an energising impact, powering us to stand up and look after ourselves. It takes care of us.

But anger can overrun us and take us into survival mode when it is not required. When that happens, our emotional reaction interferes with clear thinking and there's a risk of 'hot-headed' behaviour, which is impulsive and rash. We will become fixated on a threat, lose situational awareness and develop clouded judgment.

Though our RED system can be a source of great energy, our emotional thermostat can also overheat and blow a fuse. Onlookers can see that we will regret our hot-headed behaviour when our anger subsides, because there is no way we would have acted that way in more rational moments.

How well our emotional thermostat works – what temperature it can handle and how efficiently it regulates spikes – was set in our infancy and is now imprinted deep in our unconscious memory. So our RED reactions are not just driven by the immediate challenge but also have long roots, fuelled by buried memories that carry similar emotions. That's why our strong reaction to a relatively minor issue today can seem out of keeping with the situation.

Our thermostat operates unconsciously in every new situation we enter, and when we are performing under pressure, it becomes crucial to our emotional self-control.

Hot-headed behaviour is usually short-lived but damaging. If we have a reputation for hot-headedness, people will see us as reactive, unreliable and unpredictable, which suits few performance scenarios.

When we are hot-headed, our RED reaction causes large physical movements and coarse mental judgments. Perspective and precision give way to tunnel vision and exaggeration. The rising heat disturbs our clarity of thought and we find ourselves mentally and physically compromised for anything other than emergency situations.

Even in performance situations that require aggression, uncontrolled and unregulated anger is dangerous, because if the emotion is not matched and contained by clear thinking, we will trip up and cause problems for ourselves or someone else sooner rather than later.

Would people who know you well sometimes describe you as hot-headed? At those times your ability to think clearly under pressure is compromised: a significant handicap for yourself and those around you. If you have hot-headed moments, in those moments you failed to perform under pressure.

BLUE cold-bloodedness

So how do we corral the drive of our RED system into useful service, and avoid the hazards involved in losing control?

The good news is that being in the BLUE can mean being as forceful, powerful and aggressive as being in the RED. If we operate in a performance domain in which aggression and physicality are valuable behaviours, it is a mistake to limit our view of BLUE to being a gentle, benign, relaxed state of mind.

Let's look at an extreme form of human behaviour – violence – to understand why BLUE can be associated with intense, driven states of mind. In early forensic psychiatry, violence was said to come in two forms, equating to emotional and rational states of mind. In emotional violence, the individual has uncontrolled emotions – perhaps rage triggered by disrespect – that drive reactive, unsophisticated aggression. In rational violence, the aggressor is triggered by a desire to do whatever is necessary to get what they want, and there is a more controlled, deliberate quality to their behaviour. Some of these individuals are called psychopaths.

In RED–BLUE terms, emotional violence is RED or hot-headed, and rational violence is BLUE or cold-blooded.

Which one should concern us more? RED violence occurs only when the emotion overwhelms the individual's senses. It comes straight at us, and is crude and obvious. BLUE violence is often hidden or hard to spot, and is more controlled and devious. We can never rest easily around individuals with a tendency to

BLUE violence, because they remain dangerous even when they are not emotionally driven. Indeed, they pose such a risk because they don't feel the emotions that others feel and so have less empathy for their victims.

Hot-headed surges of aggression can be daunting but they are one-dimensional and easy to spot, and often lack accuracy. Cold-blooded individuals are more chilling.

I am not suggesting for a moment that we want to migrate violent behaviour into our performance domain – but forensic insights about extreme human behaviour can provide some clues for performance.

What does it mean to be hot-headed versus cold-blooded in a performance environment? If our performance needs an aggressive component (and this is within the rules!), then being more cold-blooded can provide an edge.

Rather than relying on RED emotion to carry us through, it might help to add the steely clarity of BLUE. Controlled accuracy beats impulsive roughness. Would we rather face a hot-headed or a cold-blooded boxer?

Nature provides similar lessons. A cold-blooded wolf pack is coordinated and cohesive. If the pack becomes impatient or hot-blooded, its effectiveness can vanish. The pack needs a *combination* of RED and BLUE to be at its most lethal.

RED passion, presence and power can help get the job done in many pursuits, but overstep the mark with too much RED and we can come across as roused, reckless and rash.

Most performance pursuits require heart *and* head, RED *and* BLUE. Viewing BLUE solely as a relaxed and laid-back state of mind is a mistake. Goal-driven behaviour is tightly connected with our left frontal lobes, the centre of our BLUE mind. RED might give us an energy boost in the short term, but for longer-term commitment, RED–BLUE balance is critical.

Consider the words that fit best for the helpful RED emotional element in your field of performance: do you look for passion, presence or power? Now consider what too much RED looks like in your field. Next, name the BLUE rational component that will combine with RED to give you the best of both worlds – do you need anticipation, agility or accuracy?

Would you benefit from adding some BLUE steel to your RED furnace?

Threshold and Resilience

When we hit our limit under pressure, our fall can be dramatic. We call this limit our mental **threshold,** the level of pressure at which we lose our capacity to remain functional. Our threshold is the moment when our RED mind – previously regulated by BLUE control – starts to over-dominate, and unwanted, irrational and impulsive behaviours take over. What everyone else sees is the erratic fight-or-flight behaviour when we get too aroused, or the flat, passive freeze response when our arousal is too low.

Every individual has a different threshold – some people can tolerate much more emotional discomfort than others. And our personal threshold fluctuates all the time, because it is affected by fatigue, our mindset, the state of our relationships, and a long list of other factors that take their emotional toll.

Anything outside our performance that drains us emotionally can lower our threshold. This could be a major life event such as a change in our relationship, job, living arrangements or physical health. Or it could be doing something else that's demanding right before we perform. If we deplete our energy reserves before we even step out to perform, we shouldn't be surprised if our threshold is lower than usual.

But just because we hit our threshold and start to mentally unravel doesn't mean that it's a one-way street. We can mentally wobble but not fold. Somehow we struggle through the difficult patch, reverse the negative process and regain mental control.

We can call this ability our mental **resilience**. It relates to our ability to tolerate emotional distress, and, if we *do* descend into unhelpful behaviours, the time it takes to regain control.

We can bend, but we don't have to break.

We can all remember days when we were trying our best but we were confronted by a series of obstacles and suddenly found ourselves launching in (**aggressive**), storming out (**passive**), or giving up (**escape**). We hit our threshold and lost effectiveness. And we will also recall days when we seemed to be able to carry on while those around us floundered.

One interesting aspect of the RED–BLUE story is that what we might think is our threshold actually *isn't*; we are probably capable of more. When it comes to discomfort, our mind gives up before our body.

This is common knowledge in military circles, and is put to use in selection courses, where candidates face a series of gruelling physical tasks that gradually take their toll mentally. Although experience shows that many candidates could cope with more, many decide to give up. That means they could also decide to stick in there. It is in that moment that they either meet their threshold and give up, or show resilience and move past it. That people can go further is demonstrated by extraordinary survival stories, in which people somehow struggle through unimaginable journeys to save their own lives following accidents in the wilderness.

If we want to reach the top of our profession or pursuit, our threshold and resilience are likely to be crucial. If we can tolerate more than the rest, or the same amount for longer, then our resilience will take us to places others cannot reach. That might mean taking on more difficult cases as a medical specialist, rising up to lead a sports team when those around us begin to buckle, or remaining clear-thinking in combat when others go cloudy. In all of these scenarios, the individuals still experience discomfort, but rise up despite, or even because of it.

In my experience, people are surprised when they suddenly grasp that everything they've invested time and effort in in the name of performance was about making themselves feel more comfortable. The most common request I get is for techniques to *take away* anxiety and tension. It comes as a revelation when I suggest that it's not about trying to *reduce* the level of discomfort but about learning to *face* it. For those used to pursuing the comfortable life, walking towards discomfort (running is too scary) opens up a new world.

When we appreciate the power of being more **comfortable being uncomfortable** than others, we actually become *energised* by the challenge of discomfort.

Adopting an approach of walking *towards* the pressure – embracing it – does not mean that we like the pain and stress, just that we appreciate that pain and stress will definitely stop other people – which will allow *us* to be the one who remains standing. We can understand how our threshold and resilience change dynamically in different situations by revisiting the **face and find, fight–flight,** and **freeze** reactions introduced in Chapter 2. The three reactions can be understood as a **Mental strength sliding scale,** which describes our reactions to pressure situations.

For our purposes, Level 3 is occupied by the **face and find** reaction, Level 2 by the **fight–flight** reaction, and Level 1 by the **freeze** reaction. We can achieve constructive Level 3 reactions when – despite the discomfort – we still feel safe enough to face the challenge and find a way through it, remaining aware, clear and on task (IMP-ACT). If the challenge becomes too threatening, we become defensive and try to get out of the

MENTAL STRENGTH SLIDING SCALE

CLEAR THINKING
Overview / Overcome

TRUST

3 FACE–FIND

Free

Challenge

2 FIGHT–FLIGHT

Aggressive-Escape

Threat

1 FREEZE

Passive

Trapped

FEAR

DEFENSIVE THINKING
Overload / Overwhelm

The Mental strength sliding scale gives us a sense of how we are reacting to a situation.

situation, either by becoming aggressive or trying to escape. And if we feel trapped, we freeze and become passive, shutting down any constructive behaviour.

We all move up and down the Mental strength sliding scale, depending on our threshold and resilience. Seeing this simple scale in our minds can help us to recognise our own reactions to pressure and discomfort and the extent to which we are remaining constructive and engaged, or becoming defensive.

Using the **Mental strength sliding scale**, reflect on the last three occasions when you faced significant pressure. At what level did you manage to operate? Did you remain engaged, positive and productive, or did you slip down the scale and start to become defensive or even passive?

RED and BLUE: Lessons from Children

A sweet insight

In the United States in the early 1970s, Professor Walter Mischel carried out a now well-known psychological experiment using a shrewd design. Today we know it as the Marshmallow Test.

Four-year-old children were asked to sit at a table in a barren room. Each of them had a marshmallow on a plate in front of them. They were told they could either eat the marshmallow now, or they could wait and be rewarded with a second marshmallow. What the children didn't know was that they would have to wait 15 minutes: an eternity for a child of that age facing temptation.

This set up a mental struggle within each child between their hot RED emotional system, which wanted to eat the sweet straightaway, and their cool BLUE thinking system, which tried to delay instant gratification in favour of a bigger goal. Would BLUE control be able to inhibit RED craving? Which was stronger?

The children either ate the treat immediately, tried to wait but quickly gave in, or stuck it out for the full 15 minutes. And later studies – including other ones that followed groups of children into adulthood – revealed interesting outcomes. In the long term, young children who had shown better 'executive control' by holding out for 15 minutes in the test (or by equivalent measures) had, overall, better physical health and better academic and work histories.

Psychologists also discovered that, rather than being a fixed ability, emotional regulation could be developed as a skill. When they tracked the Marshmallow Test children over time, they found that the children tended to continue with their original behavioural tendencies. But with simple interventions – such as distraction techniques – the researchers could increase a child's capacity to cope with the emotional struggle.

One approach was particularly symbolic. Children were invited to imagine the treat wasn't real but a picture with a frame around it, which seemed to cool their desire and increase their ability to place their attention elsewhere. Children who had been unable to resist the temptation became able to delay reaching for the reward for 15 minutes. The researchers said this was due to the children being able to use their imagination to step back from the treat, which reduced their sweet craving. Learning the skill was immediate – not a lengthy, complicated procedure. The key was the 'step back' component to get some mental distance from the source of their discomfort.

For parents, the message is this learnt: few things are more important for our children than the gift of emotional self-control, which can be taught.

For the rest of us, the message is equally clear: if stepping back out of the RED is a concrete skill that young children can learn, then we too can learn it.

What a sweet insight.

Finding our 'purple patch'

Several years ago, I gave a 20-minute talk to a primary-school class about RED and BLUE. Afterwards I received a pile of suspiciously similar thank-you letters from the pupils. But one stood out, because it was quite different.

This particular ten-year-old girl told me how, on the evening of the talk, she'd been invited to a party where she knew she would encounter some children who'd been bullying her. She described how she had decided not to go, but realised that she had put herself into the RED. So she put herself back into the BLUE head, went along, and faced up to the bullies. She added that she would like to promise me she would be 100% BLUE for the rest of her life, but, thinking about it, decided she would probably be mainly **'in the purple'**!

As children occasionally do, her account cut through adult clutter to uncover deeper insights.

First, there was no mention of blaming the situation, or other people. She simply saw her RED reaction and changed her behaviour. It was *her* mind, and if she was in the RED then she must have put herself there. Which also meant that she could move herself back out of RED and into the BLUE. Her mind, her responsibility. What could be simpler?

Second, there were no complaints about how hard it was to move from RED to BLUE. All she needed was the picture in her mind of the RED and BLUE states and she moved *herself*. We adults overthink and complain, because we want others to do it all for us. Age has given us language to talk our way out of actually having to do it for ourselves. While adults trail behind, drowning beneath blame and excuses, children just get on with it.

Third, the young girl showed sophisticated insight in accepting that life is complicated, and that in the majority of situations she would experience a mixture of RED and BLUE – hence she'd usually be in the purple. This absolute gem of an idea caused me to change the way I present my RED–BLUE mind model.

But rather than regarding purple as a compromise – which was how the ten-year-old saw it – we can instead see purple as our ideal mental state. For performance under pressure, we require both the energy of RED and the clarity of BLUE to reach our potential. We need to operate out of our mental **purple patch**.

At the biological level, this means that our RED limbic system is active but under control, and our BLUE rational system is providing a beneficial feedback loop. Despite a degree of discomfort, our emotional system is regulated. Our RED and BLUE mental circuits are in sync.

We traditionally associate the colour purple with respect and achievement: royalty, clergy, academia and the military all wear purple robes and medals. Likewise, purple can be symbolic of *mental* achievement under pressure.

This ten-year-old girl captured the essence of the RED–BLUE mind model. When we're faced with life's tricky problems, it's often our mental approach that blocks the way forward. Children remind us of the spirit of high mental performance: simplicity and learning by doing.

If a ten-year-old can hear a 20-minute talk about RED and BLUE then immediately apply it to a tricky bullying situation, then adults have no excuse. If we find the suggestions in this chapter too complicated to use, it's because we've chosen to make them that way.

Under pressure, do you think you can tell whether you're too RED or BLUE, and adjust your state of mind and behaviour by finding your mental purple patch? If you're inclined to start complaining that it's too complicated, or making excuses and casting blame on others, pause for reflection.

Even if you don't like to admit it, your answer must be 'Yes', because a ten-year-old did it with ease.

SUMMARY OF CHAPTER 3 CONCEPTS

Context	RED–BLUE Out of Balance	RED–BLUE in Balance
Perception	Threat	Challenge
Mental activity	Overthinking	Connecting
Attention	Split attention	Dual focus
Behaviours	Aggressive–passive–escape (APE)	Aware–clear–task (ACT)
Pressure source	Expectations–scrutiny–consequences (ESC)	Intention–moment–priority (IMP)
Experience	Overload and overwhelm	Overview and overcome
Mental movement	Fixation	Flexibility
Performance attitude	Worry and regret	Curiosity and interest
Time frame	Past or future	Here and now
Relationship to pressure	Mentally captive	Mentally free
RED–BLUE connection	Caught in two minds	Single-minded
Mindset	Judgment	Movement
Quality of actions	Hesitant/impulsive	Decisive/incisive

CHAPTER 4

THE RED-BLUE TOOL

If we're not mentally prepared for pressure, we're vulnerable. We'll either restrict ourselves to performing only when conditions are favourable, or we'll be playing a dangerous game. To perform well under pressure, it's essential to have the right mental techniques.

In this chapter I'll take the principles of RED–BLUE balance and translate them into a practical tool that will place us in a good mental space to perform. I've also included breathing routines and exercises to refine our use of the RED–BLUE tool.

Later in the book we'll look at other techniques we can use *before* we perform (to strengthen how we use the RED–BLUE tool), and *after* we perform (to help us return to normal). They'll be just as relevant whether we're usually faced with chronic stress or with acute moments of pressure.

You don't have to use all of the techniques, all the time. You'll probably find that the core RED–BLUE tool plus one or two other techniques will suit you and your situation best.

If you arranged the RED–BLUE tool and the related techniques along a timeline, it would look like this:

Name of Technique	When to Use
Mental blueprint	*Preparing* to perform (or *reviewing* our performance – mental blueprint with a twist)
Three circles	*Days before* we perform
ICE	*Days or minutes before* we perform
RED–BLUE	*While* we perform
Offload	*After* we perform

Let's start where the action is – in the middle of our performance – by looking at the RED–BLUE tool. Then we'll be in a position to consider how to prepare for performance, and also how to review and learn from it, and wind down after it's over.

The RED-BLUE Tool

RED or BLUE? Decide. Do!

This is a three-step tool that we can use to develop stronger emotional self-control and to feel and think clearly under pressure.

Anna is a secondary-school teacher facing a struggle as she tries to get her class to pay attention. The school has a culture of poor discipline, the class has been difficult and rowdy all lesson, and to top it all off, Anna received some difficult news about her mum's health this morning. Now, a student has made a rude comment about her behind her back. She feels a flash of anger rise up, and she feels the urge to react verbally to the student and the class in general.

Three things will help Anna in this moment. First, she has to recognise her volatile emotional state and get it under control, otherwise she'll say something that she later regrets. Second, she needs a fresh perspective, because if she sticks with the same combative attitude, conflict will occur sooner or later. Third, she has to re-engage with the class, but in a more effective way, or the lesson will be unsuccessful. Take away any one of these steps and her performance as a teacher will fall away. This is performance under pressure.

How can Anna do all of this? By silently talking herself through the three steps of the RED–BLUE tool.

RED–BLUE TOOL

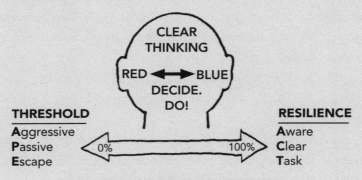

The RED–BLUE tool leads to emotional control, clear thinking and effective action.

Step 1: 'RED or BLUE?' – Anna mentally steps back and pictures a line that is RED at the left end and BLUE at the right end. She asks herself the question: 'RED or BLUE?' To answer this, she needs to locate her emotional state on the line. Is she in the RED half, the BLUE half, or the middle? She silently names her reaction 'RED', and immediately points herself back mentally towards the middle of the line. She doesn't want to lose her RED drive and energy, but she does need more BLUE clarity right now. Immediately she feels more in control of her reaction. She has completed Step 1 in 10 seconds.

Step 2: 'Decide' – Anna visualises a small RED frame fitting tightly around her and the class. She says to herself: 'Decide.' She sees the frame expand to become a much bigger BLUE frame containing new information. Different angles spring into view. She knows the rude student has a tough home life; the tough news about her mum's health has put her on edge, which is not the class's fault; and she suddenly remembers a complaint made against her because of a previous incident in class. Better information, allowing better decision-making: another verbal outburst is not a good idea! Instead, Anna decides to *disengage* from the battle with the student and *engage* the whole class. She has completed Step 2 in ten seconds.

Step 3: 'Do!' – Anna silently instructs herself: 'Do!' She walks to the front of the class and addresses the students in an even voice, setting out the purpose of the lesson, the time remaining, and her expectations about the tasks she wants the students to complete in that time. She emphasises that they'll need to conduct themselves in a respectful manner. She has completed Step 3 in 10 seconds.

- **Step 1: 'RED or BLUE?'** – mentally step back, see the RED–BLUE line and where you currently sit on it, and point yourself in the right direction.
- **Step 2: 'Decide'** – frame the scene, zoom out, see the bigger picture and decide on a more effective response.
- **Step 3: 'Do!'** – mentally re-engage and step into the situation, paying attention so you can take effective action.

All up, the RED–BLUE tool took Anna 30 seconds to complete. She simply took it one step at a time, and in no time at all she had completed the three steps. She stopped overthinking and overreacting and got back on task, avoiding the unsavoury pathway she was headed down.

The three steps helped her avoid three major mental performance traps. The first step of naming and recognising her mental state avoided an ill-judged, emotional response. The second step of reframing the situation helped her avoid getting tunnel vision, or being caught in two minds. The third step of resetting and the transition into action helped her avoid becoming stuck and wasting time.

The first step is crucial, because if we lose emotional control, the next two steps become impossible to do well. The decisiveness of our first step will depend on where we are on the RED–BLUE spectrum. If we feel like we're under control emotionally but can feel the pressure mounting, our mental task is to hold our nerve. If we feel like we've already lost control and are slipping deeper into the RED, our mental task is to get a grip.

The final step – a commitment to act with conviction – focuses us on the quality of our external behaviour and gets us moving. We can add detail to the decision through the second step, but it's vital that we don't stall. Instead of being hesitant and trying to *convince* ourselves we can do something, we need to jump straight to decisive action.

We can act with conviction no matter how we're feeling. And once we get moving, the external picture changes quickly and our feelings soon follow. In this context, 'Fake it until you make it' is good advice.

Positive action is much more powerful than positive thinking at clearing our head. We've seen that RED cannot be switched off in the face of threat, and trying to ignore it with simplistic BLUE thinking just gives it more fuel. Looking in depth at our own mental processes is also unhelpful, because it diverts us from our external task. It's time for performance, not therapy.

Instead of trying to think ourselves into feeling something we don't, we need to skip to action and get on with it.

Lucia is a musician about to play a solo at a major public event. She is playing with the orchestra but she can see her solo looming and can feel her confidence waning. She recalls a clumsy mistake she made during her last solo. Worry about repeating the error fills her head, a signal that she is at a RED turning point.

But she's anticipated this moment of doubt. This isn't the time to try to convince herself with positive thinking. Instead, she uses the RED–BLUE tool to *decide* and *do*, refocusing on her physical connection and feel for her instrument. She bypasses her temporary worry and loss of confidence and skips straight to acting with conviction. She once again becomes single-minded, and as her solo begins, her confidence comes flooding back.

We can use the RED–BLUE tool at any time, in any place. Because it is a silent mental tool, we don't need to feel self-conscious. Even in front of crowds, no one can see what we are thinking.

The RED–BLUE tool leaves us in control, because it doesn't tell us what to do. It just returns us to a good mental space by allowing better emotional control, better information, and better actions. It can't guarantee a successful outcome, but no tool can do that. It simply provides us with what we need in the moment. In a nutshell, it gives us clear thinking under pressure.

So when should we use the RED–BLUE tool? First, when we notice we're physically tense or mentally stressed and our emotional temperature is too high (too RED). Second, when we notice we're slow or passive and our emotional temperature is too low (too BLUE). We can use it as often as we like – we can never have too much emotional regulation. Whenever we feel like we are acting too fast without perspective, or too slowly without commitment, the time is right.

We can also use the RED–BLUE tool to prevent a slow build-up of emotional tension by running regular checks on our mental state during the day. A good habit to develop is to do a RED–BLUE check every time we move from one task to another, or from one work space to another. Multiple brief RED–BLUE emotional checks and adjustments will raise our emotional awareness and reduce the emotional burden we carry through our day, making emotional spikes much less likely.

Even if we operate in an environment where things move fast and we don't have time for the three steps, using the first 'RED or BLUE?' step can instantly clear our head enough to prevent rash actions when we feel overloaded and overwhelmed. When we are familiar with the tool, our unconscious mind can run the process for us as long as we kick it off.

Think of a recent stressful situation, either personal or professional, when you acted in an unhelpful way. Imagine the situation around you as you saw it at the time. Go back inside your body and mind as they felt at the time – just as far as you want to. You want to remember the situation, not re-experience it.

Compare how the same situation might have worked out if you'd followed the three RED–BLUE steps.

First, mentally step back from the situation to locate your position on the RED–BLUE spectrum and rename it silently: **RED or BLUE?** Did you show any unhelpful APE behaviours? If you'd used the RED–BLUE tool, you could have caught yourself losing emotional control and pointed yourself back to a RED–BLUE balance.

Second, remind yourself of the way you perceived the situation at the time. Imagine actively expanding the imaginary frame around you to get more of an overview – what angles re-emerge? How might that have changed your decision-making about the best course of action at the time?

Third, reflect on your actions at the time. What decisive first step could you have taken with that clearer overview in mind?

Can you see how the outcome rested to a large extent on your mental sharpness under stress?

When we become skilful at using the RED–BLUE tool, the three-step routine can make us feel energised by challenges rather than burdened by obstacles, allowing us to move toward and through uncomfortable situations with composure.

Build your ability to think clearly and act decisively under pressure.

RED or BLUE? Decide. Do!

Mental Movement: Step Back, Step Up, Step In

A great way to ingrain the **RED–BLUE tool** in your memory is to add an imaginary physical movement for each step: **Step back, step up, step in.**

- **Step 1: step back** and see the RED–BLUE line, and where your reaction to the situation currently sits on it.
- **Step 2: step up** to a higher performance plane, gain an overview of the situation.
- **Step 3: step in** onto the higher plane and take action.

STEP BACK, STEP UP, STEP IN

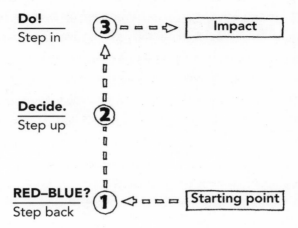

Do!
Step in

③ = = = ▷ [Impact]

Decide.
Step up

②

RED–BLUE?
Step back

① ◁ = = = [Starting point]

Mentally step back to gain emotional control, step up to see better options, and step in to take the initiative.

This movement pattern is so basic that it imposes next to zero mental load on us. All we need to do is imagine the first movement and the remainder of the RED–BLUE tool will follow naturally.

I must admit I use this pattern myself, because it's so easy to remember under pressure, and the physical movements seem to have a magical effect by getting us out of the overthinking trap. The three movements, and the images that go with them, are ideal for running our mental laptop screen.

Here's how Anna, our distressed teacher, might have used the **Step back, step up, step in** sequence. First, when she felt the urge to release her verbal outburst, she would have mentally stepped back: a mental movement in the *opposite*

Step back, step up, step in counteracts the RED behaviour patterns of fight, flight and freeze. **Stepping back** neutralises our urge to confront someone or something, or simply to flee the situation. And **stepping in** is ideal for forcing ourselves into action when we're frozen or passive. The movements highlight the fact that we are mentally stuck and not moving, and therefore actively not performing. To counteract what can be a very strong physical urge to react or stay still, we can make our mental movements equally sharp and forceful to snap us out of that state. Meanwhile, **stepping up** reminds us that to improve, we have to move from our current plane to a higher level.

It doesn't matter what the situation or obstacle is in front of us. As our position changes, so do our perception and the options we can see – and our physical body reflects that RED–BLUE balance.

consistent with that level are allowed – what springs to mind? And finally, imagine having to step in onto that plane of performance, where you need to get going immediately – what will be your first task?

How the RED–BLUE Tool Works: Rename, Reframe, Reset

RED or BLUE? Decide. Do! describes *what* to do to think clearly under pressure. And **Rename, reframe, reset** is the three-step mental procedure that describes *how* to do it.

Rename, reframe, reset supports the basic RED–BLUE tool and the **Step back, step up, step in** sequence by making clear the mental task behind each of the three steps. Beneath **RED or BLUE?** sits **rename**. Beneath **Decide** sits **reframe**. And beneath **Do** sits **reset**.

Rename requires us to name whether our emotional state is more RED or BLUE. This task might seem simple – and it is – but it has a powerful biological benefit. It fires up the three most important BLUE mind functions, which we met in Chapter 2. First, we have to visualise the RED–BLUE line, which switches on our BLUE mental laptop screen (our **working memory**). Second, we have to step back and think about our own state of mind, which activates our powerful **metacognition** function (thinking about thinking). And third, naming the colour activates our **language** function.

We can make this triple BLUE circuit boost occur naturally, in a few seconds, simply by carrying out the silent **rename** process. Best of all, we don't need to remember all the functions being activated – all we have to do to reap the rewards is silently name our colour, RED or BLUE! Being able to quickly recognise and name our state of mind takes the edge off what we are feeling, settles us down, and gives us back mental control and choice.

Remember Anna the high-school teacher? In the middle of mounting tension, she was about to have an emotional outburst. In that moment she mentally stepped back to see the RED–BLUE line flash up in her mind, immediately saw that she had gone deep RED, and held her aggressive outburst back. Her mental movement stopped her physical action – shouting out.

The second step – **reframe** – requires us to picture an expanding frame around our situation to deliberately reverse the tunnel vision of a RED emotional state. RED activation causes us to narrow in and fixate on the threat, at the expense of awareness of our broader environment. This state of mind doesn't help most performance scenarios.

Moving quickly from a small RED frame to a larger BLUE frame means we will naturally see two or three angles re-emerge, so we need to trust that they are relevant. They were probably always there; we just lost sight of them through tunnel vision. The objective is to be more *objective* and see the same situation from an overview standpoint. This step is completed when, after a quick but deliberate look at the bigger picture through the BLUE frame, we see and commit to a better course of action by making a clear decision.

Anna's **reframe** step allowed her to see the rude student's bad home situation, the upsetting news she had received that morning and the complaint she had received about an outburst towards a student in the past. She immediately realised that removing her attention from the disruptive student and trying to re-engage with the class was a smarter move. Once her mind started moving in that direction, it didn't feel hard at all. She decided to address the class as her first step.

The third step – **reset** – requires us to get out of our head and into action, but in a more constructive way than previously. It's a reminder not simply to default to our standard behaviour and repeat what we were going to do in the first place. Resetting engages our BLUE mind in planning and goal-setting, to further restore our RED–BLUE balance. It also slows us down if we were too aggressive, frantic or impulsive, and speeds us up if we were too passive or were procrastinating.

> Anna **reset** her intent by choosing not to take the bait and react to the rude pupil, but to speak to the class as a whole. Her actions were deliberate, composed and thoughtful, which settled the class.

Any time we start to feel overloaded, we can use **Rename, reframe, reset** to help step our way through **RED or BLUE? Decide. Do!**

Breathing Routines

Chest and belly breathing

Once we understand how our breathing is related to our RED and BLUE systems, we can further refine our RED–BLUE routine by paying close attention to our pattern of breathing.

There are two basic types of breathing pattern that we all use: **chest breathing** and **belly breathing**. Learning to shift from chest to belly breathing can take our RED–BLUE routine to another level.

Chest breathing occurs when we go into RED overdrive, typical of a fight–flight reaction. Under threat, our breathing increases in rate and our chest hyper-inflates with each in-breath as our body prepares for immediate exertion. Or, if we go into a freeze state, our chest, neck, arms and abdomen tense up and our breathing becomes shallow. Sometimes we even hold our breath.

Both are forms of chest breathing, one with *increased* chest movement to allow more physical movement, and one with *reduced* chest movement to help us become still.

In contrast, **belly breathing** is controlled by our diaphragm, the powerful primary breathing muscle that separates our lungs from our belly. When our diaphragm contracts, it moves downwards to create space for our lungs to expand, at the same time pushing our abdominal organs downward. As our pelvis creates a bony barrier below, our abdominal organs have nowhere to go other than to push outwards in all directions, which is why our belly seems to grow.

Belly breathing can occur when our abdominal muscles are relaxed, which allows the abdominal organs to move outwards. If we are tense and in a RED overdrive state, we hold our belly tight and the diaphragm can't move fully downwards. A good way to see belly breathing is to watch infants, who are not yet self-conscious about the expansion of their bellies.

Our two lungs are pyramid-shaped, which means most of their volume and blood supply is in the lower third of the lungs. This is also where they exchange the most oxygen and carbon dioxide. Belly breathing – especially through the nose – allows greater access to these regions, while shorter, shallower chest breathing restricts it, which can make a 5% difference to our oxygen uptake with each breath.

> When you feel tense, place one palm on your chest and one over the middle of your belly. Which one is moving the most? If you're breathing through your chest, the hand on your chest will be moving in and out while the hand on your belly will be relatively still. This is because your abdominal wall is tense, stopping your diaphragm from working.

> Relax your abdominal muscles and watch what happens to your breathing: it should become deeper and more rhythmical as you change to belly breathing.
>
> Here's a simple way you can do this when you're performing so no one notices. When you feel tense and notice you're breathing through your chest, place your hands around your waist just above your hip bones, so you can feel your abdomen on each side. Point your thumbs to the back and your fingers to the front.
>
> Relax and soften your tummy muscles and allow your belly to expand as you do three belly breaths. With each breath, notice how your expanding belly pushes your fingers and thumbs out and apart.

While chest breathing is linked to our hot-headed RED system (through our sympathetic nervous system), belly breathing stimulates our soothing BLUE system (through our parasympathetic nervous system). If you're in a room full of people under stress, you'll notice shallow, rapid breathing all around you. Some people even unintentionally hold their breath when they get very tense. In contrast, belly breathing can quickly dissolve tension and clear our mind.

One common unhelpful breathing pattern under pressure occurs when our in-breath is longer than our out-breath, which over-inflates our chest. To reverse this tendency, To reverse this tendency, time your breathing so that your out-breath is one more count than your in-breath. You have to tailor this to your circumstances, so that, for example, when you're working hard physically you might be counting to two while breathing in and three while breathing out. When we're exerting ourselves physically it's normal for us to use both chest and belly breathing, but we can usually still use the counting routine to encourage more breathing from the belly.

Regulating our breathing regulates our emotions. Breathe well, perform well.

Three breaths

Composure under pressure is priceless – and three breaths are all we need to achieve it.

> Take three belly breaths, with your out-breath at least as long as your in-breath. On each in-breath, place your hands on your waist above your hips and feel your belly expand. To make this more effective, imagine a wave of air flowing in through your nose and throat and down your spine, reaching the base of your spine before circling back to your centre of gravity, 5 centimetres beneath your navel.

Sometimes we'll have to carry out the RED–BLUE steps during a momentary break in our performance, or even on the run. Limiting each step of the RED–BLUE tool to a single breath in and out maintains a brisk pace. Our breathing becomes the conductor, and we have to keep in time.

Let's start from the baseline of a normal adult resting rate of 12 to 16 breaths per minute, or around five seconds per breath cycle. That means our RED–BLUE sequence is completed in about 15 seconds. (You'll have to adapt this to your own circumstances and physical state.)

Rather than worrying about getting each step done perfectly, the idea is to do what we can within one breath cycle and keep moving until we complete the three steps. Knowing that the sequence is brief should give us a mental lift. Just think: in only 15 seconds, we can improve our mental and physical state under pressure! We can run through the steps even faster if we're pressed for time, because our RED mind can move at unimaginable speeds. It's our conscious mind that might appear to struggle.

Don't worry if it takes you some *time* to get the *timing* right. At each step, any accuracy we lose we'll make up for in mental movement. Once we are mentally unstuck and on the go, we can pick up on some of the details we missed earlier.

The three-breath routine is an effective way of regaining composure when we're under pressure, even if we *don't* match it up with the RED–BLUE tool. In fact, this routine is the fastest way to reset our RED–BLUE balance. Use it alone, or in tandem with the RED–BLUE tool, to adjust your physical and mental state under pressure.

The eyes–hands–feet breathing routine

This is a variation of the three-breath routine that some athletes have told me they find useful. It uses the same basic structure of three belly breaths, with our hands placed on our waist at each in-breath. Here's the new part.

On each out-breath, shift your attention to focus on a different body part.

First, your **eyes**: as you breathe out, soften your focus and look into the distance so you have a wider view of your surroundings, taking in the background and peripheries all at once.

Second, your **hands**: as you breathe out, notice which set of fingers is tingling more – right or left?

Third, your **feet**: as you breathe out, notice which set of toes feels more connected to the ground – right or left?

The eyes–hands–feet sequence moves our attention from top to toe, allowing us to reconnect with the whole of our body.

Using our eyes to look into the distance activates our BLUE parasympathetic system and calms our emotions. (We saw earlier that RED arousal is increased by direct, held eye contact but reduced when gaze is diverted off people and into space.) In a RED fight–flight state, blood flows towards our large muscle groups in preparation for major exertion, and away from the extremities of our body like our fingers and toes. Placing attention back on those areas can redirect blood flow into a more balanced state.

An indirect benefit of this sequence is that it emphasises body parts and sensations to counteract the overthinking trap. Our thoughts tend to drag our attention into the past or future, while physical sensations can only occur in the here and now, so the eyes–hands–feet routine helps get us beyond our thoughts and connecting with our senses in the present moment.

Although the routine suits athletes well, there is no reason why other performers can't use it in their own fields. We can quickly regain control of our body and mind while sitting around a boardroom table, or while dealing with a grumpy two-year-old at the shopping centre.

A solid and reliable three-breath routine is a strong tool to have in our back pocket for performance under pressure.

Exercise: Self-Awareness

Here's a simple exercise that allows us to draw a line between the situation we're in and our reaction to it. This gives us mental control because it gives us the power to choose.

> Draw a vertical line down the middle of a blank piece of paper to create two columns. Call the left column SITUATION and the right column REACTION.

Choose a recent personal scenario when you felt under pressure and your performance was mixed. In the left column, write down words that describe the *external circumstances* involved. Depending on your activity, this might involve comments about the opposition, the score, what other people said or did, or a negative media report.

In the right column, write down several words that describe *your reaction* to the situation. Try not to explain why you behaved the way you did; simply list your feelings, thoughts and behaviours at the time. Note down both RED **APE** behaviours, and constructive BLUE **ACT** responses.

This exercise provides a clear external–internal division between the situation and our reaction to it, and shows how the RED–BLUE tool can give us mental choice and control. It also forces us to take responsibility for our own reaction. No one else was responsible for it; it was driven entirely by our perceptions and decisions.

Many people allow the facts of the situation and their reaction to become confused. The RED–BLUE tool is powerful because it forces us to take ownership of our thoughts and feelings. The very first step – **RED or BLUE?** – demands that we look at our own reaction as distinct from the pressure within the situation.

Top performers *choose* their reaction to any situation, rather than feeling like the situation is forcing them to behave in a certain way. The last thing we want is to give up our power to choose. If we're not self-aware, then how can we alter our reactions? It's often far more comfortable *not* to be, but that isn't the pathway to performance under pressure.

Exercise: The 'Stuff-Up Cascade'

If we start to get confused about which mental path we *should* be taking, clarity is just around the corner. Let's reverse the process of the RED–BLUE tool and design the perfect **'stuff-up cascade'**, a path that will lead us to certain failure.

Once we can see the best way to undermine all our good intentions, we simply need to do the opposite. We've probably already been down this road – right now, our RED brain is probably murmuring faint hints about past performances when we stuffed up good and proper.

A team sportsperson might describe their stuff-up cascade for a game as follows:
- Don't anticipate – react blindly.
- Either hesitate or be impulsive.
- Worry obsessively about mistakes.
- Overthink the situation.
- Focus on the scoreboard and imagine what it will be like to lose.
- Don't initiate change, wait to get a lucky break.
- Randomly try new things for the first time.

You get the picture. Knowing how *not* to do things tells us how to do them well.

Imagine you are a corporate leader; your stuff-up cascade for an important team meeting might involve:
- having no agenda and completely winging it
- not addressing the purpose of the meeting at the start
- mixing up facts and opinions in a random manner
- jumping around between topics

- seeing team members as threats
- attacking anyone who disagrees with us
- taking any form of debate as a personal slight

Has anyone who works in an office environment *never* been in a meeting like that?

Creating a humorous stuff-up cascade allows us to stay detached from such a horror show – while recognising that we regularly do a lot of these things for real.

If we can put together a stuff-up cascade so easily, how come we can't prevent ourselves from doing those same things when it counts? We know all about what to do and what *not* to do in theory – so why doesn't it play out that way in real life?

The stuff-up cascade is most useful when we get a fuzzy mind and start losing our bearings. It gets us back on the right track in a hurry by showing us the pathways we definitely do *not* want to go down. It helps to declutter our mind.

It also alerts us to two common mental blocks in performance under pressure: being **vague**, and being **passive**.

If we are **vague** about what we want to improve and how we're going to do it, we shouldn't expect to build anything to admire in the mental space.

Likewise, if we routinely adopt a **passive** position and see unfortunate things as happening *to* us instead of arising straight from our personal decisions, we will always be on the back foot and never reach our full potential.

The stuff-up cascade works in the same way as the **self-awareness exercise** we've just looked at. It helps us realise that we, personally, are responsible for our actions. We're capable of making our own decisions about a situation (performance), but instead we often choose to let the situation control *us* (submission). When I ask a performer who is complaining about a poor outcome to teach me how to perform poorly, it forces them to accept that *they* caused their stuff-up cascade – no one else!

Three of the most telling words in the performance lexicon are 'responsibility', 'accountability' and 'ownership'. The moment I hear this triad is typically the moment I realise I am *not* in a high-performance environment. People who are at that level are just too busy being responsible and accountable and taking ownership to *think* of those words, let alone *say* them. Rather than *talking* about it, we should just do it.

When our mental resolve wavers, if we quickly go through a silent stuff-up cascade then all will become clear: we are actively contributing to our own downfall. The stuff-up cascade works because it points out precisely who is responsible for our mental performance.

Reflective Listening: BLUE–RED for Others

Up to this point we've focused on using the RED–BLUE tool to help ourselves regain emotional self-control in uncomfortable situations. But is it possible to use the tool to help *others* get hold of their emotions when they get out of hand?

> Ian is a senior executive involved in a tense situation with Ben, a colleague at work. Ben has just stormed into Ian's office to confront him about something Ian said in their leadership team meeting this morning. Ben claims it left him feeling exposed and looking unprepared in front of their boss. It's clear he's extremely angry.

What's the best way to handle this kind of situation? In short, avoid getting into an argument. Avoid taking on their problems.

Stand your ground. And while we attempt to do that, help the other person process their emotions. That sounds like a lot to manage.

When people get angry, they're usually defending, protecting or avoiding something personally significant. Anger is their natural response to the emotional pain. Anger is helpful when it energises us to take care of ourselves, but it's unhelpful if it makes us lose control and spills over into aggressive behaviour. There's a big difference between feelings and actions.

> In this case, Ben thinks Ian has damaged his reputation. He's in the RED, acting aggressively and wanting to pick a fight. His hot-headed state means he's lost the clarity of BLUE, and a reasoned discussion won't be possible until his emotional intensity drops enough for him to be able to reflect and consider alternative points of view. At the moment, he's mentally stuck in his irrational view: he's outraged because he thinks Ian has deliberately slighted him.

Our best strategy in this situation is to try to sensitively activate the other person's BLUE system, because it will help cool their RED emotions. We can't ignore the RED, or argue it away, because dismissing or criticising our colleague's attitude will be like throwing fuel on the fire.

Here's a healthy, robust approach: we reflect back to them a brief description of the situation (which activates BLUE) and their reaction to it (which recognises the presence of RED). The BLUE comment comes first because BLUE activation will help cool their RED intensity, and separate their reaction from the overall situation. This approach mirrors the self-awareness exercise we just looked at.

Ian might say, 'So this is about our team meeting this morning to look at which option to take?' (The BLUE comment.) 'It sounds like you have some strong views about what was said.' (The RED comment.) He's listened carefully to Ben's words, separating his comments into the situation (BLUE) and Ben's reaction (RED), and reflected them back to Ben. This is *reflective listening*.

The BLUE–RED sequence is the key to helping the other person move into the BLUE. Making a standalone RED comment – 'You seem angry' – deprives them of the cooling effect of BLUE on RED, and can easily provoke an even more intense reaction.

Our task is to watch the other person and listen to each of their comments, and decide whether it's RED, or is becoming BLUE. We keep making RED–BLUE reflective statements until we detect a BLUE shift, a comment that seems more logical and less intense.

Ben might respond to Ian's first RED–BLUE reflection by saying: 'Yes, you're right! Your comments made me look stupid. How dare you make me look bad in front of the CEO!'

Ian sees that Ben is still in the RED, so his second reflective comment is: 'OK, I made some comments about the different options [BLUE situation] and now you're angry [RED reaction].' Once again, he uses a brief RED–BLUE sequence to separate Ben's reaction from the situation.

Ben replies: 'I just couldn't believe the way you pulled the rug out from under me! My team really wanted Option A but you persuaded the boss to go with Option B, and now I have to tell my team that all their hard work was for nothing!'

It's clear that Ben is still RED; he's dropped a level and is becoming more coherent, but he's not ready for rational debate just yet.

In response, Ian says: 'So your team worked hard for Option A and my team worked hard for Option B [situation], and you're angry with me for making a case for Option B [their reaction].' Ian has simply reflected back Ben's comment, and has avoided becoming judgmental or defensive.

Ben then responds: 'Well, when you say it like that, I guess I couldn't have expected you to do anything else. You just did the same thing for your team that I was trying to do for mine. And perhaps Option B *does* have some things going for it. I just don't know how I'm going to break it to my team after all their effort ...'

Ian notices the BLUE shift – a move to a mostly rational response – and realises he can now engage with Ben in a more logical way to solve the problem. He replies, 'Yes, they were both good options and both teams worked hard, but in the end we had to make a choice. Now the decision has been made, I wonder if there's some way we could get our teams to work together on this project?'

RED–BLUE reflective listening is especially helpful for conversations like this one, involving emotion, conflict and confrontation. We focus on listening and watching carefully instead of arguing, so there's a much better chance that the other person will feel heard. By inviting the other person to respond we give them space to process their own emotions – and often to ventilate – rather than trying to do it for them. We assist them in processing their emotions until they move to a more reflective position. And we hold our ground by not engaging in impulsive explanations or accusations, or hasty apologies. When the other person is still emotional, the time is not yet right for our logical opinions.

A useful rule of thumb is that it often takes three emotional comments from an individual before they lose enough intensity to make the BLUE shift. Until they are more reflective they will not be able to see or hear what we are saying, so it will be wasted effort, or more likely will inflame the situation.

The BLUE–RED reflective technique avoids the common mistake of immediately trying to fix the situation by taking on responsibility for the other person's feelings. Their feelings belong to *them*, and *they* are the ones who have to feel them before they can let them subside.

Another trap is trying to be too clever or specific by interpreting our colleague's emotional state. Simply saying that they seem to have strong views or feelings or they seem to be angry is enough. Telling someone who is emotional that we understand how they feel is asking for trouble. Simply ask what their view was about the issue, or how they saw it. This is a discussion, not therapy. Also, try to listen carefully and reword what they say to avoid simply parroting back their words, which can be seen as patronising.

This technique is a good example of the **Rename, reframe, reset** technique. We are renaming their words, reframing them within the RED–BLUE structure, and reflecting them back so that the other person has to reset and do their own emotional processing. By separating the situation from their reaction, we help the other person own their reaction and see a bigger picture. We also help ourselves, because the RED–BLUE structure will insulate us from being intimidated or accepting *their* view of the situation.

The BLUE–RED reflective listening technique can be used for any emotional or challenging discussion. If you're a parent, it works well with teenagers, because it avoids lecturing as if you know best.

Listening is the most powerful form of communication. The BLUE–RED reflective listening process involves giving the other individual our full attention and keeping the focus on them. It's surprising how powerful it is for people to experience being listened to fully, because it is so uncommon.

What would those around you say about how you handle tense emotional discussions? Do you let emotions interfere, or are you able to stay sensitive and balanced? In high-pressure conversations, do you rename reframe, reset, or do you reload, re-aim, re-fire?

PART 2

PREPARING TO PERFORM – LAYING THE GROUNDWORK

All serious daring starts from within.

Eudora Welty, author (1909–2001)

CHAPTER 5

CREATE THE GAP

The Performance Gap

Here are three questions to answer. Just go with your initial gut response for each.

1. Do you want to get better at what you do?
2. Have you reached your full potential?
3. Do you have a clear picture about what your next level of performance looks and feels like?

In my experience, the majority of people answer Question 1 with 'Yes', Question 2 with 'No', and Question 3 with 'What are you talking about?!'

If you answered in a similar way, unfortunately you're unlikely to fulfil your potential.

Here's why.

First, pretty much everyone says they want to get better; there's no cost in saying that we want to improve.

Second, hardly anyone says they have reached their full potential. For the majority of people this is an easy answer and is quite accurate, and the minority who have reached their highest level are understandably reluctant to admit their best days are behind them.

Third, people who enter their 'performance space' each day with a clear picture in mind of what a better version of themselves looks like are the exceptions rather than the rule.

These three questions are a quick way to **create the gap** between how we are functioning now and the level at which we ideally want to function at some point in the future. Saying we want to get better shows our intent to improve, and saying we haven't reached our full potential identifies that a gap exists in our mind. But if we don't have a clear picture of what the next level looks like for us, our chances of getting there are slim.

The stark reality is that most people plateau in their career after a relatively short time. They don't improve in any significant way once they become familiar with the standard procedures behind what they do. This inconvenient fact means that saying we want to improve won't get us very far, because it won't set us up mentally to succeed.

If we say we haven't reached our potential, that's good, because it means there's another level for us to get to. In fact, reaching our full potential will probably require us to step up through *several* levels. But having potential alone doesn't get us there. I like to define potential as what is left over when we retire, so we don't want too much of it. Better to translate most of our potential into performance!

If we're quite happy where we are right now, we have no performance gap – and we're among the majority of the population.

But if we genuinely do want to improve, we need to stop being sensitive about looking at our weaknesses and vulnerabilities. Instead of seeing it as a negative thing, we need to recognise that a gap between where we are now and where we want to be is mandatory for movement.

If we think about our *performance*, we will feel comfortable. If we think about our *performance gap* – where we fall short – it feels different immediately. Unless we are uncomfortable with the status quo, we are not going to improve.

Once we accept that a performance gap is actually a *good* thing, we can start applying these principles to our own performance domain.

Technical vs mental factors

Earlier we saw that *moderate* performers tend to point to **external factors** like the weather, financial markets or staffing levels to account for weak points in their performance. On the other hand, *leading* performers tend to look towards **internal factors** to work out where they need to improve. These internal factors could be either **technical** or **mental**.

Whatever our activity or line of work, we will have technical factors that we need to be competent at to perform well. But there will also be mental (or human) factors, such as clarity of thought and effective decision-making. Over the decades I've observed a curious contradiction. From business to sport, there is a strong bias towards the technical – things that are easy to grasp, see and count – at the expense of the mental, which is hard to grasp, more invisible than visible, and frustrates those who want to quantify it.

Ironically, the margins on technical matters are usually small, and the outcomes are relatively visible, concrete and predictable. The technical factors often don't fluctuate much from day to day, or even week to week. Meanwhile, the human factors – intangible and variable mental skills like making a critical decision or seeing the next move in the heat of the moment – are often underappreciated. The very things that fluctuate the most, and make the biggest difference, tend to be the least resourced. Just look at how, for example, a sporting organisation is usually resourced: plenty of managers, coaches and technical experts, but very little attention paid to psychological input.

This theme holds horizontally across pursuits from medicine to the military, and vertically, from whole organisations right down to specific individuals. I've consistently found that even leading performers are more impressive technically than mentally. And why shouldn't that be the case when they've spent thousands of hours doing technical training, hundreds of hours doing physical training, and often less than ten hours – sometimes zero – doing specific mental training?

I see two main reasons for this. First, it's just easier to deal with the concrete and the measurable, even if everyone is doing much the same thing and there is little to be gained in the way of competitive advantage. Maintaining a technical focus keeps us away from mental matters, which suits those who might quickly become less comfortable if the spotlight were redirected towards their leadership, teamwork or emotional reactions. For most of us, it seems technical vulnerabilities are more palatable than mental ones. Having something wrong with our *technique* is easier to accept than having something wrong with *ourselves*.

Second, it's easy to dismiss what we can't see and don't understand as less relevant and reliable. But I think it's a serious error to conclude that just because the mental world is more elusive, it's less valuable.

There are usually plenty of individuals in a field who are *technically* exceptional, but far fewer who are mentally exceptional. And *very* few are technically *and* mentally exceptional.

If we now look to create the gap for ourselves in terms of human factors, what do we see? How would our mental skills need to improve for people to see that we are operating at a new level?

Feedback vs feed-forward

The obvious method is to start with our **current reality** then look at our **future potential**. And the best way to look objectively at our current reality is to take on board the **feedback** we receive from others.

Unfortunately, the feedback we tend to hear loudest is negative criticism of our shortfalls. Receiving criticism can be painful, and often makes us feel threatened and defensive. Consider the emotional toll of things like performance reviews and 360-degree feedback.

When we're faced with criticism and obstacles, mental movement is difficult. When we feel hurt, the natural reaction of our RED system is to act defensively, rather than making use of this potentially valuable information. The feedback process works for the minority – but for the majority, it doesn't lead to improvement, and for many, it sets them back.

But what if we worked *backwards*? What if we started out by focusing on our future potential – our next level of performance – *then* looked at the current reality – what is already working well, and what is missing? Because this approach involves looking into the future first, it has been called **feed-forward**.

The feed-forward process is a powerful alternative to standard feedback. One key difference is the different underpinning biology. As we've seen, the feedback process triggers our RED mind from the outset, driving defensive reactions. However, the feed-forward process activates our visual, forward-thinking BLUE mind by constructing a positive image of how we want our future to look and feel.

The second difference is in the way feeding forward helps us see our current reality. Once we have a solid, appealing picture of our future, looking at current obstacles that are holding us back is not just more tolerable, it's actually energising.

An effective feed-forward leaves us uncomfortable with the status quo and restless to get moving. If we want something deeply, and we can identify what is holding us back from achieving it, removing those obstacles becomes a priority. Discomfort with where we are now is converted into energy to move. And combining the BLUE image of our positive intention with our RED discomfort in staying put provides the magic.

When it comes to creating the gap, **feed-forward** trumps **feedback**.

Three building blocks to create the gap

In this chapter, we'll commit to a personal **feed-forward**. We'll look at three building blocks – **pressure, intent** and **reality** – that will help us work out our destination and develop a route to get there.

To ensure that this route is as direct as possible, we need to work out what pressure we will face in our performance environment and work backwards from there. If we don't start with our performance context – **pressure** – the gap that we create will lack meaning.

If you're a team athlete, start on the grass with your opposition two scores in front and dominating the game. If you're an entrepreneur, start in the boardroom in the middle of a tense negotiation. If you're a teacher, start in the classroom facing a rowdy, distracted class on a hot Friday afternoon. This makes it personal to *you*.

The second building block is our **intent** – how well we want to perform under the pressure. This is where we spend time building a realistic, challenging and emotionally engaging picture of what our next level of performance looks and feels like. Without it, we have no direction or commitment.

And thirdly we need to determine our current **reality**. This means focusing on our current level of performance – teasing out what is working well and what is holding us back, technically and mentally, externally and internally.

Identifying where we are right now creates a performance gap between our current level of performance and the level at which we want to perform. With a clear performance gap in mind, we'll be primed and ready to move.

Pressure, intent and reality form an indispensable triad for moving our performance level. If we're not able to provide a clear, succinct description of our personal performance gap, then we're not really serious about our performance.

1. Pressure: The Performance Environment

The pressure equation

Pressure has a structure. Challenges in different fields might look very unlike each other, but the way they create pressure has common threads. When we get hold of the strands and work out how they interweave, we can start to get a grip on the *anatomy of pressure*.

THE PRESSURE EQUATION

Pressure arises from a combination of external factors, which creates a sense of internal discomfort.

Imagine a surgeon needs to perform an urgent, potentially life-saving operation. The pressure placed on her arises from **high stakes, uncertainty, small margins, fast changes** and **judgment**. We can call this the **pressure equation**.

The **high stakes** include the patient's health status and ability to work, all just for starters. The **uncertainty** comes from the possibility of mistakes and complications. The **small margins** are the millimetres between vital anatomical structures, and the limited time frame for getting the job done. **Fast changes** kick in when a slip-up occurs or the patient's condition deteriorates. And throughout the process there is judgment from all angles – the anxiety of the patient and their family and friends, the close scrutiny of the surgical team, the watchful eye of colleagues and hospital managers.

These strands don't sit in isolation but compound to form a formidable ball of pressure. High stakes start the ball rolling. Uncertainty on top of high stakes immediately ups the ante. Small margins exaggerate the uncertainty. Possible fast changes amplify the small margins. And judgment aggravates everything.

We can find the same combination of strands across different performance situations. Depending on our career, life might not be at stake, but our employment, health and self-esteem might be. Surgical complications might not be on the horizon, but sudden emergencies, traffic jams, bad weather and other people's behaviour all sit outside of our control. The margins might not involve surgical millimetres, but tight time frames, fluctuating exchange rates, scoreboards or clocks. Clinical deterioration might not be at risk, but poor handgrips on vertical rock faces, deadlines met or missed, or contracts won or lost can change the tone of the situation in the blink of an eye. And judgment might not be directed at the surgeon but at us, from a posse of selectors, teammates, bosses, colleagues, customers, media, family, officials or the general public.

Take a moment to identify a key challenging moment on your own performance horizon. Pay attention to the conditions you'll face by considering the anatomy of pressure. To what extent will there be high stakes, uncertainty, small margins, fast changes and judgment?

The pressure equation starts to allow us to see the context of the pressure we face. Lower stakes, more certainty, wider margins, slower changes and less judgment all reduce the pressure in a situation. The opposite dynamics merge to create pressure in a flash.

It's clear that pressure transcends territories.

A tough day

To bring the pressure equation to life, we can imagine a tough day when it seems like everything that *can* go wrong *does* go wrong. We may not operate in an area where slip-ups mean potential fatalities, financial devastation or emotional trauma. But if we assume that the uncertain event actually happens and we breach our small margins, what fast changes can occur, what is at stake, and what judgment will result?

Every junior doctor could construct a tough day list from their experiences of being on call: working while suffering from a virus; friends having fun on the weekend while we are on call; staff sickness that leaves us short-handed; poor sleep because of sick children at home; conflict with a senior colleague; tension from a demanding patient; computer systems down, meaning information is unavailable; and a sense of overload as our pager announces the arrival of even more patients, while hospital staff give us surly responses because we are moving too slowly.

> To deepen your feel for how pressure works in your own environment, take a minute or two to jot down a list of things that could happen to you to make it a tough day. How does this compare with the tough day of the junior doctor?

The crossover will be obvious. Tough days often come about less from technical factors and more from human or mental factors – the difficult interactions, circumstances and obstacles people face no matter what their environment. As we've seen, technical factors often grab our attention because they form the signature markers for any field, but it is often the mental factors that create pressure.

Notice how your tough day contains mental elements that are not so much rare visitors as constant companions – the norm rather than the exception.

No one is exempt. You have your performance environment and I have mine, and although the conditions in which we operate vary, the human factors like fatigue, feeling rushed, conflicts, overload and distractions have impact across the board. (In Chapter 13 I describe a series of typical days under pressure; you might see a lot there that's familiar.)

When I've worked with groups on improving performance over the years, here's a question I've often asked them: 'If you could choose when to have major surgery, what day of the week and what number on the operating list would you go for?'

The people in these groups – surgeons included – have tended to arrive at the same option: second on a mid-week list. Most rule out Monday (surgeon possibly getting over the weekend) and Friday (fatigue, eagerness to get away for the weekend), and first on the list (let the surgeon warm up on someone else to get their eye in) as well as last (fatigue, rushing to finish). We hold surgeons in the highest regard, but whatever the reality of wait-list data we see them as human too, and therefore vulnerable to the same human factors that cause performance drop-off in us all.

Tough days through human factors are predictable and unavoidable. They are part of our landscape. As we create our mental picture of the context where we intend to perform, we need to make sure the human factors take centre stage. (The **three circles technique** in Chapter 7 will help us do this.)

Regardless of our level of performance, pressure has currency in our life. It decides the outcome; it can hold us back, or it can help push us forward. If we want to reach our full potential, our relationship with pressure will have to change.

A clear picture of the origins of pressure in our performance environment is our first building block in creating the gap.

2. Intent: How Good Do We Want to Be?

Now we have a clear picture of our challenging context and the pressure we'll face, we can work out how we want to perform within that context. Are we serious about reaching our full potential? Just how good do we want to be?

Other people can impose expectations from without, but only *we* can set our intent from within. The key is to avoid a **mismatch** between the level of pressure we face and the mental level we operate at.

A lot of my work is pointing out inconvenient mismatches between the outcomes people claim they want and their actual behaviour, which falls short in predictable ways. If we compromise on our mental habits, we shouldn't be surprised when the intended results don't occur.

Here's a handy **scale of mental intent** used by some athletes. Don't be put off by the sporty language; it can easily be applied to most fields, even if you're not in a competitive environment.

MENTAL INTENT

TT?   Training to ?
TTW   Training to win
TTC   Training to compete
TTT   Training to train

The scale of mental intent allows us to make a choice as to where we want to position ourselves in terms of performance.

What's your line in the sand – how good do you want to be?

- Are you training to **train**?
- Are you training to **compete**?
- Are you training to **win**?

If we were **training to train**, we would be content with being one of the many. If we joined a gym, we would do an initial assessment and work out a training programme, but we wouldn't stick to it, and we would regularly miss days. We would lack discipline and commitment. We would be a 'sometimes' performer.

If we were **training to compete**, we would set out to be one of the best few performers in our domain. If we joined a gym, we would do regular fitness reviews, adjust our routines accordingly, and turn up reliably. We would be disciplined and committed, although we would have our limits. We would be a 'most of the time' performer.

If we were **training to win**, we would set out to be the single best performer in our territory. Being second-best would not be acceptable; we would be driven to get right to the top. In the gym our attendance, attitude and commitment would stand out from the rest. We would look for any small angle we could find to help us edge ahead of others. We would especially look at our vulnerabilities to identify and correct any weaknesses. We would be resilient, adaptable and 100% reliable. We would be an 'always' performer. Training to win means being committed to constantly learning and adapting.

I find it useful to add a further category to the scale.

Above **training to win** I would add a further category for those who wish to stay at the forefront of their field of performance. I tend to leave the specific word open for people to decide on themselves – **training to '?'** – because the word should resonate for the particular field. **Training to dominate** might work in some sporting codes (in the sense of dominating the performance domain, not other people); but training to master, lead or excel might appeal more in other fields. Whatever word we use, some people are not satisfied with being the best or leading just once – they want to be the best in their field or lead again and again, to create a legacy. They have a hunger that is unquenched by success, a preoccupation with performance details, and a willingness to make substantial sacrifices. (We'll look at this mindset in Chapter 10, on mastery.)

At this level, we can find **'legends'**, those rare individuals who are determined – and have the opportunity – to become the best of their generation. They're able to redefine the challenge and recreate the method, finding different ways to break new ground. It is deep within their psyche to be on top or to extend themselves beyond perceived limits. Sacrifices and risks are givens. Their names may come up when people discuss who is the greatest of all time in their field.

In addition to this level, a coach I know well has suggested – with me in mind – that two further categories are needed, but at the other end of the scale. First, **pretending to train**, and, right at the bottom, **turning up**. Charming!

A common mismatch I see in sport is athletes who claim they're training to win, but have mental habits more in keeping with training to compete or even training to train. They always get *found out*.

Individuals and teams who operate with a champion's mindset are less common, and stand out through their actions more than their words. They always *find a way through*.

> Take a few minutes to identify where you want to sit on the scale (in keeping with your technical ability). What would that level of performance look like (BLUE) and feel like (RED) under pressure? There's nothing wrong with training to train or training to compete, as long as you're fulfilling your potential. There's also nothing wrong with training to train and not trying to improve. But this book is designed for those who aren't satisfied with things as they are. If you want to go up a level in your performance, then your mental habits will have to go up a level as well.

We need to translate the outcome we're after into a concrete mental picture – like a short scene from a movie. What would it take for all our colleagues to agree that we were operating at 'the next level'? How would we be acting and relating to people? We need a mental image that is challenging but realistic, so it pulls us upward.

Within our performance context of **pressure**, once we've set our **intent** we have our second building block for performance under pressure.

3. Reality: Our Performance Line

Let's return to the surgical scenario we looked at to understand the anatomy of pressure. Imagine you need urgent, potentially life-saving surgery because of acute abdominal pain. On a **performance line** from 0 to 100% – in terms of real-world, not hypothetical, performance – at what level would you like your surgeon to perform?

When I use this scenario with groups, no one is ever prepared to go much lower than the full 100%.

What if you were informed that only an inexperienced surgeon is available locally, but a surgeon at a hospital two hours away is as good as they come? A transfer would cause discomfort and an increased risk of serious complications (including death). How low on the performance line would the local surgeon have to be before you would consider a transfer?

Most of us would accept a 99% level to avoid all the potential consequences of the transfer. At 98%, again, most would stay put. But as the number gets lower, our discomfort in accepting the local surgical performance increases, until we finally make the tough call.

Through years of using this exercise, I have seen remarkable consistency, with group members usually calling out 'Stop!' at around about the 80% mark.

The message is clear: when we have our own skin in the game (even in our imagination), we demand the very highest level of performance from others. Because the stakes are so high, we want the performance to be of the highest standard too. Pilots, paramedics, extreme athletes ... all must perform at a high level each and every time. Significant drop-offs would mean serious consequences.

But even for highly trained performers like these, there are performance differences between individuals, and each individual also has their good and bad days. Ideally the level of performance stays above 90%, but under no circumstances should it fall below 80% in these high-stakes activities.

Let's call 80% the cut-off for 'high performance'. Let's also nominate 90% as the cut-off for 'world-class performance'. Remember, the scale is about *actual*, not potential, performance.

My experience has been that people in high-stakes professions (especially where lives are on the line) have a good sense of whether they are worse than, about the same as, or better than their colleagues.

In some fields – particularly the arts – the quality of performance can be very subjective, and we're not trying to reduce everything to a simple number. But rather than dismissing it as a futile exercise, we need to make an effort to look at our performance more objectively. If we can't position ourselves in relation to any reference points, we are confining ourselves to the performance plateau.

Most of us are adept at making everyday decisions based on comparisons – the best coffee, the best holiday spot, the best school – but we somehow quickly lose this ability when we look at our own performance level.

Keep it simple: who are the best operators in our field? Where do we sit in relation to them? If we find that difficult to measure, we can consider our reputation – given to us by other people. *They* usually find it easy to make the comparison, even if we don't.

It might be difficult to say where we sit without any reference points, but the moment we introduce other markers – comparing ourselves with others – the task becomes easier.

Take 10 seconds and position yourself on a performance line for your own occupation or pursuit. Where do you sit?

This is a rough-and-ready, gut-instinct estimate, not a lengthy intellectual exercise. But it forces us to rate ourselves, which makes an abstract concept like performance suddenly seem – and feel – very real indeed.

If you scored yourself above 80% or 90%, then the chances are you are very accomplished in your field, maybe even on a world scale, but then small margins would still carry a lot of significance – perhaps the difference between winning and coming second. If you scored yourself at 80% or less, you categorised yourself as a moderate performer because you fell short of the 80% high-performance cut-off. (We have a strong bias to rate ourselves favourably – 50% is not 'average' on the scale because nearly everyone sees themselves as being above that mark.) And if you scored yourself below 50%, it means you have plenty of room to move.

(Being classed as 'moderate' or below usually causes a strong reaction. The fact that a lot of people are immediately uncomfortable with this shows how quickly we can become defensive in the face of perceived judgment. But I always remind people that *they're* the ones who've given themselves that rating, not I. Are they uncomfortable because they don't think their own assessment was accurate and fair? Or because it *is* accurate, and it hurts for this to be pointed out?)

The performance line is useful even if we don't see ourselves in a competitive environment. We can still rate ourselves in terms of the contributions we make to performance in whatever terms we see as relevant. If you work in a health service, think in terms of your reputation for patient care compared with the reputations of your peers. If you work in a government department, think in terms of your reputation for high-quality, well-timed advice, and for working effectively with people in other departments. If you work as a teacher, think in terms of your reputation for the classroom culture and learning environment that you foster, compared with others.

The performance line can also be tailored to our situation to avoid unrealistic comparisons. Not everyone operates on a global scale. If you're a keen amateur footballer, then compare yourself with the best amateur footballer in your region placed at the 100% mark, not Pele. If you're a single working parent with three young children, struggling to keep your family functioning, then compare yourself with someone in a similar situation, not a film star. Always rate your performance within a meaningful context.

Although our score on the performance line is our own estimate, it invites us to be more objective by determining where we sit in comparison to others. We find it hard to make *free-floating* judgments, but we can be surprisingly fine-grained with *relative* judgments. The performance line converts vague performance descriptions into a specific position on a line, something that we can see and refer to.

At this point you might be feeling some discomfort, which is a signal that the process is working. You are moving away from the comfort of general performance chatter to the discomfort of a more specific probe into your performance.

Drawing a performance line moves our performance thinking from the general to the specific. It sets up a constructive internal debate about what might need to occur for us to move up the performance line. What is working well, and what is holding us back? Confirming our strengths first usually makes us more open to reflecting on where we are falling short.

Inconvenient facts

When we look at what is holding us back, we need to consider both *external* and *internal* obstacles. As we saw earlier in the chapter, most of us find the external factors a lot easier to recognise. We have no problem blaming our performance shortcomings on the traffic, the weather, or other people – but find it much harder to put them down to our own short fuse, impatience, or a lack of concentration.

To identify our *internal* obstacles we can look for **inconvenient facts**, those uncomfortable truths about our performance that we don't usually admit to. The word 'inconvenient' seems to strike the right chord – not too strong but not too weak. And calling them 'facts' means we can't deny them.

In my experience, most people find it easy to complete the sentence 'I'd like to become a better performer, but if I'm being honest, it's an inconvenient fact that ...'. It produces some candid observations that until that point were missing from their performance gap thinking.

A tennis player's inconvenient fact might be that they have a lower-than-average winning percentage in tie-breakers. A salesperson's inconvenient fact might be that they've never met their quarterly forecasts. A politician's inconvenient fact might be that they repeatedly give contradictory statements to the media on key policy topics.

In each case, the person's ability to perform competently is not in question. But when they're faced with additional pressure – a tight match, a sales deadline, a searching media question – a personal vulnerability has been exposed and they've fallen short. In each case, the inconvenient fact has identified a clear target for improvement.

Relabelling our weaknesses as 'inconvenient facts' helps break through our myths and illusions about our performance, by gently drawing our attention to the areas we typically avoid.

So put the third performance under pressure building block in place: in our field, where do we sit on the performance line?

Scale of mental impact

The Scale of mental impact below provides a 10-point scale that you can adapt to your own performance field. Each number represents a step in the scale that must be earned. No cheap talk allowed. If the scale of mental intent we saw earlier helps you to describe how good you *want* to be, the purpose of the scale of mental impact is to help you to work out how you are performing mentally *right now*.

The 'entry level' is at number 5. This is the level of rookie performers: plenty of energy and some skills to boot, but lack of experience means their decision-making under pressure may be inadequate.

Consider your performance in three main areas: attitude and level of commitment (RED energy); quality of decision-making (BLUE clarity); and quality of execution (RED–BLUE balance). (Adapt each of these so it's relevant to your field.)

You can move up *or* down the ratings. And there's no guarantee that you'll only move upwards. There's also no guarantee that top *technical* performers will be top *mental* performers.

Potential: Create the Gap and Seek Out Pressure

At this point, we have three essential reference points – **pressure, intent** and **reality** – that will create a personal performance gap and help us put the RED–BLUE tool and related techniques to use.

We have potential – more to give – but unless we find ourselves in the right situations, it will remain hidden inside and never see the light of day. In that case, we will follow the majority onto the performance plateau.

Scale of Mental Impact		
Level	Title	Description
10	Legend	Within top three in field for the decade. Generational standout. Redefines attitudes to their field. Affects the whole situation through their presence. Awe-inspiring.
9	Master	Within top three in field for the year. International standout. Training to dominate. Consistently inspires behaviours in others that raise the standard. Always humbly learning and adapting.
8	Standout	Reputation in field for turning up under pressure. Training to win. Behaviours stand out from the rest, motivates others through their presence.
7	Strong	Leads under pressure. Training to compete. Contributes without being prompted, shows lots of initiative, always constructive.
6	Solid	Reliable under pressure. Contributes when prompted, some initiative, sometimes constructive.
5	Entry level (rookie)	High energy and competency but sometimes indecisive or rash under pressure. Training to train. Uncertain or reactive but well-meaning.
4	Unreliable	Consistently poor in one area – energy, clarity or accuracy. Sometimes negative, a burden at times.
3	Avoidant	Consistently poor in two of three areas – energy, clarity, accuracy. Goes missing in action, weak link, consistently negative.
2	Disengaged	Consistently poor in three areas – energy, clarity and accuracy. Pretends, gets by. Makes excuses and blames others.
1	Saboteur	Divides and diverts others. Ill-intentioned. Energised by interference and conflict.

Where do you currently sit on the scale of mental impact?

If we're serious about reaching our full potential, then we need to become comfortable with performing under pressure. We know that this is dangerous territory, because pressure can break us down instead of building us up. But we can't break through our current limits without operating in a demanding environment, which forces us to dig deep inside ourselves.

Potential is derived from the Latin word *potentia*, meaning 'power'. Pressure has the power to pull us up or push us down, but our reaction to it can also be powerful. Without powerful moments, we will never reach our potential.

The pivotal question for us is: **pressure – friend or foe?** If we adopt a **train to win** approach, we'll embrace the challenging moments because they offer opportunities to learn and excel. Instead of being the enemy, discomfort will be welcomed because it extends us into new territory.

Pressure does not respect social status – it respects mental resilience. Pressure differentiates between those who have a mental edge and those who haven't. The best keep going, while those who are just very good do not.

If our intention is to stand out, pressure is a good thing. How we respond to it is what will set us apart, and without it, success will be elusive, because everyone can perform well when they're comfortable. If we are aiming high, pressure and the performance gap are essential – they will become our driving force.

The performance gap is created simply by contrasting the way that we want to perform under pressure (the scale of mental intent) with the way we are performing now (the scale of mental impact).

We now have a mental performance gap. And what we need next is a mental blueprint to *bridge* that gap.

CREATE THE GAP

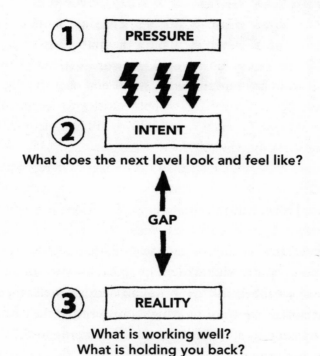

① PRESSURE

② INTENT

What does the next level look and feel like?

GAP

③ REALITY

What is working well?
What is holding you back?

Seeing our performance gaps creates the space
we need to move and improve.

CHAPTER 6

BRIDGE THE GAP – THE MENTAL BLUEPRINT

The **mental blueprint** is a preparation technique that will allow us to **bridge the gap** we've just created using **pressure, intent** and **reality.** First, *create* the gap. Second, upgrade our blueprint for different areas of mental activity to *bridge* the gap. Creating a gap gave us the space for movement between where we are now and where we want to get to – and the mental blueprint technique gives us a simple structure for working out how to get there.

The mental blueprint can also be used to review our *last* performance and make adjustments to prepare for our *next* performance.

When we're in a high-pressure situation, the **mental blueprint** acts as a prepared foundation for what is unfolding around us. Rather than working out our reaction when we're right in the middle of the drama, if we have our blueprint already in place it means we don't have to waste energy under difficult circumstances. It means we're much more likely to hold our ground.

A house that is built with strong foundations can withstand a storm. Building a strong house in the middle of a storm is a terrifying prospect. Forewarned is forearmed.

The Mental Blueprint: Our Script for Success

A mental blueprint is a working template we carry inside our mind for every action we perform. As we've seen, our first mental blueprints were formed from countless interactions during our first two years that are now imprinted deep in our implicit memory; they drive how we relate to others and how we react to facing discomfort. We've essentially been building blueprints for every task in front of us since then.

For everyday tasks that we are very familiar with – especially simple routines like making coffee or tying our shoelaces – our mental blueprint is largely unconscious. Some scripts are largely physical or technical, such as kicking or throwing a ball, driving a car, or using a scalpel or firearm. The movements have been absorbed into our brain as habits, coded in the basal ganglia, alongside our limbic system. In normal circumstances, we don't notice any mental effort in accessing the script to carry out the action; our mind can run it through without any assistance. It's automatic.

For actions that are more demanding or less familiar, our existing blueprint will fall short. We have to consciously build our mental map and use it more deliberately to get the task done. It's far from automatic.

A mental blueprint consists of three elements:

1. **Mindset** – our mental attitude towards the task (the **feeling** element)

2. **System** – our structural plan for the situation (the **seeing/thinking** element)
3. **Skillset** – our execution of the task (the **doing** element)

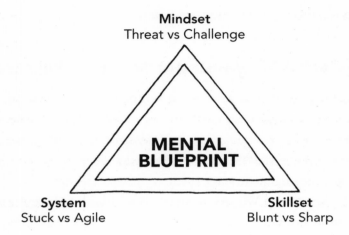

It's helpful to think of a blueprint as a triangle. **Mindset** goes in the top corner, **system** bottom left, and **skillset** bottom right.

To perform a task successfully, we need the right motivation, strategy and execution. Our mindset drives our level of emotional self-control and motivation. Our system provides an overview that shows us what to do next. And our skillset allows us to get the job done.

A mental blueprint for crossing a road would use a **mindset** of caution and seriousness because of the danger. Our **system** would involve looking right, looking left, then looking right again to get a picture of the traffic situation. Our **skillset** would involve adjusting our walking speed to allow for the speed of the traffic, or taking extra care when it's raining or when we're crossing a road at night. Try crossing a busy road in difficult conditions without an effective mental blueprint.

This kind of blueprint usually operates semiconsciously and without great mental focus, but we can use the same template to organise our approach to performance under pressure, when greater concentration is required.

Our blueprint would focus on a part of our performance where we've identified a clear gap – not so much a general area as a specific task. It's important that we work on this blueprint in bite-sized chunks, one element at a time. We'll make faster progress when we don't try to develop everything at once.

Paul is a young nurse with just three years' experience working on a general medical ward in a large city hospital. He's shown some initiative in looking after very sick patients, and has been asked to stand in for his unit manager and run the shift for the next two days.

Paul has no management experience, and is nervous about being responsible for the whole unit and having to supervise more experienced colleagues. He decides to upgrade his mental blueprint for nursing management.

He adopts a **mindset** of remaining composed no matter how stressful the situation becomes, and being decisive when necessary. He builds a **system** by drawing up a shift timeline and checklist of the nurse manager's tasks so he doesn't miss anything important. And he develops his **skillset** by asking more experienced colleagues what they've learned from managing a unit.

Paul finds the increased responsibility challenging but stimulating. His management timeline and checklist turn out to be invaluable in keeping him one step ahead as the unit becomes busy. The advice from senior colleagues is helpful as he deals with situations where several important things happen at once.

Sandra is a college student about to sit her final written exams. She has previously performed badly in exams due to anxiety, poor essay-writing skills and lack of time management. She is determined to do herself justice in her last set of exams, so she focuses on upgrading her mental blueprint for essay-based exams.

She commits to a **mindset** of remaining calm and composed throughout each three-hour exam, and carefully managing her time, especially when she comes across difficult essay topics. She develops an easy-to-use **system** for planning each essay, based on simple ways of structuring the opening, middle and ending. And she works on her **skillset** by practising opening and closing sentences for mock essay topics, because she has found she gets stuck and wastes time on these.

Sandra finds she manages to stay relatively calm, even though her friends say they were thrown by the difficult essay topics. Her essay plans keep her answers relevant, and her opening and closing sentences keep her moving.

Sandra and Paul both operate in very different worlds, but by deliberately building their mental blueprint in specific areas, they are training their minds to come up with the right responses, decisions and actions when the big moments arrive.

Pinpoint an area where you have an obvious performance gap. What one thing could you change about your mindset, system and skillset in that area that would make the gap smaller?

If you're struggling a little to come up with an area to focus on, think about where you sit on the **performance line**. What's the difference in practice between someone at the very top of your field and where you sit right now? What mental features and behaviours do *you* lack that make *them* stand out from the crowd?

Now that we have a personal example of a mental blueprint for one aspect of our performance, we can look more closely at each of the points of the triangle – **mindset**, **system** and **skillset**.

1. Mindset: Threat or Challenge?

Changing our **motivation** is the starting point for upgrading our mental blueprint. It comes first because our motivation starts in our RED mind. Feeling comes before thinking.

Motivation is the force that leads to movement. If we choose a situation and make a commitment to moving *towards* or *away from* it, we've refined our **mindset**.

If we see a situation as a **threat**, it will create tension and anxiety, and we'll look to get out of it as soon as possible. But if we see the same situation as a **challenge**, it will energise and excite us and draw us in with vigour.

When we're in a crisis situation – think accidents or medical emergencies – a composed mindset is essential for survival. When we face hardship such as chronic illness our mindset influences our experience of the situation. When we're faced with major change, like getting a new boss or manager, or moving to a new city or country, our mindset will establish whether we let events get the better of us or *we* get the better of *them*.

But a positive mindset is just as important in more ordinary situations. A sportsperson might see media duties at a major tournament as a burden to bear, or as an opportunity to embrace as they represent their team with enthusiasm. A businessperson might regard endless travel as a hardship, or as a rare chance to experience different places and cultures. Having a work colleague who is ill could be a millstone around the neck, or an opportunity to cover a different area, gain valuable experience, and build team spirit.

In each case, adopting a more constructive mindset gives us emotional self-control, which will help us react positively when we come face to face with pressure.

One classic challenge mindset is the **underdog**. Their opponent is technically or physically stronger and has more potential to inflict damage. So the underdog must make up for the deficit in ability by being mentally prepared to fight to their limit, because anything short of that will expose them. The underdog's ferocity comes from knowing they are vulnerable.

Consider the opposite to the underdog – the **favourite**. This role is so often a poisoned chalice in sporting contests because of the *lack* of threat or challenge. It's hard to reverse a mindset like being tagged the favourite, because it's grounded in our RED emotional system, which operates in the here and now. Any images of *anticipated* success make our RED system feel that success has already occurred. The favourite's technical ability doesn't change but the way they perform does, because their unconscious mindset can whisper success, so they begin to lose their drive. (We'll look at this more a little later.)

Then there's the **champion's mindset** – the attitude of **training to win**. We've seen that in order to move forward we have to learn to be **comfortable being uncomfortable**. Rather than avoiding the most uncomfortable parts, champions identify their greatest vulnerabilities – where they feel least comfortable – and place intense focus on those aspects.

In contrast, time and again individuals and organisations flail and fail when a never-ending series of discomforts compounds to generate a **threat mindset**, signalled by complaints. They don't want to be there, and their mindset, taken into the performance arena, soon makes that a reality.

It's also important to make sure our motivation is coming from the right source. The key issue is whether we are driven from *within*, or whether we require pressure from *without*.

Looking back at what we learned in Chapter 3, under pressure, are we driven to **ESC-APE**, or to have **IMP-ACT**?

Being internally driven allows us to commit ourselves fully to the moment, because we're not relying on others to take us there. When we program ourselves to step into uncomfortable moments with composure, we have a greater chance of feeling in control and maintaining a grip on our emotional reaction. Astronauts and flight crews famously train to remain calm under pressure by simulating threatening scenarios. Relying on others will take us only so far.

Uncomfortable being comfortable

One level up from the champion's mindset is the **warrior's mindset** – the attitude of **training to dominate** (or training to master or lead). The warrior craves the test and wants to rise to the challenge. Only in the most demanding scenarios can they truly see how far they can go. They will seek out such challenges – with deep respect – and head straight for them.

The warrior mindset can be applied to gentler, non-combative pursuits because the same principles of fearlessness and truth hold. If we work in a creative field, it can be frightening to show others what we've produced – a work of art, a stage performance – because of possible judgment. But the warrior follows this path with the calmness born of simply accepting themselves for who they are and being curious to see how far they can go by constantly refining their performance.

These people want to face the greatest mental challenge and not flinch. For them, pressure is their territory of choice. Without the discomfort that comes with pressure, differences in mental strength can be hidden and it is anyone's game. Apply discomfort, and only the warriors are left standing. Discomfort is essential to their progress. In short, they are **uncomfortable being comfortable**.

As we've seen, we can't raise the level of our performance unless we're **comfortable being uncomfortable**. But the warrior mindset takes it a step further. When we're **uncomfortable being comfortable**, we're not just comfortable when discomfort arises, we're also *un*comfortable during those periods of comfort in between.

The power to change our mindset is much more than playing with words; it's a shift in psychology that takes our biology with it. *How* we see our world changes the way we experience it.

A powerful example is the life of Jewish psychiatrist Viktor Frankl, who survived four Nazi concentration camps and later wrote compellingly about his experiences. He argued that identifying our 'why' – our cause – can allow us to transcend even the most extreme hardships. Our work (performance), our relationships or even our struggle can bring deep meaning to our life.

From his own experience in the camps, and the experiences of those around him, he saw that interpreting the same situation in a different way can change how we feel and act. Instead of focusing on his suffering, he saw his traumatic experiences as an opportunity to learn. His own suffering immediately lessened as he used it to gain insights into how humans cope in such extreme circumstances.

He wrote that humans have the power to choose their response to any situation, no matter how great the hardship. This dovetails with what the RED–BLUE tool teaches us about how to separate a situation from our reaction to it. If we're capable of choosing our reaction in the most extreme situations, it follows that we can do so in less extreme, but still pressurised, environments.

And applying this principle is how those with the **training to dominate** mindset get ahead. It's not that they *like* discomfort, but they certainly like what it brings – the opportunity to stay in the struggle as others fall away, or become preoccupied with their own suffering. Instead of turning their attention inwards and fuelling their discomfort with a 'poor me' loop, these high performers focus on their external task, and allow their internal discomfort to gradually subside.

Frankl wrote that not only is there power in knowing our 'why' – the greater cause that we are pursuing – but it is also important not to pursue a life of complete comfort, because then we'll lack drive. He believed that carrying some tension – not being satisfied with the current situation – is mentally healthier than being tension-free, and can allow us to reach a higher level of effectiveness.

This completely reverses the standard thinking about comfort and its role in human performance.

This ability to reappraise a situation and find new meaning in it comes from our BLUE mind, especially our **left pre-frontal cortex**. We learned in Chapter 2 that our RED mind regulates our emotional state first and foremost, but then hands this information over to the BLUE mind for further reflection, before it is passed back to our RED mind for final processing. Our BLUE mind has the power to name *and* find meaning in a situation. Words and interpretation go hand in hand with our emotional regulation, which makes sense of all of our experiences.

When we're faced with a difficult obstacle, we have a choice of responses. We can focus on our internal suffering – or we can focus on the challenge, find meaning in that, and remain committed to the task at hand. And both choices lead to very different outcomes.

Our basic RED threat mechanisms will kick in straightaway, but we can revise our reaction through giving the obstacle a name and a new, more appealing meaning. That way, we're controlling our RED reactions through deliberate BLUE reflection.

Doing this in the middle of a struggle is the role of the RED–BLUE tool. But doing it ahead of time through the mental blueprint technique – more precisely, through changing our mindset – is an even stronger strategy. It will raise our **threshold** and **resilience** so we can meet the next challenge with our mindset already primed.

Even in the moments of greatest hardship, we have choice. Once we accept that, it opens up new doors to high performance, because we take more responsibility for the decisions we make every day.

Strive and thrive

Returning to Frankl's extreme example of human endurance, the ultimate question is not success or failure, but the nature of our response. For genuine warriors, the attitude they show in the middle of the struggle is far more critical than the outcome.

We saw in Chapter 3 that the root cause of RED **fixation** on regret or worry is being unable to face the outcome of losing. BLUE **flexibility** means *learning* from our performance rather than judging it.

With a **strive and thrive** mindset, we aim to do our best, no matter what the situation. We strive if we're leading and clearly going to win; and we strive if we've fallen behind and are clearly going to lose. Our reaction keeps us focused on the task – the process of getting where we want to go – and not on the question of whether we're going to get there or not.

A **win or lose** mindset will make us anxious and tense under pressure. A strive and thrive mindset will keep us energised and increase our chance of success. Just defining ourselves in relation to other people will not allow us to explore how far we can personally go. It will inevitably lead to a performance plateau.

But to reach our full potential we can't just consider the level we want to get to. We also need to look at the trajectory – how quickly we want to get there.

To get there efficiently and without delays, we must deliberately place ourselves in testing situations. The more we extend ourselves, the more we learn. By facing consistent challenges and monitoring how they affect us, we accelerate. And if we always manage to pass the test, we're not setting ourselves hard enough tests.

We can win or lose and never meet our potential. If we focus solely on winning and losing then we're ensuring that will be the case. If we focus on reaching our potential, set demanding tests, then strive and thrive, we've *already* won.

No one can meet all challenges. We keep our mindset positive and don't lose our spirit, even when we fall short. We commit to the next test, regardless of our last result. With this attitude we become emotionally balanced and resilient.

If we're unable to face unfavourable outcomes, we're limiting ourselves to a world of underperformance. If we face challenges with a strive and thrive mindset, we're on the fast track to fulfilling our potential.

> If you reflect on the big moments in your performance history, to what extent have you been mentally tied up in the outcome? Did you manage to enjoy the moment because of the thrill or gripping nature of being stretched to your limit? Or did you leave yourself vulnerable by narrowly defining yourself in terms of win or lose?
>
> What is your **mindset** for chasing performance – are you a winner and loser, or someone who extends themselves to the limit and, in so doing, *happens* to win or lose?

Our mental blueprint starts with our mindset, which recognises that we are in an emotional relationship with a pressured task. By working on our relationship with pressure beforehand, and committing to it even if we expect adversity, like all relationships, it will become stronger, allowing us to hold our nerve.

2. System: The Power of Sequences

With our **mindset** now simmering away, the next step in developing our mental blueprint is to put in place an effective **system.**

The word 'system' probably sounds daunting, but it's simply a plan that is broken down into connected parts. As we learned earlier, we've been making sense of the world all our lives by forming scripts, or systems, for how things work. We have systems for getting dressed, eating, washing and just about everything else we do. These systems are powerful, helping us interpret the world and guiding our responses. Developing a system is completely natural, so we can develop a system for a performance task too.

Let's return to the examples of Paul, the nurse, and Sandra, the college student. Both of them will be able to perform better when they can maintain a working overview of their performance. While he's covering for his manager, Paul needs a simple system that keeps him on track with standard routines, while helping him cope with unexpected situations. Sandra needs a simple system that helps her stay on time and maintains the structure of her essays. Neither will be well served if they get stuck on the detail and lose track of the bigger picture.

To build a pressure-proof system for our mental blueprint, we need to:

a.   Build a practical sequence
b.   Add in 'What if?'s

a) Build a practical sequence

The simplest system of all is the **sequence.**

Short sequences are BLUE brain heaven, engaging it on just about every level, and strengthening all the special BLUE brain abilities we learned about in Chapter 2. They use **logic, language** and **numbers,** because they're based on named and numbered parts. They are kind to **working memory** because they group information into small, connected segments. And to see where we are in a sequence, we need to consider a broader perspective, which activates our **metacognition** (our ability to think about thinking).

You might notice that many of the techniques in this book, such as the **RED–BLUE tool,** have a snappy, three-step sequence built into their structure. Like a physical salute, short mental sequences can snap you to attention.

We can use this innate ability to help us think clearly under pressure, by building simple mental sequences ahead of time. In high-pressure situations, they provide mental short cuts that allow us to make quick judgments. We don't have to use up our mental horsepower in the middle of a stressful situation, because we already have these sequences ready to go. When we lose our way or need a nudge in the right direction, like maps, short sequences reorient us quickly. They tell us where we are and what to do next.

Using short sequences like **timelines** is an ideal way to structure our performance plans. A timeline is a visual cue that helps us distinguish between what is in the past, what is happening right now, and what is in the future. Presenting a sequence in a visual way boosts our ability to call it up into our working memory. The capacity to imagine time as a line is almost universal.

Paul found that preparing a basic timeline of tasks for his nursing shift kept him on track as things got busy. Likewise, Sandra found that preparing a timeline and an essay structure based on a sequence kept her on point. While Paul and Sandra are focused on a task, the sequence or timeline sits quietly in the background, but as soon as they pause for a moment to reflect, it's instantly available to remind them where they are in the scheme of things. It helps them stay organised.

Sarah used a three-part sequence for each essay: Step 1 was the essay opening, Step 2 the essay body and Step 3 the conclusion. She prepared essay plans for seven topics using this structure so that each plan had a sequence of two possible opening statements, seven main bullet points for the essay body – each with examples and facts – and two possible conclusions, so that she had a selection of sentences and lines of argument that she could choose from to suit the essay question. Sarah was delighted to find three essay questions that matched her plans well, and by following her sequences achieved her best grade.

Sequences don't take action *for* us – the plans won't organise the shift for Paul, or write the exam for Sandra – but they certainly drive our perception of what we see in front of us, help us get our bearings, and guide our thoughts and actions in that moment in a helpful way. If Paul becomes preoccupied by the needs of one patient, or Sandra becomes lost in one paragraph of her essay, returning their attention to their sequence or timeline will quickly get them back on track.

Examples of sequences are found everywhere in the world of performance. Sometimes it's so vital not to miss important steps, and the risks are so extreme, that checklists are produced to reduce the number of thinking errors, as for flight crews and surgical teams. In fact, in some ways the purpose of a checklist is to allow you to work your way through potentially overwhelming situations *without* thinking; just working your way from step to step is enough.

In these situations, **checklists** – simple, prepared and practised sequences – can become essential mental blueprints for survival. No good in constructing such a checklist in the middle of the emergency; it's the fact that it's been prepared beforehand and we've already become familiar with it that makes it effective when the time comes because the structure gives us immediate orientation and mental space to adjust and be flexible. Checklists are particularly helpful if we use them repeatedly.

In the sports world we see another form of prepared sequence: pre-shot **rituals** and **routines**. Watch a rugby player before they kick a ball, a tennis player before they serve, or a golfer before they play their shot and you will see prepared sequences in action. A golfer, for example, might have a pre-shot routine that includes standing behind the shot and visualising the path of the ball; identifying an intermediate target to aim for; taking a deep in-and-out breath; adopting their posture; taking one practice swing; checking the intermediate target; a further in-and-out breath; and then playing their shot while focusing on the 'feel' of the ball. These personal rituals provide a solid, familiar structure that the person can follow almost unthinkingly, so it helps protect their mind from straying and interfering with their game. It creates a kind of bubble around the individual so they're not distracted by the pressure, keeping them in the BLUE and warding off intrusive RED thoughts.

Now that we have a short sequence in place for a personal task, we can make it more pressure-resistant by adding in '**What if?**'s.

b) Add in 'What if?'s

Unfortunately, things don't always go according to plan, so it makes sense to stress-test our **sequence** by challenging it with '**What if?**'s.

'What if?'s involve looking ahead, anticipating the main things that could go wrong, and planning a response: 'If things go according to plan, do X; but if *this* situation arises, do Y.' It means we'll have a helpful prepared reaction to an unwanted situation, or even a *worst-case scenario*.

What if?'s are BLUE mental shortcuts that we can choose to follow or not, as the situation demands. Our RED intuition will help us decide whether to use them in each case. They're ideal for uncertain performance conditions when we don't want to think through all the complexity. It's time for performance, not paralysis by analysis.

Paul might foresee that two urgent situations could occur at the same time, so his 'What if?' could involve delegating responsibility for each situation to a senior nurse, so he doesn't get tied up in either one and can continue overseeing the unit as a whole. Sandra might anticipate that there could be an essay question on the exam paper she feels less confident about answering. Her 'What if?' might involve doing the easier essays first to gain confidence *before* she goes back to tackle the more difficult option.

No one can predict every eventuality, but by developing robust 'What if?'s, we bolster our performance sequence and make it more resistant to pressure. Our mind becomes used to adapting our basic sequence to suit the conditions, so that even if we haven't prepared for a certain turn of events, we've already developed skill in maintaining RED–BLUE balance and holding our nerve.

Putting it all together

Reacting randomly to whatever appears will sometimes work out for us, but more often it won't. Using effective systems in high-pressure situations speeds up our reaction time. When we are actively looking for cues with a familiar mental tool, we'll be alert and controlled. When we are reactive and *not* trying to anticipate what lies ahead, we're much more likely to display unhelpful **APE** behaviours.

Most of us have good systems for our areas of *technical* expertise, but in my experience even accomplished performers are found wanting when it comes to the *human* elements. Most people are competent at drawing a diagram of technical aspects of their role, but all at sea when I ask them for a diagram of the mental elements (which is why I've written this book!).

If we spend time developing simple systems for our most challenging areas of performance, it will pay dividends in terms of our ability to see the reality in front of us, anticipate the consequences of various actions, and decide the right path to travel down. We shouldn't cross the road without one.

Under pressure, this will enable you to **find your move**.

3. Skillset: Using Rough Conditions to Smooth Our Skills

In building the mental blueprint for our next level of performance, once we have our **mindset** right and our **system** in place, we can concentrate on the performance itself. Our **skillset** is focused on execution – what we need to do, and how to do it accurately.

Under pressure, the default, one-size-fits-all approach is more comfortable, because it requires less effort. But skilful performance is about being able to adjust your delivery every time, rather than being tempted to revert to a standard procedure.

To be an exceptional performer we have to pay attention to the detail so we can make small adjustments to deliver a better outcome. Top performers are intrigued by small variations, because by making the necessary adjustments, they can achieve the perfect balance. The exceptional performer doesn't just carry out the task, they nail it.

The ordinary salesperson runs through their routine more or less by rote. The exceptional salesperson still uses a general framework, but tailors each comment to the individual client.

The ordinary waiter treats every table the same. The exceptional waiter develops an interest in the people at each table and personalises the service.

The ordinary babysitter goes through the motions with each set of children. The exceptional babysitter connects with each child, and balances fairness with a personal flavour.

What needs to be adjusted will vary according to the situation. The salesperson explores their client's unique situation and emphasises the relevant benefits of their product, rather than robotically listing product features. The waiter approaches each table with their mind open to understanding personal preferences, and adjusts their behaviour and timing to deliver a special experience. And the babysitter engages with each child with genuine interest and adjusts their tone to match.

Whether it's the emphasis, timing or tone, small adjustments have a large impact on the situation.

The skilful performer needs **sharp skills**, not **blunt techniques**, and the surprising secret to developing these is the same no matter what our pursuit: abrasion.

In the same way as a knife-edge is ground on a whetstone, our skills are honed by being exposed to harsh situations. Practising them in isolation will lead to routine performance. Rehearsing them in demanding circumstances forces us to adjust and develop them.

The skill ladder

Developing our skills is like climbing up a **skill ladder** that has three rungs. Level 1 is basic **technique**. Level 2 is **skill**. Level 3 is **pressure**.

On Level 1, we first break our technique down into smaller, more manageable parts and keep refining each part through practice. A tennis player might practise his serve throw. A chef might practise making the sauce for her new dish. A manager might rehearse his opening comments for a presentation.

Then all the parts are brought together into a coherent whole, but still in isolation. The tennis player practises his full serve, without an opponent. The chef prepares the new dish from start to finish, but not for customers. The manager gives the complete presentation, to an empty room. Constant *whole-part-whole* repetition makes the process so familiar it's automatic.

On Level 2, **technique** becomes **skill**. In performing a technique, our focus is on running through a standard procedure. In executing a skill, our focus is on engaging with our immediate circumstances – making specific adjustments to have the most efficient impact.

On this level, we learn to adapt our technique to a simulated situation. The situation is not demanding, but it's realistic. It must resemble the scenarios where we want to improve as closely as possible. The tennis player practises his serve against a less skilled opponent. The chef prepares the new dish and serves it up to her family. The manager gives his presentation to a group of friends.

Finally, on Level 3, an element or two of **pressure** is added. The tennis player serves in a practice match against a respected opponent, and they restrict themselves to only one serve per point so they have to get it right first time. The chef invites a fellow chef with a reputation for high standards and biting criticism to her restaurant to taste her new dish. The manager presents to a senior colleague renowned for her honesty.

Levels 1 and 2 refine techniques into skills – first in an isolated, then in a controlled setting. Level 3 introduces real-world challenges and demands adjustments.

In some scenarios, like sport, there is far more time spent in preparation than performance. But that doesn't mean the skill ladder is irrelevant to time-poor situations where there's little opportunity to practise.

A shop assistant might develop his management skills by spending five minutes each day practising how to deal with suppliers instead of customers. At Level 1 their focus is on building brief checklists for calls to a supplier for different parts of the supply sequence: leading up to, during and after a shop promotion of the supplier's special range of products. Level 2 of

SKILL LADDER

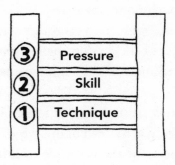

The skill ladder reminds us to polish our technical foundations and to pressure test our skills.

the skill ladder involves practising these calls with an experienced colleague who is familiar with how suppliers function. And at Level 3 the shop assistant practises calls with a senior colleague where there is an imaginary dispute or conflict with the supplier, which puts pressure on the shop assistant.

Practice in environments where there is *moderate* stress can prepare us for *high*-stress situations. As long as the training scenario engages us emotionally, it allows us to work on controlling our emotions *while* we're performing the skill.

Take rehearsals, for example: a tried and trusted method of preparing for a stage show. The last rehearsal takes place in full costume to closely resemble what it will be like on opening night. This has a big effect on our mental condition – people get more anxious at dress rehearsals – which is great practice for the real thing.

Coaches and players in sports teams often claim it's impossible to fully recreate the pressurised environment of, say, a final with 100,000 people watching. But what would happen if those in high-stakes occupations adopted the same attitude?

Flight crews practise dealing with challenging situations in a simulator. It's generally accepted that this innovation has led to a marked decrease in crew-related errors. Yet the crews are fully aware that they are going into a practice scenario, not a real plane with real passengers. They spend years training to increase their emotional control in strenuous, confronting situations.

We've seen that **uncertainty** is a core feature of pressure. When crews go into a simulator, they're not sure what they'll face. And then, just when they feel they have the situation under control, a new twist is unexpectedly thrown in to test their ability to adjust *during* their performance.

A well-known military mantra is that the plan survives only until first contact with the enemy; after that, it's impossible to predict exactly what is going to occur. Special military and police forces train so that their basic technical expertise is rock-solid, then immense physical pressure is applied to lay bare their ability to deal with changing circumstances, both personally and as a team. Level 3 pressure training is taken to new heights, even though it falls short of real combat.

The message is clear: when we can't recreate the conditions in which we'll perform, there is value in approximating them, especially by being creative in introducing an emotional element at Level 3 of the skill ladder.

We need to work our way through *all three* levels – up and down the ladder – to sharpen our skills and polish our performance, so we'll be able to stand up under pressure. Neglecting Levels 1 and 2 will mean our foundations aren't reliable. Neglecting Level 3 means we'll be vulnerable when adjustments are required.

I've noticed a tendency for individuals and teams to practise at what I call 'Levels 1½ to 2½'. Most of them appreciate the need to test their skills, but do so only in a limited way. Ordinary performers might break down their technique to some extent, but exceptional performers become engrossed in the detail. They isolate and refine tiny adjustments *and they* practise in red-hot environments (yes, RED-hot).

If we only develop BLUE brain habits, we will be vulnerable when our RED brain kicks in. We want to be able to perform BLUE brain functions – thinking clearly, seeing the options, focusing attention – when our RED brain is activated.

Fine-tuning our balance and timing

Sandpaper is used to take the rough edges off a surface. The finer the grade of sandpaper, the smoother the result. The same thing happens as we **fine-tune** our skills: exposing ourselves to rough conditions is a powerful way of upgrading our skillset.

So how do we do this? With **balance** and **timing**.

The skilful tennis player strikes the ball with perfect timing – not too early, not too late. The skilful chef bakes their dish for just the right amount of time – not too little, not too much. The skilful speaker delivers the punch line at just the right moment – not too soon, not too late. The skilful trader sells the shares at just the right time – not too early, not too late. And the skilful parent attends to their angry child at just the right moment – not too early, not too late.

In all cases, skill is a matter of balance and timing. Thinking ahead and pinpointing the key timing issues will give us a perfectly balanced performance.

When we're crossing the road, the skill comes with adjusting our timing according to the circumstances: altering our pace to allow for the speed of the traffic, slowing down when it's raining or we're crossing a road at night. The skilful operator is closely focused on the world around them, and constantly making the necessary shifts to get the right timing and therefore the right outcomes.

External focus requires inner balance. When we're distracted by worrying thoughts, a negative content loop or other mental clutter, we cannot be as connected with our environment.

Our sense of the perfect balance is impossible to describe, because it comes from our senses and emotions – our RED brain – and that goes by instinct and feel, not words. But what we will most definitely be able to say is whether we are going too fast or too slow for our environment, or in what particular way we are out of balance. It's difficult to describe what we *do* want, but fairly easy to tell when it isn't quite right.

Our thinking minds are often poor at describing physical sensations and feelings in an accurate way, because that is asking the BLUE brain to do a RED brain job. But what the BLUE brain *can* pick up on is relative judgments. The right RED brain can send the message 'Too little' or 'Too much', 'Too fast' or 'Too slow', and the BLUE brain can picture that easily, put words to it, and make the adjustment.

We know when we have too little time to cross a road. We know when our dish has too little seasoning to bring all the elements together. And we know when we are too tense to perform our sporting movements fluently. In each case, if we're a skilful operator, we'll make an adjustment to our **mental blueprint**.

The strong operator – who has a **champion's mindset** – will make adjustments during their performance. And the *standout* operator – who has a **warrior's mindset** – will make the adjustments during the *toughest moments* of their performance.

When we're focused on balance and timing, we're not focused on the mechanical steps of how to perform a task – that's best left to our unconscious RED mind. We're not even thinking about our timing and balance, because that would be *thinking* about the task rather than doing it. All we're doing is setting our focus, allowing ourselves to perform, and noticing the small variations in our immediate environment. As we go we make micro-adjustments that allow us to get our RED and BLUE minds in sync.

Rather than being a source of pressure, the **small margins** and **fast changes** in our external environment become critical information that keeps us engaged, so we'll continue making adjustments and achieve that perfect balance.

Once we have that perfect balance in mind, our mental blueprint is completed.

Putting It All Together: The Penalty Shoot-out

The penalty kick in football (soccer) is a classic pressure test. In training, professional footballers can kick a ball 12 metres accurately enough to score the majority of times. But put them into a situation where they stand arms-across-shoulders with teammates at the halfway mark, then have to take a long and lonely walk up to the penalty spot, where they are confronted with a goalkeeper who is trying to mess with their mind, while the world is watching in a championship knockout game ... and a simple task becomes a genuine mental challenge.

The penalty shoot-out has all the elements of the perfect **pressure equation** (Chapter 5). The **stakes** are **high**: this moment affects not just the player but also their team and their club or country. There is genuine **uncertainty** in penalty shoot-outs: no one knows what will happen. There are **small margins**: hitting the post is not good enough. There are **fast changes**: right now the team are on top, but if the player misses they'll be on the verge of elimination. And all of this is occurring within a cauldron of **judgment**. The three components of judgment (**ESC** – Chapter 3) are also present. There are **expectations** that professional players should be able to score; massive **scrutiny** from teammates, staff, fans and commentators; and **consequences** not only in terms of the immediate win-or-lose outcome, but also in terms of future reputation.

Despite the foreseeable pressure, many coaches and footballers pay scant attention to practising penalty kicks. They haven't developed a **mindset** that will help control their emotional reaction, a **system** to anchor their attention, or a **skillset** that allows them to fine-tune their basic techniques.

Consider how a football coach might develop the mental blueprint of their players to help them deal with this situation.

First, the coach can ask each player to develop a personal penalty routine just as a professional golfer has a pre-shot routine. The routine has three main elements: a brief opening settling breath to clear their mind and calm their body; a personalised system of approach to the ball and set-up that provides a familiar and repeatable sequence of movements; and a selection of three different penalty kicks they have practised and like executing, with at least one option to the left and one to the right – high or low, passed or driven – to give them choice.

Then, the coach can use repeated scenario training involving two teams competing against each other at the end of training to mimic match conditions, so that the players have to rehearse the whole process of the penalty shoot-out just as they would in a game, including walking from halfway to take their penalty kick in front of everyone else.

Whatever our performance field, we can build and practise a mental blueprint that will serve us well when we have to walk up to the spot.

Exercise: Sharpening Our Mental Blueprint

Now our mental blueprint is in place, we're almost ready to go. But first, let's check that we have the technique down cold by doing the following exercise on a blank piece of paper.

- Choose a particular performance situation you find uncomfortable. At the very top of the page write **PRESSURE** and beneath it name the situation and write down three words or phrases that describe the pressure involved.
- Underneath that, draw a line across the page. Write **INTENT** above the line, and below it write down three words or phrases that describe what people observing you would actually see and feel if you were performing at the next level up in that situation.
- Draw a second line across the bottom third of the page, write **REALITY** above it, and below it write down three words or phrases that describe what is currently working well in this situation. (The lines create a visual gap, which boosts your BLUE brain power.) Then put a + next to them. Now write down three words or phrases that describe what is holding you back. Put a − next to them.
- Now draw a mental blueprint triangle in the middle of the gap between **INTENT** and **REALITY**, and label the corners **MINDSET**, **STRUCTURES** and **SKILLSET**. Below each label, write down one action you could take that would help you bridge your performance gap.
- Once you've completed this process, you've **created a performance gap** and then upgraded your mental blueprint to **bridge the gap** for that uncomfortable situation.

If we're able to work through the exercise without having to refer back to the material earlier in the chapter, we're ready to use the mental blueprint technique to form plans of action that will work and stick: we are primed to perform under pressure.

PERFORMING UNDER PRESSURE

Never confuse movement with action.

Ernest Hemingway, author (1899–1961)

CHAPTER 7

PRE-PERFORMANCE TECHNIQUES

So far we've met the basic **RED–BLUE tool** (Chapter 4), which we can use at any stage during our performance, and the **mental blueprint technique** (Chapter 6), which we can use when we're preparing to perform, to enhance our use of the RED–BLUE tool. (As we'll see in Chapter 12, we can also use it for review.) Now I'm going to introduce two handy techniques that we can use just before we perform:

1. The **three circles technique** – use in the *days* before you perform
2. The **ICE technique (intensity, clarity, execution)** – use in the *days or minutes* before you perform

These techniques suit situations where there's a clear build-up to our performance. But even when our performance is more constant, there are usually moments when we need to step up and perform at a higher level. An air-traffic controller or executive assistant will always need to be on their game, but there will be key moments when the pressure is really on – when there's a mayday call, or an important meeting. In these moments, their ability to perform under pressure makes the difference.

In situations where we have to sustain attention over extended periods of time – and often fight off boredom – pressure also arises. The draining effect of looking at an unchanging picture for a long time can also disrupt our focus.

Both acute pressure – when the intensity can be *overwhelming* – and chronic pressure – when the intensity can be *underwhelming* – can have an impact on our performance by distracting our attention. The **three circles** and **ICE** techniques will help us prime ourselves to perform.

The Three Circles Technique

The **three circles technique** quickly organises our thoughts into a visual format that separates what we *want* to focus attention on from what we *don't*. The tool is most useful **in the days before our performance**, when we want to take our mental blueprint and tailor it to a specific situation. If our performance is continuous, it still pays to remind ourselves what we should be focusing on, because it reduces the chance of lapses in concentration. For that reason, even though the three circles tool is primarily a preparation technique to help us sharpen our focus of attention, once the three circles are in place they also can provide a useful visual snapshot we can refer to in our minds *during* performance to redirect our focus when we go off track.

If you're like most people, you get stuck by fixating on things that are outside your control, which is a great way to drive yourself deeper into a RED state of mind. Fortunately it becomes very easy to avoid this problem once we're clear about where our attention should be.

Here's how the three circles technique works.

1. Take a blank sheet of paper, draw a circle in **RED** on the left-hand side and write **CAN'T CONTROL** above it. For one minute, make a list inside the circle of factors within your next performance that you *can't* control. These could include the weather, the traffic, sudden emergencies and other people's reactions.

2. On the right-hand side of the page, draw a circle in **BLUE** and write **CAN CONTROL** above it. For one minute, make a list inside the circle of factors within your next performance that you *can* control. You might include your emotional reaction, your mental focus, your preparation, your response to unpredictable events, your ability to adjust to small changes in your environment, and your review process afterwards.

3. In the middle of the two circles, draw a third circle in black and write **CAN INFLUENCE** above it. For one minute, make a list inside the circle of the factors in the **CAN'T CONTROL** list that you can *influence*, even if you can't fully control them. Add in any other factors you can influence but not control that come to mind. You'll probably find you're able to include several things you initially thought you *couldn't* control in the middle circle. For example, you might leave the weather in the **CAN'T CONTROL** circle, but put other people's reactions in the **CAN INFLUENCE** circle, because you can influence other people's reactions by the way you behave towards *them*. If you move an item from **CAN'T CONTROL** to **CAN INFLUENCE**, cross it out in the **CAN'T CONTROL** circle.

The three circles technique shows us how much of our valuable time and attention we squander. The main trap is getting caught up in factors that are outside of our control and offer no performance gain. It's a futile activity, but most of us do it anyway, because those CAN'T CONTROL items usually carry significant emotional charge. We might not always be able to

THREE CIRCLES

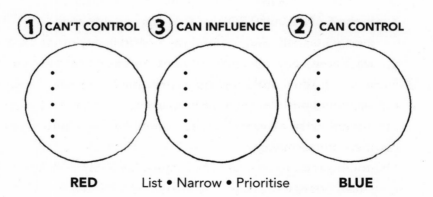

(1) CAN'T CONTROL **(3) CAN INFLUENCE** **(2) CAN CONTROL**

RED   List • Narrow • Prioritise   **BLUE**

The three circles sequence helps us to focus on things we can control or at least influence, and avoid becoming fixated on the things we can't.

control people's behaviour, but we often can't stop ourselves from reacting with frustration or anxiety. As we've learned, physical and social threats trigger our RED system to focus on our survival, even when we're chasing BLUE-minded goals. And our RED system is primed by threatening incidents from our past. Old emotional memories interfere with modern-day objectives.

Because our BLUE mind works using spatial and visual elements – like a laptop screen – when we use the three circles technique we not only create *visual* boundaries, we create *mental* boundaries too. By focusing our attention *only* on factors that are within our control or influence, we will easily spot when our attention slips over into the CAN'T CONTROL circle.

We should only allow ourselves to pay attention to the middle circle to the extent that it's useful. Reflecting on the items in the right-hand, BLUE circle will give us a lot more benefit. But advanced performers will pay *some* attention to the CAN INFLUENCE circle because those factors will still have a subtle impact.

The three circles technique, then, is a visual attention controller that shields us from emotional diversions. We see them, we know they are there, but we simply redirect our attention. If we allow our attention to drift onto the RED items, half of our mind will be trying to keep doing the task, and half will be caught up in a negative content loop. Our split attention will cost our performance.

The three circles technique uses colour-coded circles to get a dose of BLUE clarity back into the energised RED picture. And because it's quick and easy to use, it's much more likely we'll use it consistently in our preparation.

Focusing on the CAN CONTROL and CAN INFLUENCE factors means we'll quickly see changes in the situation because we've anticipated them, and we can act accordingly. Our actions will have an impact because they relate to things that we *know* we can control or influence.

Before a big performance event our lists will be ready to go in five minutes, quickly leaving us feeling mentally organised and on top of things (although you can take longer if you find the three circles technique suits you). They can be constantly updated as our performance draws closer.

We can draw up a new three circles page for each new performance; some items will probably be repeated but other items will be specific to each event.

By constantly repeating this mental process, we'll develop a tight connection between our perceptions and our actions. We will be getting performance gains through subtle adjustments and adaptations.

Consider the reverse process, when we *don't* prepare and haven't anticipated the variables that will be relevant to our performance. We'll have no clear idea of which factors we can or can't control. During our performance we'll be confronted by a mass of unpredicted factors. We'll adopt a reactive, unstructured and unplanned approach to a raft of dynamic changes in our environment.

The two options are starkly different.

If you tend to get diverted by things that are outside of your control as you prepare for a performance moment, the three circles technique will give you immediate focus of attention and the foundation for stronger mental performance.

Use the *visual* boundaries to create *mental* boundaries. Use the three circles technique consistently, and change from being reactive and random in your mental preparation to being consistently well prepared and able to take things in your stride.

Variation: Mr Three Things – Expect the Unexpected

This is an offshoot of the **three circles technique** that uses the same principles to help us avoid being derailed by sudden events that seem to happen when we least need them.

Last-minute illnesses and injuries, family dramas, or unusual circumstances that no one saw coming, have the potential to knock us off our stride. There's a very human way of reacting to these surprises: by catastrophising.

So how can we deal with these unexpected events? Simple: expect them.

Ask people how often these unexpected events occur, and they usually say, 'Oh, all the time.' Which immediately raises an obvious question: if they happen 'all the time', why are they unexpected?

To confuse matters even further, there are actually *two kinds* of unexpected events: *expected* and *unexpected*.

'Expected' unexpected events are the ones we can actually foresee, and are better described as *unlikely* events. We don't want them, but we know they are possible and so we could actually plan for them if we were being thorough.

'Unexpected' unexpected events are the kinds of events that no one can anticipate. They can't be specifically prepared for, because they're genuinely unpredictable.

But even though we can't predict such events, we can mentally prepare for them so we're less disturbed by them when they (inevitably) turn up. Simply hoping for the best leaves us open to disappointment, shock and self-pity. But if we're vigilant, constantly on the lookout for potentially disruptive events, we'll see them early and deal with them smoothly.

In Chapter 6, we saw that we can rename 'expected' unexpected events **'What if?'s** and train our mind to anticipate them, even though we can't know what shape they will take. Calling them 'What if?'s will help immunise us against overreactions when they show up.

But rather than anticipating just *one* undesirable event, we should expect *three*.

When **three things** come knocking – especially if they sit outside our control – we simply say, 'Oh, there's Mr Three Things,' and count them off, one by one. On no account do we assume that just because we have had *some* bad luck, there will not be any further visits. No way. The next unexpected event can be expected soon – in the next few days or the lead-up to an important event – and then the third, because that is the nature of three things.

> Gary is an advertising executive who's travelling to an important meeting with a potential client. He knows the client will only give his firm the contract if his pitch is well received.
>
> He's painstakingly prepared the pitch, and is especially pleased with his PowerPoint presentation. He even left home early to give himself extra time. But he didn't anticipate the serious traffic accident that has left him stranded and the freeway blocked. He didn't anticipate that his colleague Lynn, who was coming to the meeting with him, would phone to say she received devastating family news last night and couldn't be there. And though he eventually makes it through a herculean series of traffic nightmares and turns up (late), he also didn't anticipate the technology glitch, which means the main part of his pitch is useless.
>
> Mr Three Things certainly showed up.

No one wants to go through what happened to Gary. The risk is that we lose our ability to think flexibly and creatively.

We find ourselves pitched into a RED 'poor me' loop, feeling victimised by misfortune as well as flustered, rushed and self-conscious – everyone is looking at us. It's all too much for us and we momentarily freeze.

Here's what could have happened if Gary had applied a three things mindset:

When the three things happen, he shrugs off the events as unfortunate but doesn't take them personally. He keeps a sense of perspective, and feels for Lynn with her family crisis, rather than feeling sorry for himself. As the screen goes black and his PowerPoint presentation disappears, he's aware of tension in his shoulders and a churning feeling inside his abdomen, but he keeps his focus on finding a solution.

He reminds himself that everyone faces obstacles, and it's those who cope with them best who flourish. Suddenly he's energised to show the client that the quality of his pitch can overcome any technical mishap. He's prepared a 'What if?' scenario for technology breakdowns, and has worked out a basic three-minute verbal presentation that conveys the key messages in a punchy, quick and powerful way. The client is impressed and awards him the contract.

At truly significant events – the kind that occur only once a year, or every few years – three things can even become *five* things. As we become familiar with the Mr Three Things approach, we accept that we won't remain in perfect emotional balance, but we become much more philosophical about unfortunate events. We even look forward to counting them off, feeling good that we are dealing with Mr Three Things' visits seamlessly, one by one, as others struggle to come to terms with their bad luck.

Unexpected events will keep showing up, whether we're prepared or not. It's our reaction to them that counts. Like the three circles technique, Mr Three Things keeps our attention focused on things we *can* control or influence, not on things we can't.

We know that RED moments make us more self-conscious, and we can start to go into a 'poor me' loop when we feel that others don't have the same obstacles. But if we reframe the challenge as a contest to see who deals with Mr Three Things best – and *everyone* experiences him in one form or another – our emotional self-control will be boosted. In a team environment, Mr Three Things appearances can be counted together as a deliberate shared ploy to note but avoid overreactions to unfortunate events.

Adopt a Mr Three Things mindset: anticipate, anticipate, anticipate, and become the one who's calm and clear under pressure while others fall apart.

The ICE Technique: Two Minutes and You're Ready to Go

The two-minute **intensity, clarity, execution (ICE)** routine is a quick and reliable way to get into a performance state of mind. We can use it any time from days before our performance to minutes before we start. The ICE technique leads into the RED–BLUE tool, and is the perfect way to prepare ourselves to have impact during our performance. We can use the ICE routine to calm our nerves or fire ourselves up, depending on what we need.

The ICE technique uses **three sets of three breaths, repeated,** to create a routine that is easy and quick, but long enough to bring together three key elements:

1. Intensity – controlling our level of RED arousal
2. Clarity – getting a clear BLUE overview
3. Execution – performing efficiently with RED–BLUE balance

As we learned in Chapter 4, the normal adult breathing rate at rest is 12 to 16 breaths per minute – one breath in and out every five seconds or so. This means you can go through the nine-breath ICE routine twice comfortably in two minutes. Again, you'll have to adapt this to your own capacity. Trained athletes often have lower breathing rates, and going through the routine twice might take them three minutes.

Whether it takes us two minutes or three, the routine is short, which helps us get mental focus quickly and efficiently. We have more time in the preparation phase than during performance, which is why the ICE technique takes longer than the RED–BLUE tool. But if we made it *too* long we'd lose focus, so it's better to keep it relatively brief and repeat it several times a day.

Sit in a comfortable position with your spine erect and eyes closed. (When you're familiar with the process, you can try doing it standing or walking, with your eyes open.)

1. **Intensity (Body):** In the first set of three breaths, focus on your level of RED arousal and tension. As you breathe in, imagine a concentrated ball of white light forming in the core of your abdomen. As you breathe out, visualise it spreading through your body as hot RED light if you need more energy, or cool BLUE light if you need more calm. As the light flows around your body, try to feel the temperature change as it reaches your face, fingers and toes. (It might help to imagine you are breathing air in, then pumping it around the body, as if you were using a bicycle tyre pump.) Run through this sequence three times. With these three breaths, you're switching on your RED 'body' system, which runs on physical sensations, to give you a feel for the intensity you'll need during your performance.

2. **Clarity (Mind):** In the second set of three breaths, focus on an especially challenging moment you anticipate in your performance. As you breathe in, picture yourself as a spectator, sitting in the perfect position to see the whole situation evolving. As you breathe out, imagine watching yourself deal with the situation in a decisive way to produce the perfect outcome. Run through this sequence three times. With these three breaths, you're switching on your BLUE system, which runs on images and thinking ahead, to give you mental clarity for your performance.

3. **Execution (Body–Mind):** In the third set of three breaths, focus on a crucial timing moment within your performance. As you breathe in, imagine that moment is unfolding right now. As you breathe out, imagine performing the task with perfect timing, silently marking the precise moment with a mental 'click'. Run through this sequence three times. With these three breaths, you're tuning into your RED and BLUE mind systems through the use of timing, which you can only achieve when both are in sync. Timing engages your RED and BLUE systems simultaneously, ready for the seamless execution of your performance.

Once you've repeated the full nine-breath cycle, go through the same process again, but this time double the vividness of each step.

At the completion of the second sequence, silently say the word '**Trust**'. ('Trust' is a 'feeling word' that anchors and connects all three elements, reminding us to let our balanced RED–BLUE state of mind run things naturally and intuitively.)

THE ICE TECHNIQUE

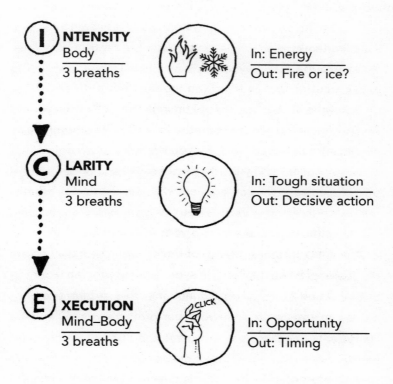

INTENSITY
Body
3 breaths

In: Energy
Out: Fire or ice?

CLARITY
Mind
3 breaths

In: Tough situation
Out: Decisive action

EXECUTION
Mind–Body
3 breaths

CLICK

In: Opportunity
Out: Timing

The ICE sequence provides a brief, repeatable visualisation
routine to prime us for action.

The ICE technique deliberately uses the sequence of activating our RED system through the body, then our BLUE system through the mind, then connecting our RED and BLUE systems through a moment of timing. We can see the process as getting us into our mental 'purple patch', with both systems primed, connected and ready to go.

Let's look at how this might work in a couple of real-life situations.

Rico is a footballer who's three days out from a cup final. He's feeling a little nervous about scoring goals on the big occasion.

Before training, he goes through his ICE routine. He closes his eyes, notes the tension in his body and breathes in, imagining a ball of white light forming in his abdomen. As he breathes out he visualises BLUE light spreading through his body, dissolving tension and calming him down. He repeats this twice, sensing a cool feeling in his cheeks, fingers and toes: just the way he wants to feel in the heat of the cup final.

Next, he breathes in and visualises a piece of play where his team get the ball and break forward on the counter-attack. As he breathes out he imagines two different options he can use to break free from the other team's defenders. He repeats this twice so he can see the options clearly in his mind.

As he breathes in to start the final sequence, in his mind's eye he sees a teammate passing the ball into his path so he has a clear line of sight to the goal. As he breathes out, he imagines connecting cleanly with the ball and scoring with perfect timing, which he mentally marks with a 'click' at the point of contact. He repeats this twice – each time with stronger feelings and more vivid mental pictures – to mentally score another two goals.

Once he has completed the first cycle, he goes through it again, this time adding yet more vividness to his mental pictures. As usual, he feels his second run-through is a definite step up in quality.

Rico completes the whole process, silently saying to himself, 'Trust.' He enjoys doing the ICE routine because it is short, simple and structured, and it makes him feel light, bright and clear. He uses it three times a day leading into a match, which seems to settle his body and mind down, reducing doubt and overthinking.

Lina is a business graduate going for her first job. She's sitting outside the boardroom of a company where she really wants to work, nervously waiting for her interview. She has five minutes before she's due to go in. She feels a little flat and lacking in energy.

She goes through the ICE routine she's developed in preparation for this moment. She does a three-breath cycle imagining a white ball of light forming then spreading fiery RED light throughout her body. Body status? Check!

She does a second three-breath cycle and imagines herself in the boardroom being asked her first question. It's a challenging question with several parts to it. She sees herself responding with calm and poise, providing an effective overview then backing it up with practical details. Mind status? Check!

Third, she imagines reaching the end of the final question, then visualises shaking the hand of each of the company partners and looking them in the eye in a perfectly timed sequence. To each handshake she adds a mental click, to create a warm but strong final impression. Mind–body? Check! She then repeats the process twice, each time going for increasingly vivid mental pictures. Then she silently says the word 'Trust'.

Lina goes through the ICE routine once more, but this time, with the mental pictures fresh in her mind, she is able to make them brighter and more energising.

She knows that events will unfold differently as soon as she enters the room, but she smiles as she notices that there are just two minutes to go and she is feeling ready to perform strongly.

A two-minute ICE routine is not something we can make up on the spot. It's something we develop and refine over time to suit our needs.

When we first start using the ICE technique, it's not a good idea to try to develop all three sequences – RED body, BLUE mind and RED–BLUE timing – at once. It's better to start with just one section and take our time to build up the mental imagery. We could stay with that one aspect for a minute or two while we mentally put the images and sensations in place. Once we have those moments identified, we can hone the routine so we're switching the mental pictures on quickly. The content should be highly personal and memorable so that it runs like clockwork in our head.

And we shouldn't worry if the visual images and physical sensations are vague as we develop our skill in using the ICE technique. The fact that it is based on repeated bursts of mental effort means that what was vague quickly crystallises into clear pictures and feelings. The ICE technique will develop our powers of concentration and stop our mind from wandering off.

Depending on our performance field, we might find that using one familiar ICE routine over and over works well for us, but equally we can create a new ICE routine for each new event to keep our build-up fresh and relevant.

The ICE technique is an ideal way to prime our body and mind for action. It's especially helpful when our final preparations are unexpectedly cut short by lateness arriving at a venue caused by traffic jams, changes in the timeline or other human factors. Once we're comfortable with the ICE routine, we'll remain unfazed by these unexpected obstacles, knowing we can be mentally ready to go in two minutes. We can also take the ICE technique into more demanding situations, such as using it on the team coach on the way to the stadium, or in the dressing room before the match – or even at half-time to get ourselves going again. And with a little imagination, we can adapt the ICE technique so we can use it as we travel to work, sit in our office before a big presentation, or rehearse a challenging conversation with a confrontational colleague. Our target is to become so familiar with the routine that we can shut out the noise of the world around us and focus with real precision for three minutes.

It is enormously reassuring to have a solid, repeatable 'go to' mental routine that quickly primes us for action. Because it's so brief, it's also flexible.

Our control over our state of mind is independent of the environment. Equipped with the ICE technique, we don't have to worry about what is placed in front of us because we know that we can front up, ready to go, in short order. Other factors may disrupt what happens *around* us, but nothing can disrupt what goes on *inside* us.

Once we develop our own ICE routine – or series of routines – we may even *look forward* to feeling the pressure mount, because we know we have a bulletproof routine that is immune to diversions.

No matter what the conditions, we'll be more than ready to go in two minutes.

CHAPTER 8

COMPLAIN OR COMPLETE – ADDING TIME PRESSURE

Now let's look at how to use RED–BLUE skills *during* our performance.

The **mental blueprint technique** provides us with the 'why?' (our **mindset**), 'how?' (our **system**) and 'what?' (our **skillset**), but it's the '**when?**' element that can really power up the technique when we perform. Reframing the way we feel about **time pressure** can make a telling difference to our ability to perform under pressure. Without the hard edge of time, it is often more talk than action.

By adding pressure, time can become our worst enemy or our best friend.

When time is our *worst enemy*, we fixate on the clock counting down the remaining minutes. With one eye on the task and the other on the deadline, everything seems to move faster as we lose our focus and composure. What seemed so easy a minute ago now seems difficult and frustrating. The time limit creates a hard reference point, so that it will be clear to everyone whether we've completed the task or not. There's no hiding place.

Lack of time creates *extra pressure*.

When time is our *best friend*, we reverse that mindset and view time limits as invaluable for driving our focus and movement. We're able to turn the tables on hesitation and procrastination by giving ourselves ultra-short mental deadlines to meet.

We put extra pressure on ourselves to make use of every *moment*, which creates *momentum*.

Most people become trapped on the performance plateau, trundling along from one moment to the next without any real desire to scale the heights, or even rise to the next level. They don't often feel like they are working anywhere near their limit and, deep down, they know they could be doing much better.

Muddling along is a very common default setting on the performance dial. Depending on our field, we can stay at that level from hour to hour and day to day, until the weeks become months and suddenly years have passed us by, and we haven't really stepped up at all. When we don't *have* to do something, we usually don't.

You might well have had moments when your boss, coach or commanding officer demanded more, but this was external pressure. In the last year, how often have you deliberately stepped up your performance when it was *you* who were driving the urgency? There's a risk that high performance will pass us by.

Now imagine that *each day*, you stepped up to your next level of performance. Not for the whole day – because for most occupations that is not sustainable – let's say for five minutes.

That's what this chapter is about. And all you have to do is step up and raise your game for **five minutes each day**.

The Tyranny of the 'To Do' List: A *Non*-Performance Tool

When I ask any group of people which of them use 'to do' lists, nearly everyone puts up their hand. And when I ask whether anyone has had the same item turn up on the list day after day, I hear groans of recognition amid a sea of nods.

This is a symptom of low performance. The dirty secret of 'to do' lists is that when we write down an item on the list, it can make us feel a little better, but that simple act also replaces actually *doing* that task for the time being. With a 'to do' list, performance is not actually required.

Instead, the 'to do' list is a universal tool for **non-performance**, because it allows awkward items to be avoided and continually relisted. The fact that there are multiple items on the list for us to juggle allows us to play mental games with ourselves. By taking on something – anything – on the list other than the biggie – our top priority – we can convince ourselves we are making progress.

WRONG.

The simple 'to do' list is designed precisely to help us with prioritising and time management, but 'to do' lists can be an act of self-deception: they give the reassuring appearance of performance, but far too commonly, they are a cunning method for *not* doing things.

The problem is that not all items on a 'to do' list are equal in terms of their emotional significance. Some are relatively neutral, but others carry an emotional charge, and the vital ones are those that carry discomfort.

Take an awkward phone call we have to make to a difficult customer. You know the type: *we've* done nothing wrong ourselves, but other people have run for the hills and landed *us* with the conversation, which we know will involve conflict.

We've put the item on our 'to do' list, then diligently written the phone number on a sticky note and placed it on the side of our laptop screen so we don't forget it. But it has sat there, staring back at us, for three weeks and counting. We haven't made the call. We've seen the sticky note every day; nothing is wrong with our eyesight. We have a phone and know how to use it. We don't need any further information. Technically, it's a very simple task, but because it's also a very awkward one emotionally we keep putting it off. We're caught up in a 'poor me' loop, and every time we glance at that sticky note, we ask ourselves why *we've* been left to deal with the situation. (This is a real example.)

With stealth and cunning, uncomfortable items work their way down the 'to do' list and onto the next one. The fact that we keep spotting it there replaces concrete action. But the emotional discomfort won't go away, and because our RED mind refuses to be silenced, it will communicate with us in the only language it has available: through our body and feelings. Putting off uncomfortable tasks creates an emotional burden that we carry around with us day after day.

How do we feel when we manage to get one of those uncomfortable items done and off our list?

When I ask a group this question, there's instant agreement. It feels fantastic! Our eyes light up and our posture changes just at the thought of it. A weight is lifted off our shoulders and we feel a sense of lightness and relief. Our positive state of mind is reinforced through the brain's release of dopamine.

Now, how does it feel when we carry out that same kind of task every day for a week?

When I ask a group *this* question, everyone looks puzzled and bewildered. Apparently it's not common to complete an awkward task every day. In fact, it's very *un*common – completely outside the experience of standard performers.

All of us agree that it would feel wonderful, but the inconvenient fact is that when I ask any group of apparently performance-focused people, no one says they have ever managed to complete the uncomfortable task on their 'to do' list every day for a week. Ever.

The cause of this rampant underperformance?

Feelings. Uncomfortable, negative feelings. Like the manager who stared at his sticky note for three weeks, we usually don't need more information or technical training to get the task done. But like the manager, we avoid doing it because of the feelings we know we'll experience during the call.

So what would happen if we made it clear to ourselves that every time we move an item down our list, we have just taken a decision *not* to perform? We've tried to cover over our uncomfortable feelings with the illusion of being too busy. We're too busy writing our 'to do' list, too busy doing easy, unimportant things on our list – the quick emails – and too busy doing things that aren't even *on* our list. We're too busy doing anything and everything but the awkward item. But that doesn't matter, because we're busy, and the busyness makes us feel better.

People usually do what is easy, not what is right. When placed in demanding situations, the standard response is to try to make the problem go away.

Our tendency to delay and procrastinate about tasks we know are important reflects a battle between our RED and BLUE minds. Our RED mind strongly influences us to do things that bring pleasure, not pain and discomfort. Because our emotional RED mind is faster, our rational BLUE mind is always struggling to keep up. When we have uncomfortable tasks that we want to get out of the way, it requires effort from our less powerful BLUE mind to control our RED mind in order to get the task done. Our BLUE mind is the one in charge of completing tasks (and making lists), while our RED mind only needs to lose BLUE's control briefly before it is diverted onto more pleasurable or entertaining things. This power imbalance explains why one in five people have been shown to be procrastinators.

We have only two choices. We can decide to make the call, or we can procrastinate and complain to ourselves and perhaps others, but never end up moving the situation forward.

If we don't move the situation forward, there's a mental block in action. But not some mysterious mental block that requires deep analysis. We can quickly unblock the situation by taking action instead of deferring it.

'To do' lists aren't inherently bad, however. The 'to do' list is either a very inefficient or a very efficient tool, depending on how we use it. If we're inefficient, it is not the tool's fault. It's *our* responsibility. Likewise, 'to do' lists are useful only if we use them for *performance*, not *avoidance*. Otherwise they turn into 'hide the uncomfortable item in the middle of the list so I can avoid it' lists.

On reflection, have you used 'to do' lists to avoid completing uncomfortable tasks? Stop avoiding and start performing, and watch yourself take off.

Enter the **micro-performance**: a five-minute window in which we either move on a task, or we don't.

Micro-performances

Bringing a sense of urgency into the current moment is called **foreshortening the future**. It's about bringing the future mentally closer to make ourselves uncomfortable about wasting time.

The usual way we do this is to imagine ourselves lying on our deathbed. What message would we give to our present-day self?

This deathbed exercise is rather dramatic and morbid, but it helps us to see that time is precious, and we may be moving too slowly and missing opportunities. It helps create a feeling that our time is running out.

A less gloomy method is to focus on foreshortening time for short periods each day. Instead of making this a constant demand, which will feel like a burden, just one short burst per day will fill us with energy.

In the longer run, our performance profile is going to depend on whether we can reset our baseline **reality**. One five-minute spurt of forcing ourselves to perform at the next level up needs to become our basic performance method. Instead of trundling along at the same level, we step up and consciously break free of our baseline – no complaints, no delays. We simply define the task and move forward.

Let's call these five-minute periods **micro-performances**.

Using micro-performances to complete an uncomfortable item on our 'to do' list once a day will transform our personal performance. The mental release of resolving emotional blocks will unlock our potential far more than ticking a single item off a list would suggest. The result is that we feel better and perform better.

Despite the effort involved in forcing ourselves to feel discomfort, a dramatic change is on the cards as we repeatedly shake ourselves free from our standard mode of functioning and continually move up to unfamiliar, higher ground. A micro-performance doesn't mean we step up in such a minor way that it would be a matter of debate whether it happened or not; it should be a solid step-up in performance so that there is no question about what just happened.

Without the five-minute time constraint, little movement occurs. *With* the five-minute time constraint, we accelerate.

Longer micro-performances are less enticing. If we had to step up for 30 minutes, we'd probably lose interest and motivation very quickly. Because our BLUE system will struggle to maintain control over the RED system, it makes sense to focus on getting things done over brief periods. Five minutes is nowhere near as daunting as 30 minutes, and it's hard to retain our BLUE control for that length of time. Our BLUE system needs conscious effort to sustain it, so a five-minute micro-performance means fatigue is less of an issue.

Take away the timing and we take away performance. Our two-minute ICE routine would take too long and our micro-performance would become a marathon. So there is no choice: we need to turn the meaning of time pressure on its head and make it work *for* us, not *against* us.

Five minutes is enough time to start on our chosen task – any task. But we shouldn't underestimate the obstacle of starting. It's common to put things off, slow things down, then land ourselves in a hurried mess when our inaction becomes overwhelming. Both delays and impulsive acts are unhelpful and avoidable.

Five minutes is a short time frame but many things can be achieved within it. If the task is far too big to finish in one go, we can break it down into smaller, less formidable chunks and complete the first one. (It could be as simple as formatting a longer piece of work, or simply taking the *first step* on a larger task.) Focusing on emotionally tough areas can be wearing, so breaking bigger tasks down into more manageable ones gives us opportunities to relax our mind and body in a way that unending stress does not. There's a world of difference between persevering on one long, demanding task and the mental boost of ticking off a series of smaller wins along the way. One feels like a struggle; the other one feels like a wave of momentum accelerating us towards our target.

In constantly ticking items off our 'to do' list, or completing smaller segments of a bigger task, we quickly see the progress and feel the movement. Micro-performances feel good because we get rid of the frustration and tension tied up in procrastination, and the dullness of the same middle-of-the-road performance, day after day.

Micro-performances work like this.

Think of a task that you've been putting off – like the manager's unpleasant phone call. Imagine someone is holding a stopwatch next to your shoulder, and as soon as you've chosen your task, they press the button. You have five minutes. You might start by complaining, ventilating, sighing or looking at your phone. Now you have only three minutes and 45 seconds left. Tick-tock.

At the end of five minutes, the task should not be in the same state as it was at the start. You've picked up the phone and made the call. You can wait four minutes if you like, but that means you have only 60 seconds to make the call. Or not.

Name the task, **time** it, and watch your performance take off.

At the end of five minutes, we can revert to our standard level of functioning, but for five minutes, we are operating at the next level up – professional, effective. Remember that the BLUE mind is linear, and loves language, timelines and sequences. The **name it, time it** approach plays to BLUE's greatest strengths.

The stopwatch is objective, a neutral reference point that doesn't have feelings, so it doesn't take our negative thoughts towards it personally. We know it's not attacking us. It's simply our timekeeper, which just happens to expose our hesitation and mediocrity.

The stopwatch over our shoulder is our mental equivalent of the whistle that a referee blows in a game of football. It lets us know when to perform and when to rest. Instead of holding an internal debate and trying to convince ourselves to get moving, the stopwatch gets us out of our head. And, as for football players, once play has started it comes at us, whether we like it or not.

We might be surprised at how much daily five-minute micro-performances accelerate our progress. Individuals and teams who prided themselves on their speed and efficiency have told me that once they introduced micro-performances, their progress went through the roof. They looked back at their earlier performance level and realised they'd actually been slow.

Once we start to master the micro-performance, it can be sobering to reflect on years of consistent but unexceptional effort that has not made its mark. There's no need to judge ourselves too harshly, but if we realise we've been chronically stranded on the same performance plane and we have an uncomfortable feeling that we've wasted time, it's a sign that we've probably sacrificed quality. This discomfort may be just the jolt we need to shake us out of our performance slumber and snap us into a life-changing series of micro-performances.

We don't need officials to control the rhythm of our own performance. We can blow our own whistle by starting the stopwatch and playing our own mental game – a nice, short, manageable one.

What would a micro-performance look like in your world – five minutes when you act decisively to start and finish a small, uncomfortable but important task you've been avoiding?

Complain or Complete

Let's reclaim the 'to do' list and make this our new rule:

> Identify one uncomfortable item on your 'to do' list each day – one with a RED emotional charge – and complete it before midday. Every day.

Let's use the five-minute micro-performance technique each morning as a personal call to action. Getting our task done before midday is important, because the clock creates a specific *cut-off point*, which also makes the task *clear-cut*.

Welcome to the **completion** mindset.

We know we have a completion mindset when our dominant habit is to **complete** tasks rather than **complain** about them. Identifying the most unpleasant task and taking that on first means we're doing so when our BLUE mind is freshest. When we tackle uncomfortable tasks first of all, a transformation occurs. Blocks are removed, and prickly areas become less sensitive as we become more skilful, and more familiar with how to address them. If we adopt a completion mindset, we'll feel different by the end of each week.

Individuals and teams who do this are often surprised at how quickly they move forward. Releasing the handbrake of emotional burdens can unleash formidable creative energy and momentum. Instead of being stalled and pushed back by obstacles, we're pulled forward by short challenges.

Limiting ourselves to completing just one unpleasant task before midday will help insulate us against emotional burnout. One per day is more than enough if it becomes a daily ritual. If we tick them off each day, by the end of our week we know we'll be in a great state of mind.

Adopting a completion mindset doesn't mean sacrificing quality. It's not an excuse for keeping busy but doing jobs poorly. That is why chasing down unpleasant tasks – which generally requires some reflection – is key. Release emotional blocks and we'll release excellence and precision.

We also need to take care not to misconstrue the completion mindset as a cover for provocative or aggressive behaviour. Challenge is desirable, confrontation is not.

Beware: the complain or complete mindset can take over our thinking. We'll know we are living the completion mindset if we become uncomfortable and disappointed when midday arrives and our task is not completed. We then go into overdrive to make it happen. Moving from a silent internal complainer to a focused external completer becomes infectious. Instead of being resistant to *starting* a task, we now resist anything that gets in the way of *completing* it!

And we'll *really* know we are living the completion mindset when events conspire against us and we just haven't got to our task, but we find ourselves eking out time at 4.45pm to maintain our perfect record. It was bad enough that we couldn't meet the noon deadline, but we simply refuse to let it slide past the end of our workday and into the next morning. We will never get that day back and it will be lost forever. So we kick into action and live 100% by our completion values.

Let's go back to that awkward customer phone call we've been putting off for three weeks. Imagine the impact if we simply picked up the phone and made the call! The sensitive issue is out in the open and able to be discussed forthrightly, feelings are expressed – some of them uncomfortable – and finally a plan is agreed on.

How do we feel now? An energy-sapping blockage has been transformed into an energising resolution. It feels great.

The positive impact of completing a task is comparable to the winner effect, in which the process of winning increases our chances of winning next time too, even if we face a harder opponent. It doesn't have to take a long time to achieve high performance. By supercharging our BLUE mind with simple names and making brief time periods very concrete, we are balancing RED and BLUE to the maximum. One success leads to the next, and the process feeds itself so that our progress is accelerated.

The complain or complete mindset can also be applied to the RED–BLUE tool and related techniques. If we understand the techniques, and find them relevant to our situation, but we just haven't got around to putting them into practice, then we can start the stopwatch on ourselves. We'll benefit from a serious dose of 'when' to stop us wasting time. If we add the stopwatch to the tool or techniques, our chances of using them go up enormously. Let's complete the techniques, rather than complain about them, and we will have added a great edge to our performance armoury.

Completing tasks is transformational, but making a personal commitment not to *complain* – even in our mind – is the real game-changer. Non-stop grumbling, moaning and criticising can take a serious toll on performance by draining energy from our environment.

We looked at an extreme form of complaining back in Chapter 3: **sulking**. When we sulk we temporarily disengage from the cause. We stop giving of ourselves and start withholding instead. Sulking is powerful behaviour that blocks performance as much as it can.

If we're prone to complaining or sulking behaviour, we need to remember it's a decision. It doesn't happen *to* us; we most definitely decide to *make* it happen. And it can be stopped in the same way as a micro-performance can be started.

First, **name it**. Recognising sulking isn't difficult, because we actively make an effort to inflict it on others; there's no point in sulking if there's no one around to punish.

Second, **time it**. Don't try to eliminate it entirely, because it will occur naturally, and it gives us a little space to make ourselves feel better (while making other people feel worse). Anything in excess of one minute can be labelled self-indulgent because our need to feel hurt and show it outweighed the needs of the group in that moment.

Limit sulking behaviour to one minute in performance environments. But if circumstances are really pressing, the time limit is three seconds. (This works particularly well for team sports.) We might complain that three seconds is ridiculously short, but I suggest this is the time limit for average performers. Exceptional performers need only *two* seconds. And *really* exceptional performers operate with a limit of *one* second. The strongest performers have the capacity to refocus as soon as they make a mistake.

Once we name it and time it, we should get ready for some breakthrough constructive behaviour when we least expect it!

Complain or complete – our choice. Once we adopt a completion mindset, we won't want to do without it.

Reflect for a moment on the past week. How would you define yourself: complainer or completer?

If you're not happy with the answer you gave, you know what to do. Start the stopwatch. NOW.

A useful way of combining the **Create the gap, Mental blueprint**, and **Complain or complete** techniques is **PRIME**, an acronym that integrates all three elements. PRI stands for **Pressure-Reality-Intent**, the three components of the **Create the gap** technique; M stands for Movement, which is the function of the **Mental blueprint technique**; and E stands for

Energy, which is the outcome of the Complain or complete attitude. We already completed the first two parts of this method when we completed the 'Sharpening our mental blueprint' exercise on page 177. Return to the exercise and add the time pressure or *when* element to your action plan, and you will have completed the PRIME method. You are now primed for performance under pressure with your PRIME personal performance profile.

The micro-performance, the reinvented 'to do' list and the completion mindset are all aspects of a special **mental blueprint**. Our **mindset** is dedicated to completing, not complaining. The **system** we use is the five-minute micro-performance. And the **skillset** we develop is in identifying the difficult task on our 'to do' list and redefining it so we can take on one manageable chunk.

Time pressure is one of our biggest weapons if we want to create a full and fulfilling life. Let's name it, time it, and allow ourselves to perform.

In the next chapter we'll look at a *companion* mental blueprint that adds *creativity*, not time pressure.

CHAPTER 9

DEFEND OR DISCOVER – ADDING CREATIVITY

From the previous chapter it would be easy to conclude that performing under pressure is all about getting the task done – while the clock is ticking.

So where does *creativity* fit in? Surely the ideal conditions for creativity are plenty of time, a lack of judgment, and an absence of consequences – pretty much everything that pressure is not? But this isn't necessarily so. As our understanding of creativity increases, we're learning that there's no single pathway leading to original thought. Many human beings have managed to display the most impressive creativity under the most intense pressure.

Perhaps some of us don't see creativity as essential to our job or activity. But *all* of us see the value of new thinking, fresh ideas and different perspectives. The fact is, there are creative aspects to *every* performance.

Perhaps creativity is an important part of what we do, but our typical day consists of tight deadlines and work overload.

Say you're a graphic designer, for instance. All your customers want original, developed ideas and they want them yesterday. You need creative juices on tap.

This chapter is about a *new* kind of creativity: developing original ideas when we have limited time or are under pressure. Let's call it **creativity for busy people**.

Creativity Under Pressure: Myth vs Reality

Creativity under pressure seems like a contradiction in terms. Creative juices flow in a nurturing, unhurried, non-judgmental environment, while high performance is all about decisive action right in the middle of a pressure situation. Pressure reduces creativity, so creativity under pressure is clearly a non-starter.

But this common assumption actually rests on half-truths. Seeing creativity and pressure as rivals, not allies, is far too simplistic a view.

In actual fact, hugely creative individuals routinely operate under pressure. Writers, visual artists, actors, musicians and other performers all face social judgment every time they display their work to the public, often working to demanding deadlines or performance schedules. What they do is *not* stress-free.

But creativity certainly isn't restricted to the arts. More broadly, creativity is finding a way to achieve an outcome when others cannot. In that sense, as I mentioned, *every* performance is creative. We might even argue that to go beyond others, creativity is essential for performance under pressure.

Perhaps the fact that different words tend to be used for 'creativity' in performance environments has hidden the potential for creativity under pressure. If we substitute 'new thinking' and 'being original' for 'innovation' and 'creativity', it sheds a new light on matters.

To be original, we have to be first. We have to break new ground. Which means we can't simply run through well-established routines. Looked at in this way, performance under pressure involves original thinking almost by definition.

Situations where there's little pressure might be one route towards original thought, but they're not the only route. Pressure can actually *drive* originality. Think of how often original ideas come to mind within tight deadlines. Think of people in dangerous situations who have found an original solution to a dire problem out of thin air, just in the nick of time. As we saw in Chapter 3, action and adventure athletes crave extreme moments because of the way they take them to a place where their creative juices are powered up like nowhere else. In these cases pressure is the accelerator, the thing that actually *triggers* the original idea or behaviour.

For those serious about performance under pressure, creativity and performance are not adversaries, but partners. Not only can creativity *overcome* pressure, but pressure might even *feed* creativity in some cases.

Those who think pressure and creativity don't mix are forgetting that creative ideas don't come from our external circumstances; they're sitting inside our head. So let's turn the tables on pressure and use demanding external conditions to our advantage. If we follow this approach, we place more importance on our mind – because that's where our ideas originate.

At the brain level, creativity is a complex process to describe. Our state of mind must be flexible, which means it must be stable. When complex systems are unstable they become rigid or erratic.

Stability means good emotional regulation, in which our RED system can keep our feelings at moderate levels, and our BLUE system can add meaning to provide perspective and control. When RED and BLUE are in balance, our brain is in a stable and flexible state, and creativity can follow.

This simple principle of emotional regulation explains why pressure typically reduces creativity. Demanding external conditions often throw our internal balance out of sync, and our capacity for creative insight is lost.

On the other hand, if we are operating under pressure but our internal environment is still under control, there's no reason why creativity can't emerge. Our RED–BLUE balance is the key.

Extreme conditions sometimes require extreme solutions, and for those who can perform well under pressure, they sometimes bring great learning.

Think of the person who is able to keep a level head in a crisis, and retain their composure, enabling them to see a way past obstacles that seem insurmountable. The extreme conditions extended them to the point where they had to be creative, and in that moment, their clear thinking under pressure was their biggest weapon. It allowed them to 'survive'.

Defend or Discover

If we're not actively focused on learning something new, it means accepting that we'll remain the same. We've seen that in everyday life this is more common than not. The tendency of most of us is to plateau in our performance.

Rather than exploring the edges of our capability to see if we can go beyond our boundaries, we fall into thinking our current way of doing things is good enough. We see suggestions that we could improve as an attack on our ability – and when attacked, we **defend**.

The origins of defensive behaviour lie in **attachment theory**, which we looked at in Chapter 2: the tendency of infants to return and attach to their secure base when they became anxious or stressed. We saw that this serves as a working template for how we approach threatening situations later in life.

In the performance context, we **defend** ourselves against uncomfortable feelings. One of the biggest sources of this kind of discomfort is when we feel our performance is being criticised. (We looked at this in Chapter 5.) As much as we know intellectually – with our BLUE brain – that feedback is essential to our progress, for many it's a painful experience, triggering a reaction from our RED mind.

This sets up an interesting problem: if most of us plateau in our performance, and to change we need to learn from our mistakes, how can we do that if we find feedback uncomfortable?

The answer lies in understanding the opposite pole of the infant's behaviour: **exploration**. The core of exploration is searching new territory, which the infant does when they are comfortable enough. Our adult performance equivalent is **discovery**: when we deliberately go looking for ways to improve.

The world of discovery has much to commend it. Exposure to new ideas and environments is stimulating and thought-provoking. Our familiar, comfortable RED habits can be examined, revised and updated by BLUE goal-setting and solution-chasing. Those with fresh perspectives are welcomed. And looking to learn from others is always on the radar screen.

The human tendency to stay within a comfortable environment is very strong, making discovery a difficult path to sustain. We hold on too tightly to our current situation, becoming **aggressive** towards other people's views, or **passive** in remaining on our own patch, or we **escape** by surrounding ourselves with people who don't truly challenge our performance. We're overly defensive, which closes down opportunities to learn.

The silo mentality keeps us within our familiar department, faculty, division or team. Anyone who enters our territory bearing expertise or a different approach is likely to be seen as a threat to our way of doing things. And going beyond our territory to see how others do it differently is also threatening.

Just like when we were infants, the more secure we are in our own identity and relationships, the more we're able to look beyond our current way of operating and see where gains can be made. In short, can we take responsibility for our actions and ask ourselves searching questions, or would we prefer to avoid the truth and cover it up with excuses and blame?

Problems also occur when the commitment to venture beyond our current territory is lip-service rather than real practice. The result is that our ideas become stale and our technique becomes blunt.

It's readily accepted in high-performance circles that if you keep doing much the same thing you'll be overtaken by those who don't. So standing still in your performance actually means sliding backwards.

For those with a **training to win** mindset, the issue of learning, improving and gaining insights is not in question. For them the pain of negative feedback is no match for the pain of failing to perform. For those who are even more driven and **train to dominate**, their quest to learn and discover takes on the feel of a pursuit or yearning that powerfully pulls them forward. Moreover, they appreciate that the power to release their potential ultimately lies *within*. Performance *levels* are less important than performance *trajectory* – the slope upwards.

When the pressure comes on, learning and improving can look like luxuries. They're often the first things to be sacrificed when resources get tight. 'We'll be all right with what we've got. We've coped before and we can cope now.'

But if we want to be able to perform under pressure, we're interested in more than just coping. Stop learning, and we can't expect to keep performing at the same level, let alone improve.

If we want to improve, we have to learn. And if we want to learn, we have to use creativity.

Creative Micro-performances: The RED–BLUE Tool Revisited

In the last chapter we looked at the **completion** mindset. But if we're interested in lifting our creativity under pressure, we'll also need to adopt a **discovery** mindset.

The discovery mindset is all about learning and improvement, based on creative thought. If we want to reach our full potential, it's essential to spend time thinking creatively about how to get better at what we do.

After we've faced the challenge of **complain or complete** in the morning, let's take on the test of **defend or discover** in the afternoon.

We've seen that the completion mindset applies five-minute micro-performances to the 'to do' list to get things done. The discovery mindset, on the other hand, applies the five-minute micro-performance approach to the Rename, reframe, reset technique, a variation of the RED–BLUE tool.

Creative micro-performances suit people who are performing in demanding circumstances and don't have the luxury of extended periods of free time. They'll still work when conditions are more favourable and there is less pressure, but they're not specifically designed for classic creative scenarios where time is unlimited and judgment isn't an issue.

Rather than painting, music and poetry, think advertising agency meeting a deadline, university student writing an essay, and architect completing a concept design. What they all have in common is a lack of time and certain judgment: conditions broadly accepted as stymying fresh thinking.

The creative micro-performance actually involves *two* separate micro-performances, with a break in between.

- **Step 1: Rename** – redefine your creative challenge in terms of a **puzzle**, contrasting the outcome you're after with the obstacle in your way. Write this down. Spend no more than **one minute**.

- **Step 2: Reframe** – on a blank piece of paper, draw a **spontaneous diagram** of the puzzle, writing down as many different angles as you can in the form of questions. Go for quantity rather than quality. Use arrows and circles to link different areas of questioning. Avoid writing down any *answers* to the puzzle. Spend no more than **three minutes**.

- **Step 3: Reset** – write down any immediate ideas or solutions. This requires you to redirect your focus from broad thinking through questions to narrow thinking through answers. Spend no more than **one minute** on this. In total, the **rename**, **reframe** and **reset** steps will have taken you **five minutes**. Together, they make up the first micro-performance.

- **Step 4: Release** – look at your diagram in overview, commit to reviewing it again for five minutes later in the day, then leave it alone and do something completely different for at least an hour, or longer if you have time available. Because you've set your intention to solve the puzzle within a certain time frame, your mind will keep processing it subconsciously with the aim of finding new approaches. If possible, take a break or do some exercise during this period, which reduces your mental load and frees up reflective capacity. If any good ideas come to mind during your 'release' period, quickly jot them down so you don't forget.

- **Step 5: Revisit** – at the time you've committed to, return to look at your diagram a second time and write down any ideas or solutions to the puzzle that come to mind. If other ideas came into your subconscious mind while you were away from the diagram copy or write them down straightaway. Spend the remainder of the time writing down solutions that you can now see. If you don't find a solution outright, generate three different promising lines of thinking. Limit your review to five minutes. This is the second micro-performance. If time permits, you can repeat the release/revisit process of the second micro-performance as many times as you like to keep looking for creative solutions.

Let's see what this looks like in action.

Fiona is a senior architect leading a major building project. She and her team are due to make a final presentation to the client tomorrow. She's just been told about a serious budget miscalculation, made by someone at her firm. It will mean substantial changes to the building's design.

She needs to find a solution that cuts costs by 20% but keeps the good features. No obvious solution comes to mind. What's needed is fresh thinking – but time is short and the pressure is on.

Fiona needs fast creativity. She needs the creative version of the micro-performance.

Step 1 is to **rename the problem** by redefining it as a puzzle, with a conflict between what the desired outcome is and the main obstacle in the way. The puzzle is how to overcome the obstacle.

In this case, the image of the ideal construction is in place but the obstacle is the need to cut costs by 20%. The puzzle is to find a new design that delivers the same functions in a simpler, cheaper format. After a minute of thinking this through, Fiona takes a blank page and writes down 'Elegant Design – Reduce Costs by 20%' at the top.

Step 2 is to **reframe the problem** so that the puzzle can be approached from different angles.

Fiona spends three minutes writing down new viewpoints and questions that come to mind. The result is a messy combination of words and bubbles and arrows. The words all have a question mark after them: Fiona isn't trying to find a solution at this stage, but is trying to find new angles and perspectives.

Step 3 is to **reset your focus** by redirecting attention from questions to solutions.

Fiona looks at all her ideas in overview for a minute and notes down any immediate ideas. In some cases this involves adjusting a solution; in other cases it means coming up with a new approach altogether. But in each case it involves a shift in focus from questions back to answers.

Two possible ideas spring to mind, which Fiona jots down, and she commits to return to the task in an hour's time.

Step 4 is to **release your conscious mind** from the task.

Fiona goes for a brief walk and does other tasks away from her desk, setting her unconscious mind a challenge to solve the puzzle in that time.

Step 5 is to **revisit the problem**.

After an hour Fiona returns to her desk. She looks at the messy diagram and copies down two further ideas that she thought of and jotted down while she was away. One of them excited her straightaway, because it popped out of nowhere and seemed like an obvious thing that had somehow been missed.

She then writes down every solution that comes into her mind over the next three minutes. She spends two further minutes thinking through the idea that appealed immediately – removing one floor from the design – before calling an urgent team meeting.

The first part of Fiona's creative process, the one-minute **rename** step, provided direction and strongly activated her BLUE mind.

The three-minute, instinctive, visual **reframe** step primed her intuitive RED mind by throwing up a broad range of concepts for potential connection. The focus was deliberately *not* on solutions, but on generating new angles and perspectives.

When the answer is not immediately obvious, ask a different question.

The one-minute **reset** process – switching her thinking away from questions and back to answers – allowed Fiona to write down any possible solutions that came to mind straightaway. Good ideas can pop into our head at any time.

The **release** stage – where Fiona set a clear time frame for unconscious processing – allowed her linear BLUE brain to consciously attend to other tasks, and her unconscious RED brain to work away on the puzzle in the background.

The final **revisit** step was also a five-minute micro-performance, this time focused on solutions after Fiona had spent an hour processing the puzzle unconsciously. She deliberately occupied herself away from her desk to give herself the mental space to be creative.

This process shares several of the features of the standard creative process, but places them within a new frame. There was an initial period of looking closely at the puzzle with some effort because it was emotionally important.

Next there was a middle period of moving away from the puzzle and focusing on other matters – called an 'incubation period' – which allowed ideas to form and grow and eventually hatch. After Fiona had defined the creative challenge with her BLUE mind, the work could be handed over to her RED mind, which worked away outside of her awareness.

During this period an idea popped into Fiona's head out of the blue, along with instant recognition that it fitted perfectly. This is often called the 'aha!' moment. Then there was a final phase when Fiona worked this idea up into a fully formed solution.

The new frame that made *this* creative process different from the standard approach was the deliberate use of time limits to accelerate creativity. While it might take time to gain creative insight, no one said it had to take a *long* time. For busy people, a five-minute priming process followed by a 30- to 60-minute incubation period is likely all the time they can spare before they need to **revisit** the creative puzzle to come up with a solution. With our linear BLUE mind otherwise occupied so it doesn't slow down our fast RED mind, the incubation period allows our subconscious processes to do the work for us.

We can use the discovery mindset when we have a specific problem to solve, as Fiona did – *or* we can use it for personal and professional development.

If you're a manager within the business world, set your mental stopwatch and spend five minutes deliberately looking for a new connection outside of your current relationships that might stimulate new perspectives and therefore new thinking for your team. If you're an athlete, set your mental stopwatch and spend five minutes deliberately trying to look at your on-field performances from different angles with a view to finding new ways to improve. If you're a skilled technician, set your mental stopwatch and spend five minutes deliberately looking at methods used in other technical fields to explore whether any of those methods could improve your own performance.

The intention in each case is not to come up with a fully formed idea but simply to generate one new angle.

Another way to do this is to remove ourselves from our usual performance space. If we work with other people, there are always opportunities to leave our workplace and connect with other people outside of our typical daily contacts. Moving beyond our normal *physical* territory takes us out of our familiar *mental* territory as well. If we set out with a discovery mindset, going beyond our boundaries will give us a fresh perspective.

Short hits of creative micro-performance can also be used in a team environment. In a classic brainstorming session, stronger personalities often dominate. In a creative micro-performance, the focus on different perspectives means the quieter, more reflective voices within the group won't be overshadowed by the louder ones.

We can even practise a discovery mindset more informally, by exploring different ways of improving without using the RED–BLUE tool.

We can see the creative micro-performance as a reward to ourselves for completing a difficult task during our micro-performance in the morning. Discovery activities tend to be more light-hearted and enjoyable than task-oriented activities – especially when they're focused on our personal development and not just on solving problems. They bring the thrill and energy of exploration. And again, the short time frame means we are much more likely to keep doing them, because shorter tasks are easier to build into habits. Creativity requires a state of mind, not a long time.

> Reflect on your last week. Did you deliberately spend time using creativity to solve a problem or develop your abilities? Would you say you have a creativity habit? Were there any instances of creativity at all?

Just like the *completion* micro-performance, the *creative* micro-performance is based on its own mental blueprint. Our **mindset** is setting out in the spirit of discovery, be it to solve a puzzle or learn and improve. The **system** that allows us to proceed is the **Rename, reframe, reset** tool. And our **skillset** consists of asking really good questions.

Completion vs Discovery

Across Chapters 8 and 9, we've met two different mindsets to help us thrive under pressure. Whether our performance is about delivering results or nurturing creativity, it's important to strike a balance between **learning** and **performing** – between **discovery** and **completion**. But because task completion is a more visible part of the performance than learning – and in many fields is also linked to revenue-raising – the commitment to learning is often lower.

Completion and discovery should never be seen as competing with each other – to pull back from either is counterproductive. They go hand in hand if you want to get better.

To understand this more fully, let's explore two different ways of thinking that achieve two different outcomes.

Two types of performance thinking

In performance situations we can think in one of two ways. Either we will be looking to **narrow down** a range of options to make a decision, or we will be looking to **widen** our thinking to increase the range of options.

It's often a trap to have too many options, because it causes uncertainty when we want to be decisive. We can avoid this by allowing our ideas to *converge* into a single option. This is called **convergent thinking**. If we want to be decisive and instil a **completion** mindset, we need to get away from the zone of uncertainty where there are many options, and decide on the one pathway forward.

At other times, it can be a trap to be too narrow in our thinking, because we may miss alternative ways of approaching the situation. We can avoid this by deliberately taking in *diverging* perspectives. This is called **divergent thinking**. If we want to be inventive and instil a **discovery** mindset, we need to get away from the zone of fixation where we're stuck on one solution, and find alternatives.

Picture convergent thinking as an *upward*-pointing arrowhead, going from a broad base up to a narrow point. And picture divergent thinking as a *downward*-pointing arrowhead, going from a narrow point at the base to a wide mouth at the top. This helps a lot in team situations, where a mixture of convergent and divergent thinking can cause confusion.

We can also picture the upward convergent arrowhead sitting *on top of* the downward divergent arrowhead, forming a diamond shape. This reminds us that performance is often a constant dynamic, where first we go wide and then we go narrow. In any given situation, it can help us visualise whether we need more options or more decisiveness.

When we're performing *effectively*, usually divergent thinking moves naturally to convergent as options become decisions. When we're performing *ineffectively*, we'll either get stuck fixating on one option, or be uncertain because we have too many options. Keeping the diamond in mind can help shape our mental activity.

It's common to associate high performance with *decisive* action, because making decisions can make you appear strong. In fact, stronger performers are often the ones willing to take on board different views from their own.

Another mistake is to assume that divergent thinking must take a long time, so it must be unhelpful when we're under time pressure. In fact, a few moments of pausing and thinking about a different way forward can prevent costly and time-consuming errors.

In a team situation, even when time is tight, the person leading the discussion can ask what people are seeing (divergent thinking through questions) then get everyone on the same page by selecting one option (convergent thinking through a decision).

A captain of a sports team, the leader of a surgical team, the commander of an armed response team, or the captain in a cockpit can ask each person for their opinion then make a firm statement about a course of action, all in 30 seconds. This is creative thinking and decisive action on the run.

People tend to have a personal bias towards questions or decisions. The most common pattern under pressure is to narrow things down too soon when we get stuck, for fear of wasting time or looking indecisive. But we can't see all the angles alone. Everyone has blind spots. It's easy to bluster through the day leaving a trail of rapid decisions behind us, without asking a single question of anyone else. If this is you, you've confined yourselves within a closed-loop environment where it's going to be difficult to learn and improve.

Even if we're an expert in our field, we shouldn't think we need to have all the answers. Asking questions shows you're more interested in learning than in other people's (or your own) expectations that you'll supply all the answers.

Under pressure, questions can be more powerful than answers. Asking questions at the right time allows us to grow, while thinking that we have all the answers is the fast track to the performance plateau.

There's a time and place both for asking questions and for making decisions. One is not inherently better than the other, but one will be more effective in any given moment. And we don't need to use both types of thinking equally; we just need to use whatever is required at the time.

This is often indicated by the nature of the problem. A sports team that is committed but not making any headway against their opposition with a particular strategy would benefit from quickly sharing alternative views by the leader quickly asking questions about what other players are seeing. Later in the game, when substitutions have been made and different players seem to have different ideas about the best way forward, clear direction through decisions will help. If we're stuck fixating on one solution, questions help; if we're uncertain about how to move forward, decisions work.

Reflect on your past week with the thinking diamond in your mind. What percentage of time do you think you've spent in the divergent half, and what percentage in the convergent half? Did you get caught in the fixation trap, being too narrow-minded? And what about the uncertainty trap, being too indecisive?

Using the right kind of thinking at the right time helps us take our performance to the next level; using the wrong kind of thinking can keep us busy without moving us forward. Switch skilfully between incisive questions and decisive answers to accelerate your progress toward your full potential.

Finding the balance

Chapters 8 and 9 have shown us that we need to develop a balanced approach to performance that has elements of *both* delivery *and* creativity. If we balance being task-focused with being creative under pressure, we will continue to perform because we will continue to learn.

If you found yourself identifying more with one chapter or the other, you may need to stop and reflect on that point, because it's providing you with an important personal message. Do you have a preference for narrowing things down to a solution, or for opening things up to new angles? Either way, a preference for one can mean a blind spot for the other. Being aware of this imbalance shows you what to watch out for during your performance, and how to adjust so that you can think clearly under pressure – either to **complete** or to **create**.

CHAPTER 10

MASTERY

My definition of mastery is 'effectiveness in all conditions, external and internal'. (This is better than talking about 'perfection', which is too rigid, implying there is only *one* best way to do something. It slows us down, rather than speeding us up.)

Mastery could also be seen as **training to dominate**, or having a **warrior mindset**. It draws together much of what we've already discussed, although mastery might resonate more for your performance field.

The key is flexibility: being able to adapt to changing circumstances quickly and efficiently. We've seen that master performers are willing to look at both external and internal factors that might be holding them back. They see them not as constraints, but as challenges. And because pretty much everyone has to deal with similar external factors, they know that their capacity to deal with their own mental state is what will give them the edge.

Loss of confidence is one of the most common things that sets standard performers apart from masters. When someone says they lack confidence, they are in effect saying that how they perform depends on how they feel. This is a particularly unhelpful mental trap to fall into, because it provides us with an 'out'. When the going gets tough, we give ourselves permission to let our standards slip. As we've seen, there are many people in high-stakes environments who don't have the luxury of stepping away from the performance table when they don't feel confident. Doctors, paramedics, flight personnel, police, soldiers and rescue workers all fit into this category.

Masters appreciate that others will blame their lack of progress on external obstacles when the real offender is their internal reaction. They appreciate being extended in different ways, especially if they have to cope with moments of doubt. The internal challenge is to deal with the doubt – the loss of confidence – and remain effective despite that state of mind.

Success – measured by the usual standards – is not necessary for mastery. Some surgeons with modest performance measures are the ones who take on the toughest cases. They risk uninformed judgment but remain solid and undeterred because they have their sights on a bigger vision.

External conditions do affect all of us at times. But exceptional performers rise above them and consistently do better than others. If we aspire to be exceptional, we need to learn to rise up when we don't feel confident. We need to become the master, not the apprentice.

Look at your performance history and consider your highlights and lowlights. Do you notice any pattern in terms of the external conditions you've faced and how you've performed? And what pattern can you see as you look at your changing mental state and how it has impacted on your performance?

Pioneering: Being First

Pioneers are captured by the idea of being first – by entering new territory. Those who follow may match their achievement but being there first is psychologically special. We all know who broke the four-minute mile, but few can name the next runner who performed the same feat six weeks later.

If we apply the pioneer spirit to our own situation, it means breaking through into performance territory we've never inhabited before.

In sport, that might mean breaking a record, but it might also mean taking our performance to a new level – a personal best. In the military, it might mean *literally* going into new territory, or it might mean taking on a new role. In all cases there is significance in extending what we've done before.

A **micro-performance** (Chapter 9) involves a brief step-up in performance, but still within familiar territory. Becoming a **pioneer** means a step-up into genuinely new terrain. Most people do not truly traverse genuinely new ground very often. Those who do are invigorated, and those moments take on special significance in their lives.

There are two basic ways in which we can become a pioneer and break new ground.

First, we can operate under *new conditions*, which forces us to face new tests, read the signs and adjust. This might mean a bigger wave, a new composition, a new organisation, a new audience or a new product. The test is in adapting our skillset to circumstances we haven't previously encountered.

Second, we might perform at a level beyond what we have achieved before: faster, more agile, calmer, more creative, more rhythmic. The test is in operating at a *new level of skill* in familiar circumstances.

Or, we can go for the double whammy: a *new skill level*

under *new circumstances*. Action and adventure athletes stand out in this regard by carrying out feats that require them to not only conquer new terrain, but also tackle a new level of technical difficulty.

Pioneers understand the risks posed by new terrain, but they are deeply driven by the challenge. In their mental world, it's better to explore new ground and fail than not to have tried at all. The exploration of new territory becomes the core source of their satisfaction. What happens is part of the story, but the outcome is less important than the exploration itself.

The pioneer is totally absorbed by the process, and curiosity keeps the focus on moment-to-moment adjustments. A surfer taking on a new wave is fully engaged in the micro-detail of their immediate environment; the result, and how they look to others, are irrelevant in that moment.

Any diversions created by internal doubt will likely come at a cost. Trust in our own mental strength is crucial. Particularly in sport, the clearly defined winning and losing outcomes form a tempting attention trap. Easy to let our imagination get ahead of the moment and taste victory when a trophy or medal is calling.

The best way to break new ground is to be deliberate. Clarify our **context** of pressure, so we know where we've already been. Define our **reality** to shake off the vague and overly generous view we often have of ourselves. Set our **intent** so we understand the limits of our personal exploration.

Pioneers are known for their mental toughness. Being able to tolerate sacrifice and hardship comes with the territory they choose to enter. They need a certain level of *ability*, but the mental side of performance determines their *durability*, and it's this quality that sets the pioneer apart.

To venture into new territory, we have to understand our abilities, but more importantly our *vulnerabilities*. If we don't identify them beforehand, the new territory will do that for us.

And that means taking a look on the dark side.

The more we want to stand out among our peers, the more we will be drawn to the part of us that holds unwanted, painful truths. Elite athletes often refer to their internal battle to overcome their doubts and anxieties – their dark side. Addressing this side of us will always be uncomfortable, but this is the only way of pushing beyond our current limits.

When darkness descends around us, it takes courage to look within us.

To become a pioneer, we need to embrace inconvenient facts so that we are brought to life by the dark side. Breaking new ground doesn't happen by accident – we need to put in the preparation if we want to fulfil our potential.

> Think hard: when was the last time you broke new ground? Don't settle for doing what everyone else does – redefine your boundaries and become a pioneer.

Wait or Take

The old saying holds true: reputations are generally earned, not made. Peers will only come to respect an individual's performance over time. But it's the way we handle those with the big reputations that will enhance our own.

The secret lies in using the **wait or take** mindset to power up our performance through ramping up the time pressure. This will challenge us to break free from procrastination and hesitation. **Wait or take** is a variant of the **complain or complete** and **defend or discover** mindsets we looked at earlier. All three share brevity, simplicity and a focus on taking the initiative. (We are not talking here about any sense of entitlement or inappropriate behaviour; just an energised, get-up-and-go attitude and willingness to take the first step *in the spirit* of the performance situation.)

In sport, how a junior team member deals with the big-name opposition players will reveal whether they have a **wait** or a **take** mindset.

Once a player has a reputation, other players will often subconsciously stand off and wait to see what they do, *then* react to it. The star player generally needs the least time to make their move – that's how they earned their reputation in the first place – and standing off and waiting just gives them *more* time. But the problem is that the other players wait to react out of respect: a mild version of being *starstruck*. It just makes the star player look even better, so that there's even more to admire.

The opposite approach – using a **take** mindset – is to understand that the big-name player needs *less* time than most and they are not going to hand over their hard-earned reputation without a fight. Instead of staying back and **waiting**, the junior player heads forward and **takes** their reputation from them. This gives the star player *less* time, *less* space and *less* acknowledgment. In effect, it shows them maximum respect by showing them maximum *dis*respect.

The junior player must expect pushback and resistance. Their initial challenge is likely to be met with a strong reaction to warn them off. So they take a second shot, which provokes an even *bigger* response. But when they go in for a third time, they send an unmistakable message: 'I'm not going away.'

If we repeat behaviour three times in a row, those who see it will expect it to continue.

The **take** mindset is found not just in sport but in all performance domains.

Bella is a junior accountant at a large international firm. Some of her senior colleagues are well known within the industry – although she hardly sees them, because they inhabit the top floor of the building. Bella understands the hierarchical nature of the industry but wants to accelerate her progress.

She's invited to be part of an interdepartmental group working on a project involving some of the company's big names. She's given a strictly supporting role, carrying out some of the legwork. Bella makes sure she performs this role in an exemplary way, but she also pays careful attention to the group's discussion, and invests time and energy after hours in doing personal research into the project, which is focused on streamlining taxation services to multinational companies.

In one meeting, when there is a lull and her colleagues appear stuck on a legal point about work visas, Bella takes the opportunity to ask if she could provide a fresh perspective. Politely but confidently she suggests that the law around work visas highlights a vulnerable point in the strategy: her firm's wish to provide better services overall to their clients might have the unintended consequence of making it more difficult to employ overseas workers and therefore reduce the diversity and flexibility of the company. This is an opportunity to take a different approach and avoid that unwanted outcome.

When eyebrows are raised, Bella adds some detail that shows she has researched the work visa implications: her views cannot be immediately dismissed. One senior partner points out that because the firm cannot change the legal context, the same situation would apply to all businesses and so their firm could argue that they are working within unavoidable constraints. Bella agrees with the point in general but suggests that the project group might like to look at suggesting clients consider using a different category of temporary visa that could transition into a work visa. This would allow her team to keep their strategy and their clients to increase both the diversity and flexibility of their workforce.

It's clear to everyone present that Bella has thought hard about the issue. The assured way she entered the discussion prompts the senior partner to ask her for a fuller analysis. He can see Bella's suggestion would help the firm avoid a potentially embarrassing situation, and at the same time provide a template that other groups could adopt across the firm. A step ahead, Bella takes copies of her printed report out of her bag and hands them around the table.

A week later, Bella is given a fast-track promotion and invited to move to the senior partner's team. She gains a reputation for being able to speak respectfully but forthrightly to senior colleagues without being intimidated by their reputations.

With a **take** mindset, the challenger brashly bursts the champion opponent's bubble of comfort and starts acting like *they* are the one with the reputation. They break the unspoken rule that says lesser performers have to stand off and show due respect.

The fastest way to *gain* a reputation is to show 'respectful disrespect' to those who already *have* reputations. Top performers privately admire those who are not intimidated and go after them single-mindedly.

The true champion will recognise the **take** mindset, because they probably have it themselves. Those with false or inflated reputations will be found out. Reputations can be hard earned but lost in an eye-blink. They are there to be taken.

Even a top performer becomes vulnerable when they drift along **waiting** for their next success to arrive. The reigning champion can adopt the **take** mindset by mentally giving away their reputation, then going out to earn it all over again. That way, they take nothing for granted.

We see the same with sports teams who feel that a cup is theirs to lose as opposed to theirs to take. When the next tournament comes along, have the team mentally handed the cup back to the competition so that it no longer belongs to them and they have to go and take it again, or do they feel they still have it and sit in wait for challengers?

The crucial mental difference between the **wait** and **take** mindsets is hunger. Top performers aren't driven by external acclaim; they're driven internally to earn the respect of their peers for the nature of their performances – and the reputation simply follows. Hunger aches deep inside in a way that pushes us on even when our initial emotional energy is spent. Hunger doesn't go away until it's sated – if we miss out, we just get hungrier.

If we see opportunity but back off, we will never go as far as those who step forward in those moments and take on the challenge. Adopting a **take** mindset puts us on the fast track to a higher level. We move ourselves off the performance plateau and put ourselves on an upward trajectory.

In taking away space, time and opportunity from our opposition we can still be courteous when appropriate. But when we get into performance mode, we need to play hard. Waiting for others or letting them go first is the same as placing ourselves second.

Take your place at the front and wait for no one. When the time comes for action, let your actions speak for you.

Pinnacle Event, or Pinnacle Moment?

There are some events we face that are *so* big they place a degree of pressure on us that more routine performances do not. They're sometimes called **pinnacle events**.

In the sporting world, pinnacle events would include the Olympic Games, the majors, world cups, world championships and the Grand Slams. But most of us will have equivalents whether we're a scientist or a soldier – special missions, national projects, elections, landmark court cases. These events carry the greatest significance because they are used by many as a measuring stick of greatness. In these events, the stakes are at the highest because our performance will publicly define us as an individual.

Because these events are regarded differently, there is a common belief that they have to be approached differently too. They are so high-pressure that they have the capacity to do things to us mentally that other events cannot.

Everyone is vulnerable to the pinnacle event. This is *not* normal performance under pressure.

So, how do we prepare for them? Here are the two alternatives most people try:

1.   Treat it as if it's a normal event.
2.   Treat it as a truly massive event.

The first strategy is flawed, because it involves trying to trick our mind into thinking that a highly *ab*normal event is perfectly normal. Even though our BLUE mind might try to trick our RED mind, our RED mind knows the truth, and it will make us pay with a really big RED response when we least want it.

Meanwhile, the second method runs the risk of making us oversensitive and overreactive to the high-pressure environment.

Isn't there *any* other option?

There *is* a third approach: focusing not on the external event, but on our response to it.

Jenny is an athlete at the Olympic Games going through the qualifying round for her middle-distance race. She sails through. Everyone knows that the crunch time is the final, but so far, so good.

At this stage it seems like there's nothing that sets this pinnacle event apart. There's nothing special about the bigger stadium, the massive crowds or the world-class competition that automatically creates pressure at this point. The pinnacle event is just an event like any other, because at this stage, the stakes are not particularly high.

But the final is where the outcome will be decided. The stadium and the things inside it will still be the same, but what will be different is Jenny's internal response.

In the final, she's in the lead and right on the edge of victory, when her mind is suddenly split between what she's doing right now and the imminent possibility of glory or tragedy.

Suddenly her vital RED–BLUE balance is precarious. Two things could happen at this point.

Her precious RED–BLUE balance could be lost as her RED system soars into high arousal. What the crowd sees is a winning athlete suddenly lose confidence, tighten up and fold.

OR she could get a grip on her RED emotion with a firm BLUE helping hand. Her RED system still flares, but doesn't get out of control. What the crowd sees is an athlete strive and thrive. It is a ***pinnacle moment***.

If we define ourselves by results, a strong **mental blueprint** will get us only so far. At a pinnacle event, in the pinnacle moment, our mental blueprint will take us straight to the outcome under threat – winning or medalling. But if we define ourselves by how we conduct ourselves under pressure, our mental blueprint will take us into pinnacle moments with relish.

At pinnacle events, seasoned professionals suddenly turn into tense and clumsy amateurs. It's only right that we're in awe of these events, but the more we build up our potential success, the more we fuel the threat of failure. If we chase the pinnacle moment, *not* the pinnacle event, we'll have the best chance of success.

Once we can face both success and failure, pinnacle moments lose their power to disrupt, and take on a power to extend and energise. We enter into a different psychological relationship with the event itself. Fear is replaced by trust that the event will do its job and provide us with a formidable test.

Choose your focus: pinnacle event, or pinnacle moment?

If you don't have pinnacle moments, you will never approach your potential.

- What have been your personal pinnacle events up to this point? What have been your pinnacle moments?
- In those moments, did you collapse under the pressure of the event, or rise up to meet your moment?

CHAPTER 11

FOR LEADERS

The art of leadership is to use pressure wisely. When we're in a leadership position, we influence the environment our people perform in, and the level of pressure we introduce is a particularly important part of this. If we don't apply pressure wisely, it means our team or organisation will not have demanding goals or appropriate supervision.

An important question for us to ask ourselves as leaders is whether we see our role as *pushing* people along, or creating an environment that *pulls* them forward. Pushing people along means that *we* take responsibility for their motivation. Developing a culture where improvement is expected, then leaving it up to *the individual* to translate that into action, creates a very different dynamic. It becomes clear who is driven from *within*, who needs to be motivated *externally*, and who doesn't really want to do much or might even be interested in *blocking* movement.

This chapter shows us how to use many of the RED–BLUE techniques we've already met to transform the way our people work: the art of balancing pressure with our team's capacity; a way of prioritising that turns avoidance into movement; and the secret of accelerating our team's progress beyond recognition through **fast leadership**.

With crucial RED–BLUE insights into what moves groups of people – and what holds them back – the door is open for us to develop a new degree of team spirit, by creating a **streamlined** organisation.

Create the Gap: Generating a Performance Culture

The idea that it takes time to change culture is a myth. That doesn't mean change always happens quickly – usually it doesn't – but without the right groundwork in place, it takes much, much longer than it needs to.

A **performance culture** can be boiled down to a single, simple idea: *everyone is focused on getting better than they are now.* Just because a team or organisation is getting better as a group, it does not mean that you are getting better as an individual. And that means everyone in the team or organisation – without exception – needs a **performance gap**.

Sporting organisations, for instance, are usually only *partially* focused on performance. Staff look at the athletes and critique them relentlessly, but they don't look at their own performance gaps with nearly the same level of scrutiny. It's easy to see where athletes sit in sporting terms because they're constantly being measured and assessed. For those in coaching and corporate roles linked to the team, it's usually much harder to find an effective yardstick. So they don't bother. They prefer to stay comfortable and safe. They assume the 'high performance' label attached to the players will automatically apply to them. It's status by association.

Another indicator of a non-performance sporting culture is the swagger we see when players have the air that they've 'arrived'.

If they have a performance gap, they have – by definition – *not* arrived. Ironically, the players who *do* see a gap and are driven to get better are the ones at the very top.

Team athletes often define themselves by being part of a particular professional league. But league membership clumps everyone together and protects them against proper scrutiny. If individuals want to get better, their mindset must be about learning, not defending their status.

Away from the sports world, it's often not as easy to assess whether we're actually improving at what we do. A common trap is to assume our performance has got better simply because we're 'more experienced'. But if there hasn't been a serious intention to improve, the chances are that we haven't improved as much as we would like to think. Otherwise, we'd get an accurate picture of true ability simply by ranking people according to age.

We shouldn't dismiss experience, but we should scrutinise harder: what *kinds* of experience have we gained? What is the *evidence* that we have been learning from it?

If everyone in our organisation has a performance gap, we have a performance culture. If only *some* people have gaps – usually the junior people – we don't have a culture of performance, we have a culture of privilege. So the change *must* start with the organisation's leaders.

We saw in Chapter 5 that most people find feedback emotionally challenging. In a privileged culture where senior people carry immunity cards, this feedback is more likely to be taken as criticism. This puts everyone on eggshells. If there's one rule for all, from top to bottom, the sensitivity of talking about performance will decrease. And when that happens, we'll feel the energy surge. In a culture of performance, these discussions are not a compulsory evil but a valued engine. They are the main pathway by which we improve.

A performance culture means, at its core, that every individual is serious about wanting to improve. Not in a 'that would be nice' kind of way, but in a deeply serious way. Everyone in the organisation needs to see and feel the gap between where they intensely desire to be, and where they are now. The more clearly they can see this gap, the more uncomfortable they will be about remaining at their current level. And in performance terms that is a very, very good thing.

As a leader, if we set the agenda and choose a performance culture, we'll be placing ourselves in a strong position to accelerate performance across the board.

Bridge the Gap, THEN *Create* the Gap: Using Pressure Wisely

Helping our team *create* a **performance gap** means applying pressure. But first, it helps to use the **mental blueprint technique** to build their capacity to *bridge* **the gap**. This avoids the risk of alienating the team by placing increasing demands on them *before* they've learned to cope with the pressure.

More pressure is not necessarily better, and less pressure is not necessarily worse. Striking the right balance is more art than science. But the mental blueprint technique gives us a practical method to ensure we're using pressure at an appropriate level.

We know from Chapter 3 that pressure comes from **expectations, scrutiny** and **consequences** (**ESC**). As a leader, we can use these three factors to encourage better performance. But rather than doing this haphazardly, we need to adjust the level of pressure to our group's ability to respond – and that's where the mental blueprint technique comes in.

We can see our team or organisation as having an overall mental blueprint that describes the dominant **mindset, system** and **skillset** within the group.

Using the mental blueprint technique for teams is not a precise, mathematical process. We could use the **performance line** to estimate the team's level of ability. For example, from a 'moderate level' starting point, we should aim to become 'good', which we can see as the next level up.

Once we've *estimated* the level of the group's mental blueprint, then *improved* it, we can introduce more expectations, scrutiny and consequences to give them the right conditions in which to *use* it.

Daniel is the foreman on a major construction site. He feels his team leaders have a complacent attitude towards health and safety meetings, which are run daily on different parts of the site. He wants to improve their performance by upgrading their mental blueprint and applying the right level of pressure.

His first step is to assess his team leaders' mental blueprint for running the meetings.

He evaluates the **mindset** of the group as hesitant and resistant. Some feel they already work in a safe way, and that the meetings are unnecessary. Others feel the meetings are repetitive and boring, and the employees are hard to engage. Others find that the negative attitude of contractors makes the whole thing too difficult.

Daniel decides that the **system** in place is not fit for purpose: there are existing health and safety protocols, but they're not being properly observed. Record-keeping is poor. Employees and contractors go ahead with their work each day having missed vital safety information because of the poor standard of the meetings – or having missed the meetings altogether.

As a result of all this, Daniel feels that the team leaders' **skillset** is low compared with their skillsets in other aspects of their job. They're simply going through the motions, without making any attempt to involve the attendees in the meetings.

Overall, he concludes that the leaders' mental blueprint for carrying out this task is, at best, in the moderate range.

Daniel's second task as leader is to **upgrade** this mental blueprint. He spends time lifting his team leaders' **mindset** by providing information about building site accidents, and the repercussions for them personally if health and safety protocols are not observed, which grabs their attention. He enhances the **system** for health and safety meetings by providing daily electronic site updates via mobile phone to each team leader, which also allows them to log attendance at the meetings. And he works on the team leaders' **skillset** by arranging for a training session by a respected expert, to stimulate his team's thinking about new and engaging ways to run the meetings.

Daniel's third task is to apply an appropriate degree of pressure to his team, to help them **bridge** their **performance gap**. This is where he has to provide a reasonable level of **expectations**, **scrutiny** and **consequences** (**ESC**). If he sets the bar too high, they'll react with **aggressive**, **passive** and **escape** (**APE**) behaviours. However, if he doesn't set the standard high enough, he won't be fulfilling his role as leader. He will have spent time and energy developing his team's mental blueprint, but not provided the right environment to make sure this led to improved performance.

To find the right level of **expectations**, **scrutiny** and **consequences** to apply, he engages the group in a frank discussion and asks them a series of questions:

- What standards do they think will give them the right level of challenge? (**Expectation**)
- How do they think their performance should be measured against these standards? (**Scrutiny**)

- What should happen when they meet the standards they want to apply, and when they fall short? (**Consequences**)

Daniel uses pressure wisely by setting standards (expectations), monitoring the team's progress (scrutiny) and following up on over- and underperformance (consequences). He communicates this using non-threatening language, and makes sure the group understand that the goal is not to catch them out, but to help them improve, individually and as a team. He knows if he portrays the pressure as the way he can provide the best environment for the team, there'll be less chance of resistance.

Every leader wants to resource their team properly and set them up to succeed. Introduce pressure first – *before* we've developed our team's ability – and we shouldn't be surprised to see **aggressive** (irritation, complaints), **passive** (complaining, doing the training but not changing behaviour) and **escape** (being busy elsewhere, sick leave, transfers) behaviours emerge. If we upgrade our team's mental blueprint *before* we introduce pressure, our team will remain engaged and thrive.

But applying pressure doesn't work well if the expectations are too high, the monitoring is too invasive, or the consequences are too harsh. If we think the group is only at the *moderate* level, then we shouldn't use a large amount of pressure that's more appropriate to a *high* level.

Likewise, if we introduce *too little* pressure, then we shouldn't expect standards to rise. If there's no difference between the group's ability and the level of pressure, there'll be no improvement. No difference, no pressure. No pressure, no movement.

But if we introduce pressure at *the next level up*, the group can rise to the challenge. That way we're **creating a gap** that gives the team space to move. If everyone understands that the performance gap is about *movement*, not *judgment*, then that movement is much more likely to take place.

Let's explore this further by returning to the example of Daniel.

Daniel and his team leaders decide that the next level up will involve a **mindset** where the leaders take collective responsibility for running a safe site, so that if one team leader falls short, the whole team is compromised. They will be genuinely committed to high standards – not just doing the minimum required to avoid problems. They agree on an intention to run upbeat meetings, as opposed to just going through the motions.

They conclude that a **system** operating at the next level up will involve regular updates from across the site. They commit to 100% attendance at health and safety briefings across the site, with all contractors accounted for at any given moment, and any important health and safety developments in their area being sent to all the other leaders.

And a next-level **skillset** will mean that, instead of doing all the talking at the briefings, the leaders will arrange for employees to contribute, to keep things fresh. They also agree to complete the training session with the expert.

At first Daniel is a bit heavy-handed. His keenness to improve the site's safety record overflows into a zealous follow-up of all missing reports and updates. Site progress slows down as his team leaders get caught up in red tape. Unpleasant discussions become more common, and relations with the contractors become particularly strained.

Daniel then backs off and lowers his expectations. He stops insisting on a perfect record, and instead he highlights and praises instances where his team leaders are able to communicate relevant information well. He takes it upon himself to communicate directly with the subcontracting firms to explain the requirements for contractors entering the site. This turns out to be the key to changing attitudes across the board.

The team leaders appreciate the way Daniel stepped in, which has removed a burden from their shoulders. They begin to report relevant incidents and activities more diligently. They start to enjoy running the health and safety meetings and begin sharing stories about how they're getting their workers involved. The building pace not only recovers but also speeds up, with a reduction in stoppages and delays previously caused by poor safety planning.

Despite the teething problems, Daniel's relationship with his team improves to the point where team leader meetings become good-spirited and never-missed events.

Leaders often tell me they don't know what their team's next level of performance would look or feel like. In response, I first ask them to reflect on what they've just said: why would any group expect to improve if they have no idea about how to get better? Insisting that you have no idea of how to improve is not a great characteristic to admit to! It really crystallises the point about working to ensure the team is operating within a performance culture.

Second, I emphasise that building a picture of the next level of performance is a creative process that requires collaboration and goodwill. It will involve suggestions, discussion, and eventually agreement. Often just being invited to participate in a conversation about 'the next level' is liberating for those who are more used to being 'told' what they should be doing.

Third, the questions the leader uses are critical, because they provide focus. For instance, asking what an onlooker would see and feel from the team if they were already operating at the next level up places emphasis on human elements – such as teamwork, communication, and willingness to address shortfalls and blind spots – and not just the technical factors.

Wherever our team sits, by helping them decide what the next level of performance looks and feels like for them and challenging them to get there, we keep our use of pressure proportionate.

If you're a leader, before you launch your next project, use the mental blueprint technique to set your team up to succeed through the wise use of pressure.

> As a leader, name a current project that is a challenge for your team. Use the mental blueprint technique to assess their mindset, system and skillset for the project. If you feel comfortable doing so, give your team an approximate category on the performance line for their ability in this area.
>
> Next, consider the level of **expectations**, **scrutiny** and **consequences** you should use for this project. On reflection, how does the level of pressure relate to your team's mental blueprint score? Are you applying too little, too much, or about the right level of pressure to allow people to perform?
>
> Finally, have you noticed any **APE** behaviours in relation to the project? Looking at the balance between your use of pressure and your team's mental blueprint, do you think you've **used pressure wisely**?

The Art of Prioritising: Subtract, Don't Add

In Chapter 9 we saw that the humble **'to do' list** can often become an excuse for *non-performance*. The most common complaint in most work environments is having *too many* items on the list, and not enough time to do them. People talk about sinking rather than swimming, or at best treading water, as more and more is added to their load. They're involved in plenty of *activity*, but often feel like they're not *moving forward*.

We've heard of a 'pity party' – well, many leaders lead by holding a 'priority party'. It's easy to ask people to 'prioritise' something, because it doesn't have any obvious impact; it simply adds another thing to their list.

But in the longer run, it *does* have an impact. Adding more and more 'priorities' creates an impossible situation. It crushes quality, it saps energy, and eventually it makes people burn out.

In some workplaces it's common to be asked to deal with six to ten 'first priorities'. Not possible. And it also makes a mockery of the term 'first priority' – it is simply not possible to do all those things 'first'. If the top priority comes first, it should be given special attention. No one can do this when their attention is scattered.

When leaders tell someone to 'prioritise' a task and they ask what they should do about all the other 'priorities', leaders often abdicate responsibility and simply ask for it all to be done. They remove nothing. They stack and run.

When adding a new task, good leaders *subtract* something first.

There's a strong correlation between the number of things people have to focus on and the quality of their focus on each one. Doing a small number of things very well, and focusing on one thing at a time, is a *much* stronger strategy than superficial multitasking. People enjoy doing things well. So let them.

When people are asked to multitask, they often sacrifice *movement* for *action*. They choose more comfortable and less crucial jobs over the ones that would allow them to make the most progress. They keep themselves busy doing non-urgent, non-important tasks.

The key difference between action and movement is *direction*. Actions may or may not allow us to make progress, because they can be erratic or even cancel each other out. If all our actions take us in the same direction, the result is movement, but if they take us in random or opposing directions, the result is interference or resistance.

'Priority' comes from the Latin *prior*, meaning 'previous' (as in English). It refers to a position in *time*, as opposed to *importance*. Some leaders struggle to decide *what the most important thing is*, when all they need to do is say *what should be done first*. Other things that are important can come later, but what job needs to be the first on the list?

We'll become a skilful 'prioritiser' when we stop confusing urgency with importance, and learn to balance the two. We must attend to the 'first thing' – the most urgent task – but not neglect the big things – the important tasks. The trap to avoid is only ever doing non-important jobs.

When an issue is not a high priority and keeps sliding down the 'to do' list, it's worth considering whether it needs to be done at all. If something is repeatedly delayed it gathers negative energy, and will remain a mental weight until it is completed.

If we're a leader, deciding what comes first and what should be delayed is arguably our most important role. We should allow people to complete tasks one at a time, feel good, then move on.

As a leader, consider how you've prioritised work for your team over the last week. Have you clearly explained which is the first priority, or have you been a serial 'priority adder'?

Would your team say they generally have a good grasp of what task should come first, and are supported when they focus on it, or would they say they're surrounded by a swarm of competing priorities and live in a world of interference?

Pay attention to making sure your team is able to pay attention. Set them up to succeed by defining the top priority, explaining its significance, and giving them time.

Complain vs Complete: Fast Leadership

Imagine the energy shift in our organisation – not to mention the progress we'd make – if we trusted every individual to prioritise one uncomfortable task before midday, every day.

Change can usually occur several times faster than organisations anticipate. But limited thinking will slow things down right from the outset. Through our RED minds, we subconsciously limit our performance so we're working within the parameters of our comfort levels. As we've seen, most people don't actively push themselves towards discomfort – and if they do, they usually still stay short of their limits.

Setting people up to succeed not only builds momentum but also lifts spirits. We can do this by personally removing obstacles that are holding our team back. We can free them up to attend to their top priority, and to use five-minute **micro-performances** to constantly complete chunks of work – especially the uncomfortable tasks. Brief, visible, repeated success stories can change the mood and culture quickly.

An executive team who considered themselves fast adopted a **completion** mindset, took on and completed a difficult item in five minutes each day, and a one-year project was finished in three weeks. For another team, one brief, difficult discussion every day led to incredible business results, day after day, without any other obvious changes.

In an organisation with a completion mindset, the needs of the many outweigh those of the individual. People complete tasks to help move the organisation forward. And they have an enthusiastic attitude: they *want* to do them, rather than being *required* to do them.

Our group may have *technical* expertise, but it's probably other things that are holding them back. As leader, if we focus our efforts on removing the *human* elements that are blocking progress, we can accelerate things remarkably. This is **fast leadership**.

Don't be misled by the phrase '*fast* leadership'. It's not about a rush to action. It's much more about calmly and consistently focusing on constraints, and removing them.

Fast leadership exposes the dangers of the performance plateau. It's easy to become complacent and assume we're moving quickly, when in fact the invisible brakes are on.

The fast leader uses the **mental blueprint technique** to generate the right **mindset, system** and **skillset**, but the catalyst that really kicks things off is time.

The fast leader decides on the longer-term vision, then quickly works backwards to define a concrete 12-month mission, and shorter-term milestones to get there. The milestones are broken up until they're down to tasks that can be completed daily using a five-minute micro-performance. Larger projects are redefined in terms of smaller tasks until they become enticing and the shackles are off. People like to tick off tasks, but if they know how these tasks feed into a bigger, captivating mission, their motivation doubles.

As visible progress occurs, and energy builds, the tendency to complain dwindles. Complaining is the great de-energiser – it kills a performance culture. When complaining stops, the suffocating blanket of anxiety and tension is lifted. Our environment literally feels different to be in.

The other big emotional blocker that creates delay is conflict. It's a natural tendency to protect a personal position at the expense of movement towards the bigger objective. When people become emotionally invested in individual agendas, they're applying the emotional brakes to performance speed. Fast leaders work to foster a high level of trust across the board. They encourage people to actively resolve their issues, knowing that people go to great lengths to avoid the tension conflicts cause. If we remove friction it creates speed.

The standard leadership speed is slow. Incoming CEOs or prime ministers will come up with three-month plans or 100-day goals, and these are often successful because the tight timeline creates deadline pressure. But how often do cultures retain this way of working long-term, so that it becomes their default approach?

If you're in a leadership position, become a fast leader. Use pressure wisely with your team by making time your friend, not your foe. Use the compelling vision – the 'why?' – to define captivating targets – the 'what?' – but combine these with tight timelines – the 'when?'. Adding the 'when?' powers up the 'why?' and the 'what?'. Spend time identifying and resolving the human factors that are blocking movement, and your efforts will be well received.

Putting It All Together: Streamline Your Way to Movement

'Alignment' is a popular catchphrase these days in the corporate world. Organisations chase it hard through strategic retreats.

Alignment involves finding a goal that everyone can agree on, and committing to work towards it as a team. The problem with alignment, though, is it gives people a general direction, but leaves them with too much room to manoeuvre in their day-to-day work. They can claim they're aligned even when they're spending time on tasks that are unhelpful, or unrelated to the primary objective. Alignment is simply too abstract to influence everyday behaviour.

Rather than considering whether our team is 'aligned', we should ask ourselves some tough questions about whether our team is **streamlined**. This will force us to look not just at the direction we're heading in, but also at the detail of the moving parts. It conjures up a clearer picture of how things fit together, so we can move as efficiently as possible towards our goal.

First, each person needs a clear performance gap in place that recognises the external and internal factors holding them back. Unless we **create the gap**, there'll be no space in which to move.

Second, we need a team **mental blueprint** that includes long-term direction and short-term priorities to **bridge the gap**. But to drive the point home, the blueprint must feature a **time** element, to bring to light any factors that might slow things down. This is where the next two steps come in.

Our third step is to power up the **'to do' list** by giving people clear priorities to focus on.

Fourth, we use **fast leadership** to instil a **completion** mindset. Fast leadership targets any friction that will be slowing down movement, and the impact on team spirit leads to inter-dependency and a shared drive for excellence and efficiency.

When there's no agreed direction, fast leadership becomes next to impossible, because there'll be no agreement about which task to focus on first. Different team members will inevitably be working towards different ends. In these circumstances – which are more common than not – teams and groups default to business as usual and people become *busy* rather than streamlined.

Streamlining reveals what's working smoothly and what needs improving to cope with turbulent conditions. The search for obstacles or points of friction becomes a helpful process, because removing these blockages and brakes causes more progress than refining something that's already working quite well. In a streamlined operation there's a clear understanding that teamwork will speed progress, while personal agendas and dramas are not acceptable.

In many organisations, the culture encourages people to actively work against each other, going out of their way make the lives of their colleagues harder. The streamlining idea exposes this behaviour for what it is. The clearest sign of a streamlined team is that colleagues work hard to *make each other look good.*

The ultimate test of your leadership lies in what happens when you're not there. When you're away, do the members of your team know how to use their performance gap to succeed under pressure? Does your team know what to focus on first, and how to work together to accomplish shared goals? If you were invisible and went for a walk around your workplace, what would the evidence say – is your team busy with actions, or streamlined for movement?

CHAPTER 12

AFTER WE PERFORM

In Chapter 7 we looked at how to put our RED–BLUE skills to work *before* we perform. In Chapters 8 to 11 we focused on how to apply RED–BLUE concepts *during* performance to support the **RED–BLUE tool**.

Now let's look at how we can use our RED–BLUE skills *after* our performance.

There are two main things we need to do after we perform. First, we want to regain any RED–BLUE balance we may have lost during our performance, especially if we became tense or worked up. Our **recovery** is as important as our preparation – but often it takes us *hours* to wind down after an event. It pays to be able to recover quickly and efficiently, or we'll end up in a chronic RED state and prone to burnout.

Second, if we're serious about improvement, we need to *learn* from our performance – otherwise we'll be missing an invaluable opportunity. If we don't **review** and reflect on our performance, we're just **pretending to train** or **training to train**. If we only review our performance *sometimes* – perhaps when something unfortunate happens – we're **training to compete**. But if we want to **train to win**, reviewing our performance must become a standard part of our approach.

We don't want a review process that just skims the surface. Nor do we want to get bogged down in a never-ending series of heavy reviews. We want an efficient but probing process that keeps us moving and improving. Ideally, we want a review process that we *look forward* to using.

In this chapter we'll look at practical methods to help us **recover** from our performance, then **review** it. We don't want to overload our post-performance period, but we do want to develop RED–BLUE skills that continue to give us an edge. Once we have these in place, we'll be able to apply the RED–BLUE principles right across the performance timeline.

Switching Off: The Offload Technique

The flip side of performance is returning your body and mind to a balanced state.

Imagine an athlete a few hours after a big event, trying to get to sleep but still feeling coiled up, tense, with racing thoughts. Their performance is long over, but it's not yet over for their mind and body. They need to quieten their busy brain and offload their tension. How can they return to some kind of relaxed state?

No one can focus intensely for a long time, again and again, without suffering from fatigue and possible burnout. When we perform under pressure, it's as important to know how to switch *off* as how to switch *on*. We need to give ourselves as much space for recovery as we did for performance. And it's literally *space* that provides a way to do this simply and efficiently.

The secret to switching off is the same as the secret for switching on: changing the way we pay attention.

The key to the **RED–BLUE tool** is that it forces us to shift our attention. Instead of focusing entirely on pressure, the RED–

BLUE tool requires us to **step back** and see a bigger picture. This broader focus gives us objectivity, puts the pressure in perspective, and just *feels* different.

The RED–BLUE tool and techniques – and the **defend or discover** mindset in particular – encourage us to balance performing with periods of experimentation and learning, and plain enjoyment. But there's also a place – especially after performances – for relaxation and recovery.

Les Fehmi is a psychologist who has spent several decades developing a method of reducing physical and mental tension called Open Focus™. He observes that how we pay attention can quickly alter our mind and body. In particular, when we have a narrow focus on *things*, our brain responds with busy activity, whereas when we focus instead on *nothing* (no-thing, or space), the brain's activity settles. There's nothing external for it to focus on, so it can switch off and enter its default mode of subconscious idling. And at the same time, our parasympathetic system allows our body to move into recovery mode too, with our system tuned to health and restoration, while blood flow around the body to drive movement slows down.

We can combine this insight with the ideas behind the **RED–BLUE mind model** to create a short relaxation routine.

The **offload technique** is a eight-minute relaxation exercise that allows us to **locate**, **activate** then **dissolve** our tension and discomfort, by increasing our awareness of space.

It's hard to allow our body to relax when our mind is still racing, so the place to start is with our **BLUE** brain, closely linked to our thinking. Mental tension often feels as if it's attached to our thoughts, which dominate our attention. Once our thinking has calmed down, we can focus on relaxing our body – closely linked to our **RED** feeling system.

Here's how it works (allow 10–15 seconds between guided imagery directions):

Sit in a comfortable position with your spine straight and eyes closed. Breathe naturally. Prepare to change the way you pay attention to the tension you hold in your body. Don't try too hard. The value of space is unique. You can't grip it, fight it or hold it. It is nothing.

1. Focus on space (*one minute – pause after direction*)
Take a moment to adjust your posture.

As you breathe in, imagine the air is filling your entire body. As you breathe out, imagine your entire body is left full of empty space.

At the same time, can you imagine the space around your body – above, in front, behind, to the sides?

Can you imagine the space inside and outside your body at the same time?

2. Head (BLUE) (*three minutes*)
Can you imagine the space inside your head, the space occupied by your mind? As you breathe in, imagine the air is filling your mind. As you breathe out, imagine your mind is left full of empty space.

(Locate) As you continue breathing in and out, notice any uncomfortable thoughts you may have. Notice the place inside your mind where you carry the most tension.

(Activate) Notice the shape of the tension. Feel within that shape to find its strongest point or region. Starting there, feel outwards to see how wide it is, how deep it is. Feel the space *around* it. Feel the space it occupies. Let it expand and fill the space inside your mind.

(Dissolve) Tension dissolves *itself*. You don't have to do anything other than to feel it fully. Move towards it. Imagine melting into it and merging with it. Imagine holding on to it, gripping it. Now imagine letting it go, leaving your mind full of space. Sink deeper and deeper into the silent stillness of your mind.

Now allow your awareness to sink down from your mind into the core of your body.

3. Body (RED) (*three minutes*)

Can you imagine the space inside your body? As you breathe in, imagine the air is filling your body. As you breathe out, imagine your body is left full of empty space.

(Locate): as you continue breathing in and out, notice any uncomfortable sensations you may have. Notice the place inside your body where you carry the most tension.

(Activate): notice the shape of the tension. Feel within that shape to find its strongest point or region. Starting there, feel outwards to see how wide it is, how deep it is. Feel the space *around* it. Feel the space it occupies. Let it expand and fill the space inside your body.

(Dissolve): tension dissolves itself. You don't have to do anything other than to feel it fully. Move towards it. Imagine melting into it and merging with it. Imagine holding on to it, gripping it. Now imagine letting it go, leaving your mind full of space. Sink deeper and deeper into the silent stillness of your body.

4. Focus on space (*one minute*)

As you continue breathing naturally, imagine the deep space, silence and stillness inside your body and mind are merging and melting into each other, becoming one, leaving you with space, silence and stillness throughout your whole being.

At the same time, can you imagine the space around your body – above, in front, behind, to the sides?

Can you imagine the space inside and outside your body at the same time?

When you're ready, take one final breath into your entire being, and as you breathe out again, notice the space inside and outside your being merge and melt together into one, forming a deep, silent stillness in space.

THE OFFLOAD TECHNIQUE

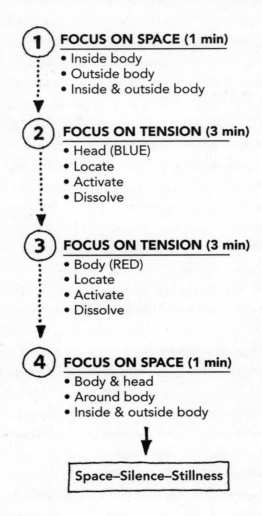

(1) FOCUS ON SPACE (1 min)
- Inside body
- Outside body
- Inside & outside body

(2) FOCUS ON TENSION (3 min)
- Head (BLUE)
- Locate
- Activate
- Dissolve

(3) FOCUS ON TENSION (3 min)
- Body (RED)
- Locate
- Activate
- Dissolve

(4) FOCUS ON SPACE (1 min)
- Body & head
- Around body
- Inside & outside body

Space–Silence–Stillness

The Offload relaxation routine allows us to identify, activate and dissolve discomfort in our mind and tension in our body.

When you're ready, slowly open your eyes.

Don't worry if you find the Offload technique difficult or abstract to follow at the start. In contrast to the techniques used before and during performance, it deliberately uses more abstract concepts, which are harder to imagine and grasp. See any difficulty in imagining the concepts as a positive sign, allow any frustration to subside, and simply allow your mind to be guided along.

Three minutes spent identifying the physical sensations inside your *head* that are associated with thoughts, and transforming blocks of tension and discomfort, is time well spent. Tension experienced in your head often moves to your body and adds to the tension already there. So another three minutes spent identifying the uncomfortable physical sensations inside your *body* allows your BLUE system to heighten your physical awareness and dissolve tension held by your RED system. Merging your RED and BLUE systems together within your inner space, and within the broader container of external space, provides a final breaking down of mental and physical barriers, giving an ultimate sense of connection that can be deeply relaxing.

Attention is the mechanism that connects our mind and body. The main objectives of the offload technique are to use our attention to localise and feel stress, stimulate it further, then release it through merging it with a broader awareness of space. The process of going towards stress and dissolving it takes us out of our performance overdrive and into a more balanced mental and physical state.

The offload technique starts by guiding us in 'opening our focus', which places our body and mind within a bigger perspective – a bigger mind – and automatically calms us. It then uses the same process to dissolve tension associated with thoughts inside our mind and feelings within our body, addressing our thoughts first because of our tendency to get mentally stuck. Finally, after opening our focus again, we're guided in merging the space inside our body and mind, returning to a broader, calming awareness, to achieve deep, authentic relaxation.

Notice how the offload technique encourages us to move *towards* discomfort, rather than trying to remain neutral or ignore it. Just as we might do this *during* our performance if we're adopting a **training to win** approach, it's helpful to do it when we're in recovery mode, because we can never switch off our RED system.

Typically we try to *avoid* paying attention to mental and physical discomfort, which is the surest way to make sure they persist! Trying to deny them only gives them power. It feeds them through fear and gives them energy through emotion. Paying attention to tension in a different way – going *towards* it, feeling it, activating it, then releasing it – reverses this process. As the fear and emotion are felt, they naturally diminish and the tension dissolves.

One key for relaxation exercises like this one is to lower our expectations. Instead of trying to release all our tension in one go, we should aim to reduce tension by just 20% each time. But if we do this, say, three times over a period of a few hours, we'll notice more progress.

Another common issue is the misconception that mind–body exercises take a lot of time and effort to carry out. The offload routine lasts just nine minutes and is easy to complete. Even brief periods of relaxation on busy days can restore our RED–BLUE balance and allow us to recover more effectively from our performance.

A third common barrier to relaxation: becoming frustrated with routines in which we're asked to think of nothing, or we find our mind wandering, which we're told to ignore or just accept.

The offload technique uses instructions to guide our attention, so we avoid falling into this trap. And to reduce mental load, the opening and closing stages use the same structure, as do the BLUE head and RED body stages.

The Offload technique uses the same principles that are built into the RED–BLUE tool: it **renames** mental stress as physical tension; it **reframes** our focus on space instead of objects; and it **resets** the balance between our thinking (BLUE) and feeling (RED) minds.

Changing the way we pay attention is the single most powerful relaxation tool we have. Use the offload relaxation technique after performances when you feel stressed to gradually release tension and rebalance RED and BLUE.

The RED–BLUE Debrief: The Mental Blueprint with a Twist

Once the dust has settled and we've regained RED–BLUE balance – perhaps with use of the **offload technique** – we're in a position to **review** our performance: a task that is often done superficially, or missed out altogether.

The objectives of a review session are to **learn** *and* **adapt**. We often focus on the learning aspect but fail to apply that to the mental blueprint for our next performance. Learning without application is for the classroom. Learning with *adaptation* is performance.

If we actually want to improve, our debrief needs to **create a gap** between our future **intent** and our present **reality**. Then we need to **bridge the gap** using the **mental blueprint technique** so that our next performance will be more streamlined in that direction.

Welcome to the **RED–BLUE debrief**, a relatively quick review process of the mental aspects of performance that can be used by both individuals and teams. To keep things simple, it revisits the technique we used *before* our performance – the mental blueprint – but adds another layer to make sure we're asking ourselves good questions *after* our performance. We can see it as the **mental blueprint with a twist**. Basing the RED–BLUE debrief on the same structures we used to *prepare* for performance makes sense, because they're already familiar to us.

As we saw when we looked at the mental blueprint technique in Chapter 6, approaching the review with the right **mindset** is crucial to the outcome. So attending to that comes first. Is our mindset **defensive**, or is it one of **discovery**? We need to be in a position to explore and apply learning opportunities, and we know that our capacity to look at potentially sensitive areas will be compromised if we're too RED.

Review sessions often take on an entirely different tone when a negative outcome has occurred. We don't have to lose to learn, but sometimes a negative event forces us to introduce a solid review process we've previously avoided. We see this when a sports team reviews their performance only after a run of losses; when a workplace reviews its safety procedures only after an accident occurs; or when new government legislation is passed to fix a long-standing problem only when something obvious goes wrong and the media get wind of it.

A good test is whether we can maintain the same constructive mindset whether the performance was favourable or not. To assist with this, the **RED–BLUE debrief** keeps the emphasis on *improvement*, not *judgment*.

Setting the tone: Feed-forward to create the gap

To set up the review effectively, it pays to use a **feed-forward** rather than *feedback*. We saw in Chapter 5 that when we **create the gap**, the feed-forward approach engages our positive BLUE mind right from the outset. Feedback has a very different feel, and often holds us back; just ask anyone on the receiving end of cutting criticism.

Human performance falls down in predictable ways when **pressure** comes to call. We start by looking at the **pressure** context in which the performance occurred, because without that, analysis loses its meaning and we run the risk of not appreciating/respecting the conditions in which the individual or team had to operate. Focusing on the overall context – the overview – activates our BLUE mind, helping settle our RED mind before we start going into more sensitive areas.

Next we remind ourselves of our **intent** – how well we set out to perform under the pressure. If we don't restate our intent, we have no reference point for assessing where we succeeded and where we fell short. Often this brief review of our intent highlights a lack of attention to this area *before* our performance, a good lesson in itself.

The third step in creating a performance gap would normally be to look at our current **reality** – identifying what is working well and what is holding us back. But instead, because our performance has already happened, we'll need to *review* the **mental blueprint** for what we *wanted* to happen. How does the **mental blueprint** we prepared compare with the **mental *reality*** of what actually occurred?

Mental blueprint meets mental reality

So our next step is to apply the **reality** questions – what worked well and what held us back – to the three building blocks of the **mental blueprint technique**. This means reviewing how we performed *emotionally* (**mindset**), *mentally* (**system**) and *behaviourally* (**skillset**).

In our original mental blueprint, the purpose of our **mindset** preparation was to give us emotional control. So in our review, we need to look hard for moments when we had good emotional control and also when we *lost* control of our emotions, when our RED system hit overdrive and we went down the **aggressive-passive-escape (APE)** track.

Here are some common examples of RED moments: sporting teams who are losing with time running down become too frantic, impatient and impulsive; workplace accidents occur when workers become bored and frustrated by safety briefings that go through the motions and end up taking short cuts and unnecessary risks; and stage performers can become overawed, tense or hesitant when they step out onto a bigger stage. In all cases, emotional self-control is reduced.

In our mental blueprint, the purpose of our **system** preparation was to give us mental clarity through the use of simple systems and short sequences. So in our review, we need to look hard for moments when we had good clarity but also for moments when we *lost* clarity – when we got caught in the detail and lost sight of the overview.

Common examples of loss of clarity include when a footballer gets drawn into a personal clash, loses sight of their role of the game plan and get caught out of position; an anxious groom finds their mind goes blank when they stand to speak; or a parent drawn into a work dispute completely forgets their daughter's violin recital they promised to attend. In all cases, situational awareness is lost.

In our mental blueprint, the purpose of our **skillset** preparation was to give us efficiency. So in our review, we need to look hard for areas in which we were both smooth and efficient and inaccurate and inefficient.

Common examples of inefficiency are when novice rowers in a race lose their coordination and rhythm and the boat stalls; executive team meetings are disjointed and unproductive; and a photographer loses the mood and connection with their subject and can't capture the perfect moment. In all cases, balance and timing of execution vanished.

The major hazard in debriefs is **hindsight bias,** our tendency afterwards to see what happened as entirely predictable and therefore preventable, when in fact that wasn't the experience of anyone who was there at the time. Because we *now* know what happened, we should have seen it coming *then*. Wrong. It's surprisingly hard to *un*-know what we know now and get an accurate picture of what it was like for those involved, who didn't have the advantage of hindsight.

Let's also not forget that this is a **feed-forward** process, the reverse of traditional *feedback*. We always start with what worked well, *then* consider where we fell short of our intent. This protects us from looking more at the negative more than the positive.

The higher we go up the **scale of mental intent,** though, the more interested we'll be in the areas where we fell short.

And the more familiar we become with the RED–BLUE debrief, the more flexibly we can use it – we can even fit debriefs in during mini-breaks in some performances.

Some team coaches use the RED–BLUE debrief in matches at half-time to work out what the team need to prioritise in the second half. Was **mindset** or **system** more of an issue? (For teams, **skillset** issues generally overcomplicate the picture, and are best dealt with individually, or in preparation for the next performance.)

In settings where the situation is constantly evolving – such as a complicated accident site, a police hostage scenario, or a live newsfeed from a major incident – it's often necessary for team leaders to have **hot debriefs** in the field while the action is still going on around them. This requires an ability to quickly enter a balanced RED–BLUE state and conduct a debrief on the run before re-entering the fray. These leaders know that if they can carry out a hot RED–BLUE debrief in three minutes, they'll feel composed re-entering tense situations where the outcome is highly dependent on their mental skills under pressure.

Searching for improvement: Strengths, weaknesses and blind spots

To take our RED–BLUE debrief up a notch, we can deliberately look for **strengths, weaknesses** *and* **blind spots**. All three areas can be difficult to talk about in a straightforward way because the people involved might feel uncomfortable talking about what they did well – through modesty – or what didn't work out – through feeling criticised. With three simple techniques we can get past the RED mental blocks that stop us from recognising areas where we can improve, and access performance gold.

First, look for the areas in our mental performance in which we met or exceeded our intention. We should be specific about what worked well to reinforce effective mental performance and to consider if these strengths can be developed even further. It is easy to talk only in general terms about positive aspects or to ignore them completely and jump straight to areas in which we had problems but we shouldn't assume that those elements will simply continue or that the people involved truly appreciated what created the positive impact.

Second, to look for areas in our mental performance in which we fell short we can ask ourselves what the **inconvenient facts** were in our performance – those unfortunate truths we looked at in Chapter 5. They often carry emotional overtones, which cause us to take the more comfortable road and skip over them. But labelling them 'inconvenient facts' – as opposed to something like 'brutal truths' – keeps our review more objective and stops us going into the RED. Plus, often we have a tendency to see something as '*the* truth' when, in fact, it is '*our* truth' or '*one version* of the truth'. Let's stick to 'inconvenient facts' – we would have preferred things to be different but they weren't – and watch a rich, productive debrief session unfold.

Third, deliberately look for blind spots. This sounds illogical – by definition, we can't *see* our blind spots – but by using the MIA questions we can take our quest for improvement up a level. We can view this method as a rigorous search party, seeking out seemingly hidden information that is actually within our grasp.

We ask ourselves: 'In this situation, what information did I **miss, ignore** or **assume**?' The MIA abbreviation usually means 'missing in action' – in our case, what *information* has gone missing in action?

We ask ourselves the MIA questions to help counteract our human tendency to avoid, explain away or miss uncomfortable things. Often it's the very things we least want to acknowledge that are holding us back the most. When we're willing to 'see' these uncomfortable truths, we're in a much stronger position to identify what we should attend to first. It's a bit like a therapist who skilfully encourages us to see aspects of ourselves that we usually try to avoid – except in this case we're our own therapist, and it's about performance, not therapy.

Like the **hot debrief**, the MIA questions also can be used *during* performance to instantly reveal important errors. An even better idea is to build stronger sequences from the start, by incorporating the MIA questions into our *preparation* phase.

Working as a forensic psychiatrist, I often used to ask myself what I was **missing, ignoring** or **assuming**, especially when things seemed to be under control. It helped me guard against complacency and encouraged me to be vigilant.

For team leaders, inconvenient facts and the MIA questions are simple but powerful techniques for probing deeper during performance reviews. They naturally lead to learning and adaptation, because it becomes immediately obvious to everyone that these areas cannot just be ignored. However, as a leader, we need to ensure these techniques are used not as weapons to attack and judge, but as incisive probes to move performance forward.

To make sure that we take the lessons from our RED–BLUE debrief and translate them into performance gains, a few concrete points are all we need. We can use the **Mental blueprint with a twist** approach to ask ourselves what we should *keep* doing? (strengths); *stop* doing? (weaknesses); and *start* doing? (blind spots), for each of **mindset, system** and **skillset**. Aiming to have one main action point for each point of the triangle – something that we will continue, stop or start doing – will keep our RED–BLUE debriefs energising, lean and practical.

RED–BLUE DEBRIEF

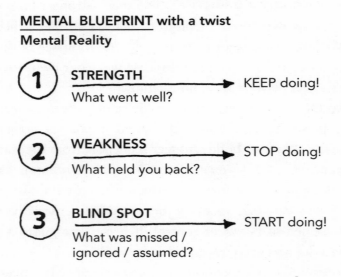

MENTAL BLUEPRINT with a twist
Mental Reality

1 STRENGTH → KEEP doing!
What went well?

2 WEAKNESS → STOP doing!
What held you back?

3 BLIND SPOT → START doing!
What was missed /
ignored / assumed?

The RED–BLUE debrief helps us to identify our mental performance strengths, weaknesses and blind spots so that we can improve.

Our Performance Timeline

The **offload technique** and the **RED–BLUE debrief** – especially when used with **inconvenient facts** and the **MIA questions** – round out our RED–BLUE performance timeline. We've now learned how to apply the RED–BLUE concepts to every stage of our performance under pressure – from preparation, through performance, to recovery and review.

After using these post-performance methods, individuals and teams quickly notice a change in their performance culture. Previously sensitive performance issues become much less prickly, and fair game for thought and discussion. Pretty quickly, people learn that a recovery process without a relaxation technique (like the Offload technique) or an honest review debrief (like the Mental blueprint with a twist) feel incomplete.

Their culture has changed: **complain** has been replaced by **complete**, and **defend** has been replaced by **discover**.

CHAPTER 13

CHAPTER 13

TOUGH DAYS

As we've learned, many of us are highly competent at the *technical* side of what we do, but average at the *mental* factors. This book has been all about developing our mental toolkit, so we can take our performance to the next level.

But if we only reach for the RED–BLUE tool and related techniques when we're in the grips of extreme pressure, we're not serious about improving our performance. If we're using the tool and techniques the way they're *meant* to be used, they should become a standard part of our typical but tough day.

In Chapter 5, we saw that no matter what activity or job we do, everyone's 'tough day at the office' is likely to be similar mentally. Whether we hold a scalpel, firearm, violin or microphone, our minds all react to pressure in the same way.

This chapter looks at a slice of life – part of a tough day – across a wide range of occupations, from a teenage student to an armed police officer. Embedded in these 'tough days' are numerous illustrations of the tools and techniques that have been introduced in this book. (Unless their meaning is clear, most of these terms have been defined in the Glossary, along with a reference to the place where they're introduced in the book.)

And just to be clear, these are *not* real stories, and any similarities between the people in them and those you know are unintentional.

If you want to take the mental side of your performance seriously, you'll need to make the RED–BLUE tool and techniques a daily habit. Use the examples in this chapter as a guide to move your mental skills from *after*thought to *first* thought.

Sales Executive

Before Tane has even stepped into his office the noise has started: his phone is buzzing with texts and missed calls. He checks his emails: an angry customer, a change in meeting times, and of course, some new **priorities** from his boss to be done along with everything else.

His **'to do' list** is brutal – too much for anyone to work through and stay mentally balanced. But he scans the list he wrote yesterday afternoon and applies his personal test, putting a **RED** or **BLUE** mark next to each item and monitoring his level of tension as he goes.

As Tane casts his eye down the list he sees a repeat offender: an item that has been on there for three days. And he knows exactly why: it's a call to his least favourite customer, who is rightly angry about a delivery that Tane's company has completely mucked up. This calls for a **micro-performance**.

He imagines the stopwatch above his shoulder and presses it, giving himself five minutes to make the unpleasant call. He steels himself by thinking about how he tends to hold himself back by staying busy, without making real progress towards his next performance level. He picks up that flicker of heat rising up through his core, revealing his irritation, and notices his neck and shoulders are tense. He takes three slow belly breaths to take the edge off his anger.

He spends three minutes making some notes, using the **Create the gap** and **Mental blueprint** techniques. He takes a sheet of paper and writes 'Call to angry customer' at the top. He writes *'Intention'* under that and briefly describes stepping up to the next level by rolling with the inevitable crossfire from the customer and dealing successfully with their issues. Two-thirds of the way down, he writes **'Reality'**, and includes a short account of his company's failures underneath. In the middle of the page he draws a triangle, and formulates his plan to put things right with a commitment to ensuring customers feel valued (**mindset**), an adjustment to the delivery process that will prevent further muck-ups of this kind (**system**), and suggestions to discuss with the customer about how to fix *this* particular problem (**skillset**). He'll need all his RED–BLUE skills to work his way through this one.

He picks up the phone, calls the customer and starts by sincerely and respectfully apologising for the series of errors and failures. He tells the customer he imagines they have some strong views. The customer certainly does – and lets Tane know – but as Tane reflects back what he's been told using the **RED–BLUE reflective listening** technique, he can hear the customer's anger subside. When he thinks the time is right, he moves on to the topics he needs to cover to clear up the situation. His notes give him all the details he requires. The call is completed in five minutes.

It's not even 8.30am yet, and Tane has already met his noon deadline for completing a difficult task for the day. He feels a sense of relief and a burst of energy as a weight is lifted and tension leaves his body.

Later in the morning Tane has to lead a team meeting about a stalled project that is making his team look bad. He needs to use pressure to get the project moving, but he reminds himself to **use it wisely** – applying pressure one level up from his team's current ability. In his head, he gives them a quick score for each component of their **mental blueprint** for this project: 50% for **mindset**, 70% for **system** and 70% for **skillset**. He concludes that the top priority is to get a mindset shift.

He spends time discussing the purpose of the project with the team. He emphasises the need for everyone to raise their game, and why this is so important not just for them, but also for the customers they serve. He senses some genuine self-reflection and a positive overall reaction from the team.

He asks the team about the standards that they would like to aim for (**expectations**), how they think their progress should be monitored (**scrutiny**), and what should happen if they get ahead of, or behind, the standards that have been set (**consequences**). He acknowledges the external pressure the team is under, and how that has led to some aggressive, passive and escape – or **APE** – behaviours.

Together, they start to break the project down into a series of smaller chunks, and Tane challenges the team to start moving on these smaller areas. He uses his gut feel to do this sensitively so they don't feel overloaded and overwhelmed. The last thing he wants is for them to **ESC-APE** under the pressure. By the end of the meeting, he feels he's managed to engage with them in an open and direct but respectful manner, and they seem much more willing to contribute.

During the afternoon Tane is unexpectedly called in to see his company's leadership team. He senses they want to question him about his delayed project, and his anxiety levels start to go through the roof. So he goes straight into his two-minute **ICE** routine. In his first three breaths, he pictures breathing white light into his abdomen and as he breathes out the light turning blue as it pumps throughout his body, and he feels his face, fingers and toes become cooler. In his next three breaths, he thinks about walking into the leadership teamroom and sees himself managing the situation with poise. He focuses on his breathing and reconnects with his body, which seemed to be somewhere else for a few minutes. And in his third set of three breaths, he imagines the first question from the leadership team and sees himself answering with perfect timing, marking the moment with a mental 'click'. This routine takes a minute, then he takes a deep breath and repeats the process, surprising himself with how much clearer the pictures look the second time around. Tane has a clear head, feels confident and has the ICE technique to thank for it.

He has guessed correctly: the leadership team want to ask him why the software project has not been moving faster. He faces their questions, which go well enough until he's caught out by one leadership team member's needling interjection. The room goes quiet, and he can see the judgment in the others' faces.

It's an uncomfortable moment. But Tane has already primed his mind with the **three circles technique**, and with the help of a quick **RED or BLUE? Decide. Do!** sequence he keeps his focus on what he can control – his own reaction – holds his nerve and manages to take it in his stride. He openly acknowledges his team's failings, but is able to describe the positive goals that were set in the meeting earlier today. Tane uses his **mental blueprint** for the project – which he has at his fingertips because he used it this morning – to provide an impressively honest, balanced but pragmatic account of what should happen from this point on.

Later, as Tane prepares to go home, he looks back on his day. He completed his uncomfortable task for the morning. He engaged his team in developing a new way forward for their stalled project. And without warning, he successfully stepped up to address the leadership team.

A series of tricky scenarios, but he has navigated his way through the day using simple mental tools that helped him think clearly in situations that might have overwhelmed other people.

He has performed his role **under pressure**.

Team Sport Athlete

Ngaire wakes at 7am and immediately thinks of the big match she has this evening. Her mind is racing, she is already tense in the shoulders and face, and she hasn't even got out of bed yet. She realises that she is overthinking things. She follows her **three-breath routine** to settle her nerves, calm her body and clear her mind.

During the morning she organises tickets for friends and family, and makes some calls including one to her manager about an appearance request that she is finding awkward to handle and has been avoiding. But she has these things completed well before her **complain or complete** cut-off time of midday, leaving her with uninterrupted time to prepare.

At the team pre-match meeting, Ngaire notices how the anxiety of a big match affects her teammates differently: some go silent, some get chatty; some laugh a lot. She notices a familiar tight knot in her stomach: a telltale sign that she is anxious, because this game is bigger than most. She quietly does some belly breathing in time with her paces as she walks across the field and gradually slows her breathing rate down.

Ngaire's coach approaches her, as a senior player, and asks her to watch over a debutante playing alongside her this evening. Ngaire prepares some simple external cues she can use with the young player on the pitch to get her out of her head and focusing on her timing, in case she starts to overthink things.

On the way to the game in the team coach, she can feel the tension among the group. Everyone seems in a kind of pre-match trance. Players retreat into their own worlds of headphones and dreams. Ngaire follows her usual habit of just watching the outside world pass by, rather than thinking about the game itself, knowing she has her routines set for the dressing room.

Five minutes before the team goes out she finds a space and starts her two-minute **ICE** routine. She enjoys the familiarity and the focus. She silently recites the word 'Trust' as she feels the energy of RED, which will give her intensity, and the clarity of BLUE, which will give her focus, come together. She visualises carrying out her opening actions in the match with perfect timing.

However, the match doesn't go as planned. With nine minutes left, Ngaire's team are two points down, key players have been injured, no calls from the referee seem to be going their way, the crowd is against them, and the clock is ticking down. Ngaire's teammates have gone either quiet or frantic, and are losing composure. She realises she has also drifted along for the last seven or eight minutes and has fallen into a **wait** mindset. She has to **take** the initiative – immediate action is needed.

First, she completes a **RED or BLUE? Decide. Do!** routine in three breaths to kick-start herself into action. She sees she must step up as a leader.

In a break in play the team forms a huddle. She speaks with composure and decisiveness. She asks everyone to keep their eyes in the game – no heads down to the ground or up to the sky – until the final whistle, because she knows that will increase the connection between them. She reminds them of the two-minute **'What if?'** routine they've rehearsed many times for just this situation, when they need to score with time almost up. She tells them to trust that process, and to increase their tempo so each player stays a step ahead of her direct opponent.

The opposition seem to have read Ngaire's strategy, and although her team might still break through the other team is gaining in strength, so Ngaire follows her gut instinct and makes a decisive call. She signals to her teammates to change their strategy again: a move that pays off when they score. One goal behind.

In another huddle, Ngaire leads her team through the **three-breath routine** before the restart. She reminds them to 'make each other look good' by supporting each other, rather than trying for the big personal play. The team are up for one last push.

But it doesn't work out. In the final seconds, Ngaire's teammate is in a position to score, but misses.

Afterwards, the atmosphere in the dressing room is strained. No one is speaking. Ngaire's mind is going over the same near-miss situations again and again – she is in a negative loop – and she feels angry at the missed opportunities.

Rather than speak straight away, she takes two minutes to release some tension through **belly breathing** and calming herself down. Her body settles and her mind clears a little. She knows she'll need to carry out her **offload** relaxation technique later on, but in the tension of the dressing room the two-minute breathing routine is as much as she can manage.

She knows emotional connections are more important for the team at this moment than words. So she moves around the change room to connect with her disappointed teammates, through knowing looks and pats on the shoulder. They stand in these moments together.

She represents the team in the media call, a daunting prospect on this occasion. She bases her responses on the simple **feed-forward** structure, speaking in sequence about what the team set out to do, what worked and what fell short, and how they tried to adjust. She understands that the media are looking for quotable angles, but she remains composed, listens carefully to the questions and does her best to answer meaningfully rather than using clichés. She looks directly at each journalist as they ask her a question and she uses a tone that is respectful.

Later that night, at home, an irritating on-field incident keeps popping into her mind. An opposition player got under her skin and she overreacted. She knows that trying to ignore this RED moment is not going to work, but now is not the time for extended post-mortems. So she sits upright in a comfortable chair and goes through the eight-minute **offload routine** she promised herself she would do.

She likes the way her busy mind quietens as she goes through the BLUE tension-dissolving sequence, and the way her body responds well to the RED follow-up. By the end she feels like she has shed about a third of her tension, her earlier irritation is forgotten, and she is ready to settle down for the night.

She has played **under pressure**.

Human Resources Director

Maria is hit by the usual barrage of 'urgent matters' that people want her to sort out as she walks into the office. A near-miss health and safety incident might have serious repercussions; and there's a message to call the boss ASAP. Oh well, some things never change!

Maria first rings the CEO, Melissa. Melissa has heard about the health and safety incident and wants an update by mid-morning, and she also wants to check on the progress of the company restructure that Maria has been working on behind the scenes. It means that many people will change their jobs, and some will lose them.

Melissa has Maria's report on the restructure, but she is briefing the board this morning and wants to check on a few details. Better still, now she thinks of it, can Maria come and give her update to the board in person at 10.30am? 'Thanks – see you there!'

Maria hangs up and immediately sees an unfortunate time clash and a tricky decision lying in wait.

She's been looking forward to the launch of a new leadership training programme she has put together. She knows it will make a difference if she's there to open the course and explain its importance to the business. It's a significant step in creating a **performance culture** throughout the organisation. But the leadership course is also starting at 10.30am.

She needs to use the **Rename, reframe, reset** sequence to help her make a decision and get her back on track.

First, she checks on her own emotional state. She finds she is feeling a tight knot in her abdomen, and has gone quiet and withdrawn: familiar signals that she is becoming anxious. She **renames** her current state: 'RED.' She breathes out, letting go of some of the tension and adding some BLUE into the balance.

Second, she **reframes** the situation with a bigger, BLUE outline and immediately sees her situation in overview. She needs to handle two urgent matters – the health and safety incident and the board meeting – and an important but non-urgent matter: the leadership course. She'd prefer to deal with each situation personally, to send the right message to the whole organisation.

Third, she **resets** her mindset, ready to **complete** three tasks, one by one, without any **complaint**, allowing herself only five minutes for each task.

Task one: the health and safety incident. Safety comes first. She walks directly to the area where it occurred, calling the area manager, Rob, on the way. She establishes the facts, checks that the situation has been made safe, and ensures that reporting and review processes are under way.

But she trusted those things to happen anyway, and her primary reason for coming was to meet with Jim, the worker involved in the incident. She asks him about his unfortunate experience: he was using a piece of equipment when it malfunctioned, causing a minor injury – though it could have been much worse. She makes sure he's comfortable still being at work. She promises to return and check in on him before the end of the day.

Five minutes – task completed.

Task two: Knowing that the best way she can support her CEO is by providing a clear, simple, compelling 'story' for the restructure, she explains to the board that programmes like this can often breed fear and resistance in employees. She uses a **feed-forward** to describe how the restructure will lead to a step-up in performance across the board. She explains what this will look and feel like for the company, translating the abstract details in her report into tangible pictures of a different team structure, with fewer employees doing the same work more efficiently. Then she contrasts this with the current reality, highlighting what is working well, and what obstacles are holding the company back. Finally, she identifies the **gap** between the **intent** and the **reality**, and summarises her plan to create movement through **fast leadership**. The exchange seems to go well, the CEO thanks her, and she leaves.

Five minutes – task completed.

She goes directly to the leadership course, apologises for arriving slightly late, and asks if she can address the group for three minutes. She explains how her appearance before the board reflects their commitment to improving performance across the organisation. They're confident that fostering strong emotional connections will lead to a more **streamlined** organisation. The leadership course is a big part of that.

She sets out the three elements of judgment – **expectations, scrutiny** and **consequences** – that this team will face in the programme, which is designed to place each of them under pressure to move. Using the **mental blueprint technique,** she explains that they have the ability to bridge the gap to rise to the challenge because of their completion **mindset**; a management **system** that brings together the team's leaders every morning to iron out any factors stopping progress; and a strong **skillset** that allows team members to engage well with customers and work through any product delivery issues.

She tells them that culture change does not have to be slow. The leaders will set the standards and remove the brakes. She feels good energy in the room: a healthy mix of willingness to step up and perform well, and perception that their current reality is inadequate.

Five minutes – task completed.

Maria heads over to deliver on her promise to speak to Jim once again. She spends half an hour talking through the incident and much more, enjoying building a rapport with Jim, and with others who join in once they see that Maria appears to be genuinely interested in their welfare and is listening attentively to their views.

Afterwards, Maria reflects on her day so far. The pressure on her has been more human than technical, but that's the nature of her job. And she can see an important truth: pressure changes people's behaviour. Including hers.

She has performed her role **under pressure**.

Endurance Athlete

Khalid rises at 5am and goes through his pre-race routine in an understated way to conserve energy. In the closing stages of his race, every ounce of stamina will count. He's pleased that his race will be starting early – 9am – meaning less time to wait around.

He finds a quiet space and goes through his two-minute **ICE** routine to set up his body and mind to perform. He likes the easy, efficient structure of the ICE technique because it gives him clarity and energy, quickly. He likes the focus on timing in the third step, because it prepares his mind to watch for sudden breaks among his competitors – too easy to miss a trick and be left behind. Fast reaction times in an endurance race sound contradictory, but he trusts the ICE technique to give him a mental edge.

When Khalid arrives at the race start area, he notices some telltale signs of anxiety. He's a little nauseous and doesn't feel like any food or fluid; as an endurance athlete, his hydration has to be spot on. But he knows what to do: he finds a quiet corner near the warm-up area and goes through his ICE routine once again to settle his body and clear his mind.

The race starts, and Khalid concentrates on falling into a rhythm while keeping an alert eye on the leaders. Races can be lost early in his sport but he responds to the initial moves of the stronger competitors with composure and decisiveness.

In the middle stages of the race Khalid finds himself at the back of the leading pack, but in increasing physical discomfort. He realised early on that this wasn't going to be one of those days when everything fell effortlessly into place – just the opposite.

He becomes fixated on the burning pain and a mental wrestling match begins. His BLUE mind is trying to tell him – in a squeaky voice – that he can do it, that he needs to focus and keep going. His RED mind is screaming out – through discomfort rather than words – that he should stop. The two 'voices' engage in a lively debate and his mind becomes busy, with pushy, negative thoughts of losing and letting people down interfering with his attempts to refocus. He feels frustrated that after all his preparation, it might not be his day. Life is frustrating sometimes.

He suddenly realises he has gone into a RED **'poor me' loop**, and over the last few minutes his rhythm has gone and the leaders have pulled away. Not too far – but he scolds himself for losing concentration.

He immediately goes into his mid-race RED–BLUE routine, to halt his slide into RED, find a way to rejoin the pack without wasting precious energy reserves, and regain his rhythm. While his body continues on automatic pilot, he silently asks himself **RED or BLUE?** He recognises that he has slipped pretty quickly into a tense RED state, but by catching himself, he is heading back to a more balanced RED–BLUE position. **Decide?** Even though he is not feeling at his best, Khalid is competitive and never gives a race away, and he decides to try to slowly find the back of the leading pack again. **Do?** He focuses on the rhythm of his breathing and his running rhythm also returns. He doesn't try to do too much – just running fluently is his immediate goal – but that is more than enough to increase his speed and he slowly starts to gain on the pack.

His breathing becomes more regular and he lets the smooth rhythm spread across his body. It would be naïve to try to recover the few metres he has lost too quickly; slowly will do it. But now he also has a plan in mind: not only to catch the leaders, but to apply pressure to them too. Too many times he has seen athletes make up ground but then fall away quickly because they haven't worked out what to do when they get there.

Important not to overthink it. Just provide his mind and body with clear images of what he is after then let them do their thing.

He goes into his race 'trance' by shifting his attention from the pain and discomfort inside his body to the world around him: the temperature of the air, the breeze on his skin, the feel of the ground beneath his feet, the sounds he can hear on all sides. The tempo of his feet focuses his attention, and in the back of his mind the pain subsides. It's a mind game; if he's in pain, then so are his opponents. Without the pain, anyone could win.

He smiles, to send a message to the pain that it is felt, but it can now take its place in the background while he attends to business.

He looks ahead, picks out a target about 100 metres ahead and estimates how many paces it will take to get there. He counts silently until he has reached his goal. He keeps repeating the process until a further 1000 metres have gone by. The simple counting process gets him out of his thoughts.

In the final stages of the race, the pace quickens and Khalid is one of five in contention. Two will miss out, three will medal, one will win. He cuts off the mental chatter inside his head about results and refocuses on the test: can he break through his previous limits?

He needs this group to take him where he has never been before. Without them, he will never explore the extreme edges of his capability. He feels a surge of respect for his fellow athletes, and a sudden sense of connection. A burst of energy follows, coursing through his body.

He uses the RED–BLUE tool again, but this time runs through the **Step back, step up, step in** version. Step 1: he mentally **steps back** and sees himself in a 'purple' state: physically pushed to his limits but loving it. Perfect. Step 2: he **steps up** and raises his thinking a notch. This helps him shift his focus from the athletes' faces to the spaces between them, and any gaps he can use. Step 3: he **steps in** and makes his move, overtaking two athletes and slowly reducing the space between himself and the leader. This is new territory, but he keeps monitoring the space between himself and the runners in front to ward off the temptation to start thinking about how he's looking and how his body is feeling. 'Spaces, spaces, spaces.'

In an exciting finish, Khalid holds off a strong challenge from the runner behind, but can't quite chase down the leader. He finishes second – but has a new personal best!

He couldn't have done this alone. He feels a flood of emotion as he realises this was his best ever race, and a new respect and gratitude towards his fellow athletes as he recognises how they need each other to push themselves to their limits and beyond. Most endurance races do not finish in this way, and any race that does is special. It may never happen again. He's been taken into fertile learning ground today – breaking through to the next level.

He has raced **under pressure**.

Surgeon

Abhi's morning just took a turn for the worse.

During the third case on her operating list, her anaesthetist has to deal with a complication and an already tight morning becomes impossible to complete. Now she's left with a choice between the two final cases on her list. Her next case is more urgent from a surgical point of view, but she's postponed the final case once already, and made a personal promise to the patient that it would go ahead today.

Her **attention** becomes **split** between the present and the future, and suddenly her current operation is not going as smoothly as it should be. She has to stop and check some of her work, which only adds to the time pressure. And she's fully aware that this case and her final two cases all have technically complex aspects.

In the back of her mind she is also replaying a brief exchange she had on her way into theatre this morning with Keith, a senior colleague. It's left her wondering whether his passing comment was actually a concealed barb about her chances for promotion. Her irritation builds.

Finally, she is also aware that Jane, one of her trainees, has a specialist exam this morning. Abhi is anxious for her to do well. Jane has failed this exam once before – which is common – but Abhi hopes she is up to the pressure today.

As Abhi continues to operate, she casts her mind forward to consider her last two cases again. There is no scope to run late, because Keith is using the theatre next, and she knows there won't be any flexibility on offer. Best not to inflame *that* situation.

She realises that she has become quiet and stopped communicating with her team. The charge nurse, who runs the theatre, is making her presence felt in the background.

Abhi doesn't want to get a reputation for being slow and not completing lists. Time for her to use the **RED–BLUE tool**.

'RED or BLUE?' A definite veer into the RED. She's feeling irritated, with a busy mind, tension in her neck and shoulders, and fluctuating concentration. But she holds her nerve, moves her feelings towards Keith and other staff into another mental compartment to deal with later on, and makes a deliberate choice to operate with a composed BLUE state of mind.

'**Decide.**' She looks at the situation through a larger, BLUE mental frame and intuitively sees the right path forward. Safety trumps promises to patients, and potential reputational damage. She knows the right thing to do is focus on the more urgent case, and place the postponed case on hold once again.

'**Do!**' With her decision made, Abhi lets the charge nurse know she is going to postpone her final case, as it's clear she won't be able to undertake the surgery in a timely and safe manner. Then she resets her focus and completes her current operation smoothly and cleanly.

In between her third and fourth cases she uses the simple **three breaths** routine to clear her mind and calm her body. With each breath, she feels a cooling wave of air flowing in and around her upper body. Then she starts on her final case for the morning.

One of her junior team members whispers that Jane is on the phone, but Abhi says she'll call Jane back later when she can give her the attention she deserves.

Some time later, Keith pops his head into theatre, which Abhi knows is a deliberate tactic to let her know he's there and waiting to start on time. She also knows the theatre staff are watching her closely to see if she gets flustered.

Abhi mentally runs through the **three circles technique** – even though she usually uses it to prepare for operations, Abhi finds that the visual boundaries provided by the circles help create mental boundaries, and it helps her refocus during the operation too. She can't control other people's behaviour, but she *can* control her attention, and she can influence the perceptions of those around her through her responses. She returns her focus to her CAN CONTROL circle, and the mental noise from the other issues dissolves. She's operating for the benefit of her patient, not for other surgeons or staff. She makes a mental note not to be bullied, to remain composed, and to rise to the occasion. No point in succumbing to the pressure – she needs to operate her way through it!

She completes her operating list, leaves the theatre in Keith's hands, and heads immediately to the ward to speak to Ed, the patient who missed out on his operation. She takes time to apologise to him, explain what happened, and commit to doing the surgery first thing tomorrow – all things being equal.

Ed initially reacts with a RED outburst, but after that ventilation, he soon makes a logical shift and agrees that he would rather wait so his operation can be performed safely, without any need to rush.

As Abhi looks back at her morning operating session, she deliberately **creates the gap** in her mind and visualises her next level of performance: being on the mental front foot through better preparation, with more finely tuned anticipation of the potential complexities within each case. It is an **inconvenient fact** – but true nonetheless – that if she had been thinking two steps ahead she could have avoided a lot of the complications that happened this morning. But now that she's faced that reality, she can move and improve.

Abhi debriefs with Jane and hears about her torrid experience of facing several tough examiners. She congratulates Jane on getting through such a thorough test. She reminds her that her training is not only about technical knowledge, but also about building the ability to **perform under pressure**.

Reflecting on her day, once again Abhi has found that the human side of her performance is as important as the technical side. Managing timelines, disruptive colleagues and upset patients in the middle of an operation can lead to loss of focus, hurting performance. Being a surgeon is complex, but it's simple mental tools that help keep her on track.

Abhi has operated **under pressure**.

Ambulance Officer

Francesca has two kinds of days in her ambulance work: routine transfer days, and emergency days. Today is an emergency day.

She's seen a lot so far in her career – road traffic accidents, violence, sports injuries, acute medical events – but not so much that she doesn't still encounter new scenarios. So she's on edge every time she's running an emergency vehicle.

And today is no exception. She's already attended a cardiac arrest, a road traffic incident, a youngster with an acute asthmatic attack, and an elderly man with confusion. But her unit has just been asked to respond urgently to an industrial accident at a plant just outside town. Several people are reported as injured as a result of a chemical explosion. She doesn't know the extent of the injuries, but it's clear they involve serious chemical burns.

Francesca has a relatively junior partner with her today, and she's never attended a chemical incident this large before. The fire service is on its way and will arrive at about the same time. Two additional ambulance units are on their way but will be 10 minutes behind hers. Francesca and Mick, her partner, are leading the way.

Francesca's mind is busy as she tries to navigate traffic with lights and sirens on. She notices that she's tense and has gone over to the RED side – lost in **'What if?'s**, overthinking, not paying attention to the road in front of her, feeling anxious and edgy and going quiet. Mick deserves more from a senior colleague. To get a grip on her emotions, she quietly runs through her basic **three breaths** routine while she drives. She imagines breathing energy and calm deep into her belly – and breathing out tension and stress.

Feeling more focused, but still 10 minutes away, Francesca radios through to the plant manager to get a firsthand account of what she and Mick are heading into. She learns that five people have received chemical burns, and although first aid is being applied, the victims are in a state of extreme pain and distress. All have visible skin damage, and two have probable eye damage. The manager is understandably distraught and keeps asking her to get there as soon as possible. Francesca requests an escort to meet them at the gate, hop on board and direct them to the accident site.

They arrive, pick up the escort, drive to the scene and kick into action. After putting on her protective equipment, Francesca's first task is to check that Mick has put *his* on correctly – otherwise, she'll be letting both him and his patients down. This is a good lesson for him to learn: during an emergency, attend to yourself first, *then* take care of other people. The gloves and mask they are required to wear make it hard to administer treatment and still be 'human' – but they are essential.

The accident site is not a pretty one: two first-aiders are helping emergency-shower five victims, but they're out of their depth and not following the correct procedure. Everyone is understandably distressed and frantic.

Francesca is relieved to see that the fire truck has also arrived as anticipated. While the firefighters establish safe perimeters, she surveys the scene more closely, and sees that several people may have incurred secondary injuries after valiantly helping their workmates.

She strides towards the first-aid officers, going through her **RED–BLUE** ritual. First, '**RED or BLUE?**' Pretty RED, to be honest! Deep breath in, deep breath out. That feels a little better ... Second, '**Decide.**' She sees that three victims are active and distressed, while the other two are stationary and quiet. Francesca follows the rule of thumb: attend to the quiet ones first. She sends Mick to the nearest quiet victim. Third, '**Do!**' She quickly walks up to the second quiet individual and identifies herself.

The patient has severe chemical burns over his upper body, but his clothes are still partly on, meaning that he's still being burned. She quickly removes his clothing, administers pain relief, and shows one of the first-aiders how to shower him properly. While he's being showered, she talks to him in a calm, reassuring voice as she explains that she is treating his eyes with eye wash before she places dressings over them. She knows he'll become even more anxious when he can't see.

She gives them a quick summary of what will happen from here. Now that his condition is stable, she's going to go and assess the other workers, but she promises to return to check on him inside five minutes. She'll be within earshot at all times, and the first-aider will remain with him.

Within four minutes, she and Mick have attended to all five victims. They've minimised the ongoing damage from chemical burns, applied the appropriate dressings and pain relief, and set up a safe zone around each victim. Two individuals have life-threatening injuries, one has major injuries but will survive, and the vision of the man Francesca first attended is at risk.

The two other ambulance units arrive and now each patient can be attended by a qualified paramedic. As the first senior officer to arrive, Francesca is in charge. She repeats the **three breaths** process to ground herself again, deliberately taking in the whole scene as she does so.

It would be easy to relax at this point and assume that everything is under control. So Francesca goes step by step through her **MIA technique**. What is she **missing**? What is she **ignoring**? What is she **assuming**? The rescue helicopter, called out because of the seriousness of the incident, has arrived to provide medical staff and additional paramedics and emergency transfers if required.

Her attention is drawn to Mick, whose patient seems especially distressed. She spends two minutes calming both Mick and the patient by talking them through the next steps. Francesca's confident, composed voice seems to settle them both down.

She calls the local hospital to make sure there are two more ambulances on their way, and does a one-minute handover to the triage nurse in the emergency department. The next 10 or so minutes seem to take forever as she and the other officers wait for the additional support to arrive. Francesca continues to rotate between the five patients, providing reassurance, time frames and simple explanations.

Even after the victims are all on their way to hospital, her work is not done: the remaining staff are still distressed and need support. She delegates responsibility for this to an experienced colleague, then seeks out the senior fire officer again to check on the overall safety of the site.

At the end of her shift, Francesca reflects on how she handled this unusually demanding situation. Despite her professional training and experience, she lost focus a few times, but those basic mental tools got her back on track. The most important thing she had to manage was her own emotional reaction to the scene; once that was under control, she was in a position to help others. She stepped up, and those around her benefited from her composure.

She has delivered emergency care **under pressure**.

Creative Director

Pressure kills creativity.

Well, that's what the received wisdom says, but that hasn't been Maia's experience at all. As often as not, Maia has produced her most original work when she's been faced with time pressure. She doesn't subscribe to the idea that creativity can only thrive in a welcoming, generous environment where everything is flexible, including timelines. And given that she's constantly having to meet deadlines, it's just as well.

Although she loves to lead, Maia also loves to create, so she's retained a hands-on role. And nearly every day she's working to a tight schedule.

Today is another one of those days. A high-profile customer needs to see something by 4pm, so they can give the go-ahead for what will be a high-profile national advertising campaign. Everything is 'high profile' – that's the point of what Maia does. Her team has set aside the morning for generating ideas, the afternoon for narrowing them down and presenting concepts, then there'll be the briefing to the client's formidable CEO. There is no place to hide.

But Maia sees an opportunity to lead *and* create under pressure. She starts by talking to her team about what they want to achieve by the end of the day, and then contrasting this with where they are now, to **Create the gap** and make them aware of what movement is required.

The **pressure** is coming from the high **expectations** from the client and their firm, the **scrutiny** is coming in the form of a presentation to the clients at the end of the day, and the **consequences** are – well, significant: her team desperately wants to be awarded the campaign!

Next, Maia sets out the team's **intent** under this pressure by describing how the presentation will look and 'feel' at the end of the day: they want to produce an upbeat, energising 45-second clip comprising three 15-second concept videos with sound bites, each offering a variation on one main 'hook'. She believes the client will respond positively to receiving a strong direction from the team in terms of the main theme, but having choice between three alternatives – confidence with flexibility.

Finally, Maia reminds her team of the current **reality**. They have the benefit of some preparation and sufficient time to complete the task for today, but this has to be balanced against two **inconvenient facts**: the team do not have a good candidate for the central advertising 'hook' yet, and her most trusted team member is away at a conference.

Maia senses that by creating the gap for her team they are eager to get going and make some progress towards their goal, at the same time as being uncomfortable with the status quo. They are ready to move – just the impact she wanted from the **feed-forward** frame she used to position the day's task.

But Maia is aware of a subtle tension in her body, and she quickly sees that she's thinking ahead to the formal presentation and the impending sense of judgment. She knows that tension is produced by feelings, and the fact that she has emotional investment in this process is a good sign: it matters. She *wants* to perform. But her level of tension is too high for her liking and she decides that the first person she should help here is herself. She uses the **RED–BLUE tool** to clear her mind before starting the team creative process. The last thing she wants is to sabotage the creative process with unhelpful RED frustration.

First breath: **'RED or BLUE?'** Definitely RED! She takes a step backwards in her mind – symbolically separating her reaction from the situation in front of her – and sees that she's gone into a **'poor me' loop** about her skilled team member being away right when she needed her most. Her negativity recedes straightaway, because she knows she hasn't got time to feel sorry for herself.

Second breath: 'Decide.' She imagines placing a bigger BLUE frame around the situation, and immediately sees that this is normal advertising life, no catastrophe is occurring, and her team will learn by observing how she deals with it all. She commits to 'stepping up' to demonstrate what composure under pressure looks and feels like: a good **mental blueprint** for them to absorb.

Third breath: 'Do!' She **steps in** and explains to her team that rather than seeking consensus, they must focus on asking questions and offering different angles to promote **divergent thinking**. This avoids the usual kind of group brainstorming session where people get in each other's way. When it comes to original ideas, she wants to give each member of the team individual space in which they're not going to be dominated by more forceful members. She recruited her team for creativity, not debating prowess.

Now she's attended to their *external* environment, Maia encourages her team to prepare their *internal* environment – their creative minds – so they'll be fertile ground for divining new connections, dissolving contradictions, and releasing inspired insights. They are ready to **bridge the gap**.

Maia uses a modified version of the **Rename, reframe, reset** tool to lead the group in a five-minute **creative micro-performance**. Spending this short period getting their minds clear avoids large tracts of wasted time, and gives them an opportunity to perform.

Step 1: **rename**. She redefines the client brief for the group as a puzzle. The client wants an emotional hook that will make their product, an everyday household item, appeal to a wide audience. Maia knows that having a puzzle to solve – as opposed to a problem to resolve – is a better bet for getting the group's creative juices flowing. She writes the puzzle at the top of a whiteboard.

Step 2: **reframe**. The group spends three minutes compiling a list of different questions, angles and perspectives, without any attempt to find answers at this point. Maia sketches out the questions and angles in rough diagrammatic form on the whiteboard as people call them out, to make it a visual task. The group look at the puzzle from different angles – exploring different time frames, word meanings and so on. Maia writes down any new leads, but otherwise the group stick to looking with curiosity at what emerges.

Step 3: **reset**. Now that Maia has turned the whiteboard into a creative flurry of small diagrams and connections, she asks the group to switch their focus to seeing whether the various components have led to any immediate ideas. She tells them not to worry when nothing much comes to mind: the reset phase is about taking their mental focus off questions and putting it back on solutions.

Step 4: **release**. Now that the group has completed their *first* creative micro-performance, Maia **releases** them from the creative task by giving them a 45-minute break. Some of them grab a coffee, some read quietly, while Maia leaves her desk and goes for a walk.

She trusts her mind to respond to this internally imposed deadline. She knows that once she has something visible to work from, her BLUE mind seems to take off and originality flows, avoiding the mental traps of freezing or going passive.

Step 5: **revisit**. After 45 minutes, Maia – refreshed from her walk and a quick catch-up with some work colleagues – reassembles the group to revisit the puzzle. As she hoped, three ideas have popped into her mind during her break, which she quickly notes down. Other members of the group share their ideas also. Next, Maia spends five minutes sketching out diagrams of each. They all feature an emotional hook that will capture the audience's attention; the product is presented in unusual but humorous ways.

By midday, the group has completed their second micro-performance with enjoyment. Maia is confident that the remainder of the day will take care of itself, the final client briefing included. Maia reflects on her morning and sees that the success of the group micro-performance has been down to her philosophy: creativity can thrive under pressure – but only when we're in the right state of mind.

Maia has learned how to deal with deadlines and use time pressure to her advantage. She used the **Create the gap technique** to frame the situation, the **RED–BLUE** tool to calm her nerves, and the **creative micro-performance technique** as a catalyst for the creative process.

She has helped her team blend the best of both worlds, balancing unconscious RED connections and BLUE creativity.

She and her team have created **under pressure**.

Coach

Andy's team has a big game this evening and his first task is to finalise the selection. He's had a restless night procrastinating about the final two places on the team. He's still caught in two minds. Selection is a core task for a coach – but sometimes he finds himself flip-flopping between players, which is a major distraction from all the other things he needs to take care of.

He decides to use a five-minute **micro-performance** and starts the timer on his mobile phone. He's narrowed his selection down to two players for each position. He starts with the most contentious decision, and jots down the pros and cons of the two players he's considering, contrasts them, and decides. Then he repeats the process for the second position, and at the end of the five minutes his team selection is complete. As always, the act of writing the two final names down releases tension. Task done.

His next task is to use the **mental blueprint technique** to plan the talk he'll give the team before they travel to the game this afternoon. The **mindset** he wants is controlled aggression. The game is an important local derby, so they need to play hard, but impulsive actions have cost them in the last two derbies. He wants controlled play and deliberate responses, not rash reactions.

To keep the strategy simple for the players, he'll ask them to adopt a **system** of counter-attacking when they gain possession of the ball. He identifies the main area of the pitch that he wants the team to focus on, and each player's role in the counter-attack. He's found that painting clear mental pictures of scenarios that will unfold on the pitch is the best way to get the team to put strategies into practice.

As usual, he'll conduct individual **skillset** discussions outside the team meeting – no need to overload all the players with information they don't need to hear. He singles out three players he thinks will be challenged by their immediate opponents this evening about how they could adjust their usual execution, in order to have a better night.

Andy completes his **mindset–system–skillset** summary and records it in his notebook and on his laptop. Task completed.

He makes a few calls to check last-minute issues with support staff and it looks like **Mr Three Things** has shown up to disrupt the game. One player has reported in sick; a second player failed a late fitness test against all expectations, meaning a late change in selection. That means one more unexpected thing is probably lurking around the corner.

Andy turns to the **three circles technique** to remind himself to focus on things that he can control or influence; becoming irritated and stuck on things outside his control will just send him into the RED. He focuses on not allowing his mind to slip into the **can't control** circle of items and sees himself regain perspective as he shifts his attention to the items he *can* control. The three circles technique always helps him adjust quickly, and protects him against overreacting to unsurprising surprises.

Satisfied that he is now on an even keel, he heads to the gym for his usual pre-game exercise routine, which will energise his body and clear his head.

At the afternoon team meeting, he speaks without notes as usual, because the **mental blueprint** structure is so simple. He talks about the **mindset** he expects, and gives examples of how that might play out on the pitch. He talks about the main strategic issues using the counter-attacking **system**, organising the players' roles into a **sequence** that's easy to follow, and providing brief footage to highlight his main points. But Andy has learned the hard way that telling the players *what* to do is only part of the story; he also needs to tell them *when* to do it. So he ends his talk by focusing on the timing of their reactions once they gain possession of the ball. Then he hands over to the team captain, who addresses them briefly before they go off to their pre-match meal.

Later in the afternoon Andy manages to get around to the three players he singled out to speak to about their individual challenges, and the adjustments they need to make to their **skillset** so they can match their direct opponents in this evening's game.

In the lead-up to the match Andy finds a quiet place to complete his preparation. He runs through his plans for injuries and substitutions so that he has every player covered, just in case. He goes over his plans B and C, two alternate **systems** he can direct the team to use if they lose control of the situation. Lastly, he writes down some key words to prompt his thinking in the post-match press conference. Satisfied that he's anticipated all the issues, he allows himself a few moments to prepare emotionally for the game.

During the match there's the usual combination of anticipated issues and unexpected dramas. **Mr Three Things** shows up again when a key player gets injured just before half-time, but Andy has anticipated changes for every position so has a replacement ready in mind. In the break, he speaks to the team about the speed of their counter-attacks; they've understood their basic roles, they're just playing too slowly.

In the second half they stick with their game plan, and although it doesn't look good for a while, they gradually get on top and end up taking out the game just before the final whistle. There's an emotional response from players, staff and fans alike.

Andy allows some time for his emotions to settle then speaks briefly to the team in the sheds, reminding them what they set out to do, how their focus and trust in the game plan benefited their play, and how holding their nerve and keeping a team focus contributed to the outcome. He lets them know he appreciates how much effort they put in.

The media interviews are the usual mixture of leading questions to draw out controversial comments, and more searching and insightful observations. His philosophy is to try to learn one thing from each media exchange. He knows that many coaches and managers dismiss this part of their role, but he respects the thinking of the more experienced media operators, and the angles they see often suggest something valuable for him to consider. He also regards these interviews as a way to indirectly convey his thinking – and gratitude – to the team.

By the time he gets home, he's tired but nowhere near ready for sleep. He's still emotionally digesting the evening's events. He reverts to his favourite refuge – reading – because it allows him to become absorbed in a different story from today's game. Within half an hour, he's asleep.

Today, he has coached **under pressure**.

Police Tactical Team Member

The callout is a sudden one – not one that Liam could have predicted.

The incident was phoned in by a member of the public who heard shots fired in a semi-rural area. Local police have confirmed that a man with a history of violence and drug abuse has occupied a house with gang associates. There may also be hostages inside. Police have sealed off all exits, but no contact has been attempted with the gang. Liam's armed police team are 15 minutes out from arrival.

Although he's a veteran of more than 200 similar incidents, Liam knows the risks are real and he's on high alert. He feels his heart racing and butterflies in his stomach. His preparation for situations like this is extremely thorough, and he trusts that it will see him through. But experience has also taught him to be aware of the impact of pressure on people: it makes them unpredictable and sometimes volatile. He never, ever gets complacent. Which means he has the edge: he's used to being hyper-vigilant, and knows the risks, but the gang members do not.

Liam's armed response team have gone through their usual detailed briefing but he spends time going through the **three circles technique** in his mind, just to reinforce his personal role. He spends a minute thinking about the things that he cannot control in this situation – the gang members' motives, their physical state and the extent to which they are under the influence of drugs or alcohol. He spends a minute going through aspects he can control, including his composure, accuracy and awareness. He then spends a minute considering aspects he can influence, including the reaction of gang members and hostages if entry to the house is made. He feels clear about the team plan and has now reviewed his personal task. Liam's switched on, connected to his immediate environment and ready to go.

By the time they reach the house, night has fallen. They silently and invisibly set themselves up in allocated positions in the farmland surrounding the house. Liam and his partner Tom check lines of sight, communication channels, and the cover between themselves and the house.

It's now a mental challenge involving polarities: extended periods of quiet inaction, followed by brief periods of rapid activity. Unchanging situations are the enemy of concentration, and immediate threat is the enemy of decision-making, so Liam's attention is disrupted both ways. The slow–fast combination can be lethal – literally. And there are so many unknowns: the number of gang members and the number of innocent people, the firearms involved, the gang's mental state. All this uncertainty builds pressure.

Time passes and the situation evolves. The team's negotiator indicates that the gang leader is losing his cool – getting anxious, shouting, making threats. Liam's team covertly approach the building and are able to gain vital intelligence. There are five male and three female occupants, not all armed. It is unclear whether any of the occupants are hostages. Six occupants are together in the main living area of the house, and two are located at opposite corners as sentries, both armed. The message is clear: the situation is complex and is likely to escalate rapidly.

Liam uses the **Step back, step up, step in** sequence to maintain surveillance while preparing for possible contact with the gang. He mentally **steps back** to check his RED–BLUE status. His personal combat sweet spot is three-quarters BLUE and a quarter RED – he needs the clarity of BLUE but he definitely needs the energy and fast reaction times of RED. He feels a little too RED, so he takes three breaths to regulate his emotions.

He **steps up** to make sure he can see a picture bigger than the gang members can. He imagines a frame around the house, then increases the size of it and examines it from different angles to see what different outcomes can be anticipated. He scans his surroundings: easy to fixate on the house and miss someone or something in the surrounding area.

As he waits he visualises **stepping in** if the situation escalates. He focuses on the fast timing he'll need so he can read what might happen two or three steps ahead. Anticipation breeds fast reaction times. And that is vital in this game.

Shots – three of them.

The team leader speaks clearly and succinctly, and all team members move as one. Incomplete information, drug-fuelled unpredictability, erratic behaviour, possible non-hostiles inside and response team members converging: a recipe for potential tragedy. Liam and Tom cover the ground efficiently, scanning in front and behind, undistracted by the explosions their team members are creating at the front of the house. The diversion works, and Liam is able to use his Taser to safely incapacitate the back sentry and gain entry.

Now there's a triple peril. He and Tom are heading towards gang members, potential non-hostile occupants and members of their own team: a potent mixture. He constantly refines his actions; each one has to be carried out not too early, not too late. All the while he's checking on his RED–BLUE balance. He relies on this to keep himself focused on the situation evolving around him. Liam and Tom carry out a **hot debrief**, quickly but calmly using the **MIA questions** to check whether they have missed, ignored or assumed anything they need to report back to the team leader. They agree no change to the plan is necessary.

After Liam reports back to the team leader, the call is made for all groups to advance and gain entry – and just 25 seconds later the situation is brought under control. Two of the assailants resisted but they were swiftly and safely restrained and all of the gang members are taken into custody. All Liam's team members are accounted for and safe. It turns out there were no hostages inside the house.

After the team debrief, Liam reflects on how rapidly events unfolded. He knows it will take his body some time to unwind after such an adrenaline-filled encounter. Through repeated, brief use of the **offload technique**, he gradually relaxes, dissolving BLUE tension from his head and RED tension from his body.

In situations like the one today it's so easy for tunnel vision to occur, for important cues to be missed and for tension to cause loss of accuracy. Waiting followed by sudden, unpredictable action produces intense pressure. But performance under pressure is the reason why he's so connected to his job.

Today, he has defended the public **under pressure**.

Struggling to Survive

Emma's focus is just on getting through the day – 'high performance' is not a world she inhabits.

She works as a receptionist at a car dealership, where her main role is booking cars in for services. But her job is shaky; she has no partner to share the load; she has financial worries to the point where her children often have to go without, compared with their schoolfriends; and she has no time or energy left in each day to invest in exercising or socialising or pursuing interests of her own.

She's angry about her situation and feels guilty about not providing more for the people she loves. Her children seem to be making some poor choices that will potentially limit them later on – all because she's unable to give them the stability and guidance they deserve.

It feels like day-to-day survival. She feels rundown and she worries about burnout. How will she keep going, day after day?

It's mid-morning at work and already she's at the end of her tether. Her manager, Brian, has demanded that she prioritise an unexpected task: a high-profile customer wants their car serviced in the next 48 hours, but the garage is fully booked for the next two weeks. She's the one who has to ring them back and say no – when it's Brian who should be making the difficult call. And he hasn't taken anything off her plate. Everything must be done in less time.

She recognises tension creeping around her shoulders and into her jaw: her personal sign that she needs to use the **Rename, reframe, reset** sequence.

She silently **renames** the tension 'RED', which allows her to step back and see her frustration at the inefficiencies in her workplace. But as she tries to teach her kids, we can always choose our reaction, and there's no point in losing control. She takes three deep breaths to settle herself.

She **reframes** the situation from a small RED frame – 'My manager is unfair' and 'I hate my job' – to a larger BLUE one – 'My manager is just a link in the chain' and 'I want to apply for promotion, so helping this customer as well as I can is the right thing to do.' The different picture in her head makes her feel much better. A promotion, while not world-changing, would definitely help. Time to show what she's made of.

She loves the mantra **complain or complete**. She **resets** herself and identifies the new top priority from Brian as the task she least wants to do. She presses the button on an imaginary stopwatch hanging over her shoulder to begin a **micro-performance**. Five minutes to finish the task. Spending longer on it would only make her feel even more irritated, tense and distracted, which would cloud everything else she does.

She spends one minute assembling information and planning her interaction with the customer, then dives straight in by picking up the phone. The customer ventilates about the two-week delay, but she does her best to empathise with them and establish rapport using **reflective listening**. At just the right moment, when she feels their RED heat tapering off, she steps in with a BLUE solution. She's taken another look at the booking schedule and can squeeze in the customer in five days' time. And she offers to provide him with a replacement car for 48 hours: not their usual practice. The customer can tell she's gone out of her way to accommodate him, so he ends the phone call sounding happy enough. Not perfect, but satisfactory.

First task completed with a minute to spare. And if she's honest, she's enjoyed the challenge of skilfully managing the situation by looking for the RED–BLUE switch. If only her children could learn to manage their RED–BLUE balance a little better …

After lunch she focuses on more creative endeavours, switching to the **defend or discover** mantra. She initiates a meeting with Sam, a colleague in the sales team. She has an idea about sending customers a text message update on their car service, in much the same way as the sales team communicate with their clients about new deals. Perhaps there's a way the two teams can work together on this? Sam seems genuinely impressed by her idea, and they agree to set up a meeting to pitch it to their managers. This could be the key to the promotion she's been hankering for.

At the end of the workday she looks back: to think she started the day feeling sorry for herself and trapped in a RED 'poor me' loop! Satisfied, she heads for home to hear all about *her children's* experiences.

At home it's Complaints Central. Her daughter Laura is complaining about one of her teachers; her son Angus is complaining about a particular coach. She feels the urge to dive in and tell them to stop, but she knows that lecturing them will do more harm than good. Some RED–BLUE skill is needed.

Both are in the RED, but Angus more so, so she starts with him.

Once again, she uses **reflective listening** to separate his BLUE situation from his RED reaction: 'You had a bad time at practice today with your coach and you're angry about it.' She reflects his words back to him twice more, and during that process his RED intensity fades. He explains that he hasn't performed well in the last two games and he'll be a reserve the next time they play. She spots the RED–BLUE switch, then discusses how he might learn from the situation and use it to help develop his game. He leaves the conversation grumbling – slightly in the RED still – but at least he's doing some BLUE reflecting on how he may have contributed to the situation, and what he can do to improve.

She repeats the reflective listening process with Laura, and learns that a test she had today didn't go so well. Emma's reflections allow Laura to step her way down from high RED to the BLUE switch: 'I guess I could have studied last night instead of going out with my friends.'

Her children have both noticed that she took the time to listen to them, and both finished calmer than they started. They also saw that she didn't complain about her *own* day like they did. Perhaps some emotional self-awareness is kicking in after all.

On the back of her gratitude for the opportunity to talk and connect with her children, a powerful new insight presents itself. Although she can't provide as much as some parents *materially*, there's is no reason why she can't develop their *inner* strength in a way that others will struggle to match. Dealing with pressure and having to think clearly in emotional situations have helped her today, both at work and at home, and passing this gift on to her children will help *them* face adversity too.

Suddenly she sees her life situation in a whole new light. Her family's adversity becomes her great cause, and therefore strength. She wouldn't want it any other way.

As she ponders this idea, she sees that what she's presenting to her children is **performance under pressure** – perhaps not the high performance we're all taught to aspire to, but performance nonetheless. Facing challenges and adversity with resilience and dignity sends powerful messages.

Although it might not have looked like it from the *outside*, on the *inside*, **under pressure**, she didn't just **survive** – she **thrived**.

CONCLUSION

Re-mind Yourself

In order to *re-mind* ourselves, we have to *remind* ourselves.

In Chapter 2 we learned that we can actually change our brain by turning *activities* into *habits*. We *weaken* nerve-cell pathways in our brain when we stop using them, and *strengthen* nerve-cell pathways when we use them more often.

But how do we weaken the biological habit pathways we *don't* want to reinforce and strengthen the ones we *do*? If it's natural to move *away from* discomfort, how do we train our brain to stay in the pressure zone, or even move *towards* it?

The single biggest mental weapon we have is our **attention**. The brain science shows us that if we focus our attention consistently and specifically, that mental pathway is strengthened. And if we ignore less helpful pathways, those pathways gradually become less efficient and less enticing. They are replaced.

It requires some persistence and repetition, but paying attention works. If we want to perform under pressure, that means maintaining our attention even when we get subconscious signals to escape. If we keep our focus on our goals and how to achieve them *in spite of* pressure, we are training, and changing, our mind.

Every tool and technique in this book is designed to provide us with a structure that helps us focus our attention in a simple, helpful direction. The techniques provide the targets for our attention to hit like a laser beam.

Hitting more and more BLUE targets, and refusing to go for the usual RED targets, means that in high-pressure situations, both our RED and BLUE systems will be firing together. We'll be surprised by how quickly our mind can achieve a RED–BLUE balance if we can only stick with it without getting overwhelmed. And that is the purpose of the tools and techniques.

If we could choose only two mental skills to use when we perform under pressure, we could do worse than using the **RED–BLUE tool** and **creating a gap**.

Without emotional control, all bets are off. Once we *have* emotional control, in order to improve we must want to search for and find our performance gap. We need one core technique for our internal world (RED–BLUE) and one core technique for our impact on the external world (create the gap).

We don't get performance for free. The techniques are simple to use, and their limitations are what we choose them to be. If we decide to use them sporadically, vaguely, randomly and reluctantly, we have already imposed our own ceiling on performance.

If we use the techniques frequently enough, our mind will rewire and remodel itself. By reminding ourselves, we will be gradually re-minding ourselves to perform under pressure – to get as close to our potential as we can. Practising for just a few minutes several times a day is enough. Don't mess around – use them, or not. Complete or complain. Discover or defend.

Under pressure, don't get caught in two minds. Two minds are better than one, so start putting them both to work, together.

When would you like to begin?

No pressure.

GLOSSARY

BLUE (pages 27–31)
The system in the **RED–BLUE model** most closely linked to thinking. It involves a broad range of mental activities, including language, calculation, logic, reasoning, problem-solving, decision-making, judgment, and the ability to *think about thinking* (metacognition). Although these functions are distributed across both the left and right sides of the brain the most advanced mental functions are more closely associated with our frontal lobes, especially the left pre-frontal cortex. (*Also see RED.*)

Bridge the gap (pages 152–178)
Once we've created a **performance gap** between our desired level of performance and where we sit now, we need to work on moving towards that new level. This is called *bridging the gap*, and is done by using the **mental blueprint technique** to increase our capacity to perform under pressure. (*Also see **Create the gap, Mental blueprint technique.***)

Comfortable being uncomfortable (pages 40–44)
This core idea says we can still be effective when we're uncomfortable, instead of needing to be physically and/ or mentally comfortable to perform well. If conditions are comfortable, it is anyone's game and everyone can perform. But for those **training to win,** the comfortable being uncomfortable mindset provides an edge, because as others fall away with the discomfort of pressure, they will be left standing. (*Also see Uncomfortable being comfortable.*)

Complain or complete (pages 208–212)
An approach to performance in which we give ourselves a choice between **complaining** about our situation, and **completing** a task within a limited time in order to increase pressure. Often this means using a five-minute **micro-performance** to complete an uncomfortable task – the one we keep avoiding on our 'to do' list – before midday. If it's a bigger task, we can break it down into smaller, more manageable chunks. Completing a task creates a positive feeling; complaining saps energy. The goal of the completion mindset is to get the job not only started, but also finished. This mindset is one of the building blocks of a performance culture. (*Also see Defend or discover, Micro-performance.*)

Convergent thinking (pages 226–227)
Deliberately narrowing our range of ideas so we can make a clear decision by choosing a single option. Convergent thinking avoids the zone of uncertainty, where people get stuck either because there are too many options and they become vague, or there is varying opinion about what to do next. (*Also see Divergent thinking.*)

Create the gap (pages 129–151)
The mental process of looking at our **pressure** context, then setting a performance **intent** and contrasting it with the **reality**

of our current performance level, to create a performance gap. If we have no performance gap, it's much more difficult to see where we have space to improve. (*Also see* **Bridge the gap.**)

Creative micro-performance (pages 219–225)
A version of the five-minute **micro-performance** in which the emphasis is on creative thinking. We **rename** our creative problem in terms of a puzzle, then use a micro-performance to **reframe** it as a diagram, and **reset** our focus by generating different questions, angles and perspectives. This is followed by an incubation period in which we **release** our conscious mind from the task, and finally by a second micro-performance in which we **revisit** the puzzle and come up with solutions. The creative micro-performance is intended for busy people who have to be creative in relatively short timeframes. (*Also see* **Defend or discover, Micro-performance.**)

Defend or discover (pages 216–225)
An approach to performance in which we give ourselves a choice between **defending** our current performance and remaining on a plateau, and deliberately setting out to **discover** new insights and learn from them. A good balance can be achieved by using the defend or discover approach after midday, to balance the **complain or complete** approach we used in the morning. Discovery *creates* energy through stimulation; being defensive *drains* energy through tension. Discovery or learning is a building block of a **performance culture.** (*Also see* **Complain or complete, Creative micro-performance.**)

Divergent thinking (pages 226–227)
Deliberately broadening our thinking so we take in diverging perspectives by asking questions and looking at a situation from different angles. Divergent thinking avoids the zone of fixation,

where people get stuck following one pathway that has ceased to be productive. (*Also see* **Convergent thinking**.)

Dual focus (pages 61–65)
Flexibly controlling our attention by alternating between an overview of our situation and a specific task or detail. Under pressure, *effective* performers maintain a dual focus, while *ineffective* performers often end up with **split attention**.

ESC-APE (pages 69–75)
An acronym that describes an unhelpful way to perceive and react to pressure. **ESC** stands for **expectations, scrutiny** and **consequences,** the process by which others judge us. Expectations are placed on us *before* we perform, scrutiny is placed on us *while* we perform, and consequences are placed on us *afterwards* – creating a cocktail of *externally* imposed pressure. **APE** stands for **aggressive, passive, escape,** three ways of responding to pressure that are parallels for the natural survival reactions, **fight** (aggressive), **flight** (escape) and **freeze** (passive). Under pressure, *ineffective* performers have an *external* focus on the judgment of others, and react unhelpfully; while *effective* performers choose to have **IMP-ACT** through a more *internally* driven and helpful response. (*Also see* **Face and find, Fight–flight, Freeze, IMP-ACT.**)

Face and find (pages 92–94)
The top level of the **Mental strength sliding scale** describing a state of mind and body in which we feel secure enough to *face* a challenging situation and *find* a way through it. This state is adaptive rather than defensive, which allows us to remain engaged with the challenge, consider options and adjust our responses, meaning that we are mentally *free*. (Also see **Mental strength sliding scale**)

Fast leadership (pages 254–256)
Using **micro-performances** and the **complain or complete** approach in leading a team or organisation, to remove friction that is slowing down progress. The focus is on setting compelling targets and identifying the human factors that are blocking movement. Fast leadership is not about frantic behaviour; it's about producing a **streamlined** team or organisation. (*Also see Complain or complete, Micro-performance, Streamlined.*)

Feed-forward (pages 133–134)
An alternative to traditional feedback, this focuses on future potential first, *then* on present-day reality. We can use it to **create the gap** between our current level of performance and where we want to be. Traditional feedback – which often focuses on current weaknesses from the outset – can make people defensive, so they're less likely to take the information on board and less motivated to improve. (*Also see Create the gap.*)

Fight–flight (pages 92–94)
The basic reaction to threat, in which animals (and humans) either become aggressive (**fight**) or try to escape (**flight**). Although it evolved as a response to genuine *physical* danger, today the same reaction (driven by our sympathetic nervous system) can be triggered by *socially* threatening events. (*Also see Face and find, Freeze.*)

Freeze (pages 92–94)
An emergency reaction by some animals to threatening situations where both aggression (**fight**) and escape (**flight**) are impossible and they are trapped. The freeze reaction (driven by the parasympathetic nervous system) involves a complete shutdown of the mind and body. Like the fight–flight reaction, the partial

freeze reaction has evolved in humans to become an extreme response to pressure. (*Also see* **Face and find, Fight–flight**.)

ICE (pages 190–197)

An acronym that prompts the three steps of a short, structured visualisation technique we can use to mentally prepare to perform from days to minutes before an event. The first step focuses on adjusting our level of intensity by imagining we are 'heating' or 'cooling' our bodies. The second step focuses on getting clarity by imagining an overview of a demanding situation and 'seeing' ourselves act in a decisive manner. The third step focuses on fine-tuning our execution by mentally picturing and feeling ourselves carry out an action with perfect timing. The ICE routine is deliberately brief to match the fast-moving nature of many dynamic performance situations, to encourage short but repeated mental practice, and to help us quickly and reliably prime ourselves to perform when time is short.

IMP-ACT (pages 69–75)

An acronym that describes a helpful way to perceive and respond to pressure. **IMP** stands for **intention, moment, priority,** an *internally driven* focus on our **intention** to improve, the way we're performing at the **moment,** and our next **priority** for improvement. **ACT** stands for **aware, clear, task**: once we're **aware** of our situation and our response to it, we can be **clear** about what we need to do, and start our next **task**. Under pressure, *ineffective* performers are swayed by *external* factors and **ESC-APE**, while *effective* performers with an *internal* focus stand up to the moment and have IMP-ACT. (*Also see* **ESC-APE**.)

Inconvenient fact (page 147)

An uncomfortable truth about our performance that we avoid because of the emotional response that it triggers. Rather than trying to identify *brutal* facts, which encourage aggressive feedback, looking for *inconvenient* facts – factors that we would rather not have displayed but unfortunately were there – seems to be more tolerable and keeps us emotionally intact. Inconvenient facts are intended for constructive honesty and uncovering of potential performance gains, not as a weapon or permission for destructive criticism.

Intent (pages 139–143)

The way we ideally want to perform under pressure. Do we want to be one of the many, or do we want to be among the best – or even *the* best – in our performance area? Our goal needs to be concrete – what would close observers see and feel if we were operating at that level? To work this out we could use the **scale of mental intent**. Our intent is the second building block in **creating the gap** between how we currently perform and how we ideally want to perform in the future. (*Also see* **Create the gap, Scale of mental intent.**)

Mental blueprint technique (pages 153–157)

A simple but effective approach to mental improvement. As humans, we make sense of the world by developing simple scripts, or mental blueprints. The mental blueprint technique allows us to create a script for a specific performance situation so we can plan how we want to feel (**mindset**), think (**system**) and act (**skillset**). It's designed for use in the lead-up to our performance, but is also an effective way of reviewing our performance, if we give it a twist by comparing our planned mental blueprint with what actually happened. This mental blueprint with a twist is known as a **RED–BLUE debrief**. The mental blueprint with a twist uses the inconvenient facts and MIA questions to gently probe for performance information that might otherwise be sensitive, thereby sidestepping guarded and defensive reactions. (*Also see **Mindset, RED–BLUE debrief, Skillset, System**.*)

Mental strength sliding scale (pages 92–94)
A three-level scale of reactions that we move up and down in a dynamic way in response to challenging situations. The scale is adapted from the physiological **fight–flight** and **freeze** reactions to threat and adapted for performance under pressure. The social engagement response, which we can operate within when we feel safe, can be termed the **face and find** reaction. It is the most constructive response, because it leaves us mentally *free* to *face* the challenge and *find* a way through it, looking at different options and adjusting our behaviour. If we start to feel threatened, we move down to the **fight–flight** reaction and adopt a more defensive response to try to bring the situation to an end. If we cannot see a way out and feel trapped, we can drop down to a passive **freeze** reaction, where we shut down and mentally disconnect from the situation. Individuals and teams can use the Mental strength sliding scale to monitor their reactions to pressurised situations, with a view to moving up the scale to enable more constructive, adaptive responses. (Also see *Face and find, Fight–flight, Freeze*.)

MIA questions (pages 272–274)
A set of three questions designed to uncover performance blind spots by deliberately asking for reflection about what might be being missed, ignored or assumed. It uses the well-known MIA – missing in action – abbreviation to actively search for *information* that is missing, ignored or assumed.

Micro-performance (pages 203–207)
A mental technique in which we imagine someone is holding a stopwatch next to our shoulder and gives us five minutes to start

a task – or not. It is closely linked to the **complete or complain** mindset and is designed to put time pressure on us to complete a task that we've been avoiding. Most of us function on a performance plateau and make few definite attempts to improve. The micro-performance is a brief period when we reverse that general trend and step up to become focused, efficient and effective for a brief period. (*Also see **Complain or complete**, **Creative micro-performance**.)*

Mindset (pages 157–163)
The first building block of the **mental blueprint technique**. It addresses our emotional attitude to a situation or task: do we see it as a threat – which will send us down an unhelpful RED pathway – or a challenge that will open us up to the constructive impact of BLUE?

Mr Three Things (pages 187–190)
A mental preparation technique (a variation of the **three circles technique**) in which the assumption is made that three unfortunate events will occur in the lead-up to a performance. It is intended as a light-hearted approach to misfortune to decrease our tendency to catastrophise. The philosophy is that everyone has misfortune and it is how we respond to runs of unfortunate events that is important, which we can always control. (*Also see **Three circles techique**.)*

Negative content loop (pages 57–61)
An unhelpful mental process in which our attention gets trapped in a cycle of negative perceptions and responses and unhelpful behaviours. We seem to get stuck on what has just happened or what is about to occur, which takes our attention away from the task in front of us *in the present*. (*Also see **'Poor me' loop**.)*

Offload technique (pages 260–267)
A relaxation technique we can use after a performance to settle our busy mind and release unwanted tension. It uses a series of guided imagery instructions to broaden our focus and increase our sense of space; identify, activate and dissolve mental tension connected to thoughts (BLUE); then do the same with tension in our body (RED); before returning to a broader focus. The offload technique takes about eight minutes to complete. (*Also see acknowledgements – Dr Les Fehmi.*)

Performance culture (pages 243–245)
A culture in which everyone is committed to improvement. This requires top-to-bottom understanding, appreciation and use of the **Create the gap** and **Bridge the gap** philosophy within the organisation. The inconvenient fact is that although most people say that they want to get better, most people are, in fact, on the performance plateau: they do not substantially improve after a relatively brief period of time within their performance field.

Pinnacle event (pages 238–241)
An event that sits at the top of our performance area in terms of its status – an international sporting event like the Olympic Games or world championships; an election; a landmark court case. They sometimes occur in cycles. We can contrast this with a **pinnacle moment**, where we don't focus on the external event, but on our response to it, using a strong **mental blueprint**. (*Also see Mental blueprint technique.*)

'Poor me' loop (pages 59–60)
A version of the **negative content loop** in which we sulk and feel sorry for ourselves, thinking and acting like a victim of circumstance in a way that is out of proportion to any negative event that may have occurred. (*Also see Negative content loop.*)

Pressure (pages 13–15, 135–139)
External conditions that make us feel like we are being mentally and physically 'pressed'. Pressure is defined as **high stakes + uncertainty + small margins + fast changes + judgment.** Defining our **pressure** context is the first building block in **creating the gap** between our current and our potential level of performance. (*Also see* **Create the gap.**)

PRIME (pages 211–212)
An acronym for the combination of the **Create the gap, Bridge the gap,** and **Complain or complete** techniques. PRI stands for **Pressure-Reality-Intent,** the basic structure of the **Create the gap** technique (although reality and intent are reversed here for the sake of the acronym). M stands for **Movement,** which is driven by the **Mental blueprint** technique. And E stands for **Energy,** which is activated by the **Complain or complete** technique. If we can quickly sketch out the components of the PRIME acronym, we are mentally primed for performance. (See *Create the gap, Bridge the gap, Complain or complete.*)

Reality (pages 143–149)
Our current performance profile, which includes both our strengths and our weaknesses. On a performance line from 1 to 100%, where would we (realistically) rate ourselves? It can help to redefine our weak points as **inconvenient facts,** and to rate our performance using the **Scale of mental impact.** Our current **reality** is the third building block in **creating the gap** between how we're performing now and what it would look like to reach our full potential. (*Also see **Create the gap, Inconvenient fact, Scale of mental impact.***)

RED (pages 21–26)
The mind system in the **RED–BLUE model** most closely linked to our feelings and impulses. It monitors the state of our internal

and external worlds, and our physical and emotional reactions. Broadly speaking, the RED system is associated with the brainstem and the limbic system, and with the right hemisphere of our brains – though this is a simplification, because both hemispheres of the brain are generally involved in processing information at any one time. (*Also see BLUE.*)

RED–BLUE debrief (pages 267–274)
An approach to reviewing our mental performance that makes use of the **Create the gap** and **Mental blueprint with a twist** techniques. The 'twist' is provided by the use of **Inconvenient facts** and **MIA questions** to gently probe for information that might be personally sensitive and therefore defended rather than discovered. The RED–BLUE debrief is designed to quickly uncover some areas of our mental performance that can be adapted and incorporated into our preparation for our next performance. (Also see *Create the gap, Mental blueprint with a twist, Inconvenient facts, MIA questions.*)

RED–BLUE tool (pages 99–125)
A three-step tool we can use during our performance to help us gain emotional control, think clearly and act decisively under pressure. In Step 1 we ask ourselves '**RED or BLUE?**' and assess whether we are mainly in the RED or the BLUE. In Step 2 we tell ourselves '**Decide**', look at the bigger picture and make a decision to act. In Step 3 we tell ourselves '**Do!**' and step straight into constructive action. You can move through the three steps at different speeds depending on your situation, but with practice it can be timed to be completed within three breaths, or about 15 seconds. By guiding you to quickly identify your emotional state and regain control ('*instant mindfulness*'), regain situational awareness, and re-engage with constructive action, the RED–BLUE tool allows you to *Hold your nerve, Find your way,* and

Make your mark. (*Also see **Rename, reframe, reset; Step back, step up, step in.***)

RED–BLUE mind model (pages 6–9)
A simple framework that describes how our minds work under pressure, and the contrasting mental pathways and related behaviours that lead to effective and ineffective responses.

RED–BLUE reflective listening (pages 120–125)
A listening technique modelled on the **Rename, reframe, reset** sequence that's particularly helpful in emotional, confrontational situations. It involves reflecting back to the other person a basic description of the situation (which stimulates their BLUE mind) and their apparent reaction to it (driven by their RED mind) using a deliberate, simple, BLUE–RED sequence. It's important to be respectful and not simply parrot back to them what they said. This sends a message that we've heard them, and gives them an opportunity to ventilate and work through their emotions, so they gradually move from RED to BLUE. (*Also see **Rename, reframe, reset.***)

Rename, reframe, reset (pages 109–111)
A way of using the **RED–BLUE tool** that describes what we're doing at each stage. In the **rename** step we relabel our state of mind as more RED or more BLUE. In the **reframe** step we picture an expanding frame around our situation that gives us an overview. In the **reset** step we set a new focus and get out of our thoughts and into action. (*Also see **RED–BLUE tool; Step back, step up, step in.***)

Scale of mental impact (pages 148–149)
A 10-point scale that describes our mental performance in terms of our energy, clarity and precision, and our influence on others.

The scale helps us to position where we currently sit in terms of our mental performance – our **reality**. Each step has to be earned following an entry at level 5, and movement can occur both up and down the scale based on habitual patterns of mental performance. The scale of mental impact can sit alongside the **scale of mental intent** to help us **create a gap** in our mental performance.

Scale of mental intent (pages 139–142)
A scale setting out levels of intended performance, possibly originating in sports psychology several decades ago. The scale contrasts the **mindset** and associated behaviours for the **Training to train, Training to compete** and **Training to win** levels. It is useful to add a further level above training to win to represent those individuals or teams who are driven to remain at the top of their field. Although initially related to sports, the wording can be adapted for other performance fields (and for sporting pursuits where the language doesn't fit well) by using fresh terminology, for example, by replacing **Training to dominate** with 'Training to lead' or 'Training to master'. The Scale of mental intent is a useful approach for establishing the fit between an individual or group's stated ambition, and their actual performance culture.

Skill ladder (pages 170–174)
A simple three-rung visual image to guide skill development training. The first rung is concerned with *technique* and basic execution and is commonly trained using the *whole-part-whole* sequence, in which a complete technique is practised, then one component is refined, before being integrated into the overall technique again. The second rung is related to *skill*, the application of techniques in varying situations to ensure adaptation and adjustment. The third rung is related to *pressure*,

the practice of skills in demanding situations to push technical and mental capabilities to their limits. A balanced approach to skill development uses all three rungs of the Skill ladder, working up and down to ensure that fundamentals are solid, but the ability to adapt is advanced. A common error is to work between levels 1½ and 2½, so that fine technical refinement and stressful pressure testing are lacking for performance under pressure.

Skillset (pages 169–176)
Execution of a task within a demanding context. To refine our skillset, we work our way up a three-rung **skill ladder,** focusing first on *technique* (basic execution), then on *skill* (making adjustments to the situation), and finally on performance under *pressure*. We practise in conditions that closely replicate our performance situation, paying particular attention to balance and timing. (*Also see **Skill ladder.***)

Split attention (pages 56–65)
A state of divided attention where our attempt to focus on the task at hand is disrupted by our fixation on an unwanted event that has already happened, or an unwanted outcome that might occur. We become distracted and diverted, and our attention becomes 'split' between the present moment and the past and/or future, harming performance.

Step back, step up, step in (pages 106–109)
Three mental movements that make the three stages of the **RED–BLUE tool** easier to remember. We imagine that we **step back** from the situation so we can see our response to it; we **step up** to a higher plane so we can see the bigger picture; then we **step in** onto the higher plane and re-engage in the situation. (*Also see **RED–BLUE tool; Rename, reframe, reset.***)

Streamlined (pages 256–258)

In a **streamlined** team or organisation, everyone shares a commitment to a clear goal and works constructively to help the group achieve this shared outcome. There is a particular focus on identifying and removing points of friction and any obstacles that are causing interference and slowing down movement towards the goal. Everyone is focused on **creating** and **bridging** their **performance gap**, and **fast leadership** is used to generate a **completion** mindset. The signature of a streamlined team is that people try to make each other look good: the opposite of what is found in most organisations. (*Also see* ***Bridge the gap, Complain or complete, Create the gap, Fast leadership.***)

Strive and thrive (pages 162–163)

A **mindset** that involves setting demanding goals, then doing our best to achieve them. Falling short is inevitable if the goals are truly testing us; we need to focus on doing the best we can then reviewing what we learned. The strive and thrive mindset can be contrasted with a **win or lose** mindset, where we're focused on results. With a strive and thrive mindset, we can succeed and learn even when we don't 'win'. (*Also see* ***Mindset.***)

Stuff-up cascade (pages 118–120)

Deliberately creating a sequence of mental and behavioural steps that will lead to inevitable failure. This technique is useful when we're feeling vague about what to do in a situation, or passive, seeing the situation as happening *to* us rather than being our responsibility. If we can work out what *not* to do, we simply need to do the opposite. A good approach to the stuff-up cascade is to get an individual or group to quickly build up a humorous composite picture of all the things that they would tell you to do if their task was to teach you how to completely mess up your performance.

System (pages 164–169)

A plan for a performance task involving a collection of parts that form a coherent whole. A short sequence – such as a timeline or checklist – is the simplest kind of system. When we get stuck in the detail of our performance, our system gives us a working overview. We can add in 'What if?'s to make our system watertight. (*Also see 'What if?'.*)

Three circles technique (pages 182–186)

A simple mental preparation technique that uses a three circle visual format to categorise potential points of attention into three categories: what we can't control, what we can control, and what we can influence. The 'list–narrow–prioritise' method provides a sense of what is most important for this performance. The visual boundaries create mental boundaries, so that we can easily detect when our attention slips from focusing on matters that we can control, or at least influence, to matters outside of our control. Although primarily used to help us to maintain our control of attention in the lead up to a performance, the three circles technique can also be used during performance to regain an impactful focus of attention when we become distracted.

Uncomfortable being comfortable (pages 159–162)

A high-performance **mindset** where we feel uncomfortable operating within comfortable parameters for an extended length of time because it shows we're unlikely to be improving. (*Also see Comfortable being uncomfortable.*)

Wait or take (pages 234–238)

A **mindset** seen in those who've mastered the art of performance. They **take** the initiative rather than **waiting** to see how events unfold. The fastest way to gain a reputation is to **take** it – through the quality of your performance. If you are in a competitive situation and faced with a high-profile opponent, rather than waiting to see what they do (which gives more time to someone who least needs it), you can show 'respectful disrespect' by giving your opponent less time and space and imposing yourself on the situation. It means remaining within the spirit of the performance code, but showing your opponent the most respect by giving them the toughest conditions to deal with.

'What if?' (pages 167–168)

A simple mental refinement of the **system** component of the **Mental blueprint technique** in which we anticipate and form a plan of action for different situations that might arise and disrupt a performance. The purpose of the 'What if?' technique is to minimise unhelpful emotional reactions and decrease reaction time in responding to the situation. (*Also see **Mr Three things**.*)

Working memory (pages 29–31)

Our ability to hold different chunks of information in our mind at any one time and manipulate them. Ordinarily, our working memory holds perhaps four or five items at any one time. Under pressure, this number is reduced, so that we might only be able to focus our conscious attention on one task at a time, and any **splitting of attention** is costly in terms of performance. (*Also see **Dual focus, Split attention**.*)

Further reading

As this book is intended as a practical, user-friendly volume for general reading rather than a technical or scientific account, I have not used references or footnotes. However I would like to acknowledge bodies of work and other important influences by suggesting further sources of reading. This is not intended to be a comprehensive list but simply a selection of books – from easily readable through to more specialist reading – that might serve as starting points should you wish to investigate further.

Allan Abbass, *Reaching through resistance. Advanced psychotherapy techniques*, Seven Leaves Press, 2015.

Jim Bartley with Tania Clifton-Smith, *Breathing matters. A New Zealand guide*, Random House, 2006.

John Bowlby, *A secure base. Parent-child attachment and healthy human development*. Routledge, 1988.

Mihaly Csikszentmihayli, *Flow. The classic work on how to achieve happiness*, Rider, 2002.

Les Fehmi and Jim Robbins, *The Open-Focus® brain. Harnessing the power of attention to heal mind and body*, Trumpeter, 2007.

Les Fehmi and Jim Robbins, *Dissolving pain: simple brain training exercises for overcoming chronic pain*, Trumpeter, 2010.

W. Timothy Gallwey, *The inner game of tennis. Revised edition*, Random House, 1997.

Daniel Goleman, *Focus. The hidden driver of excellence*, Bloomsbury, 2013.

Gay Hendricks, *Conscious Breathing. Breathwork for health, stress release, and personal mastery*, Bantam Books, 1995.

Daniel Hill, *Affect regulation theory. A clinical model*, W.W. Norton & Company, 2015.

Walter Mischel, *The marshmallow test. Understanding self-control and how to master it*, Corgi Books, 2014.

Robert Neborsky, *The collected writings of Robert J. Neborsky, Expanded edition*, Unlocking Press, 2017.

Gabriele Oettingen, *Rethinking positive thinking. Inside the new science of motivation*, Penguin Group, 2014.

Stephen Porges, *The pocket guide to the polyvagal theory. The transformative power of feeling safe*, W.W. Norton & Company, 2017.

Ian Robertson, *The winner effect. The science of success and how to use it*, Bloomsbury, 2013.

Robert Scaer, *The body bears the burden. Trauma, dissociation and disease*, Routledge, 2014.

Allan Schore, *Affect regulation and the origin of the self. The neurobiology of emotional development, Classic edition*, Routledge, 2016.

Daniel Siegel, *The developing mind. How relationships and the brain interact to shape who we are, 2nd edition*, The Guilford Press, 2012.

Chögyam Trungpa, Shambhala. *The sacred path of the warrior.* Shambhala, 2007.

Bessel Van der Kolk, *The body keeps the score. Brain, mind and body in the healing of trauma*, Penguin Books, 2014.

For more insights, information and ideas
on how to get the most out of your
mental performance, visit
www.drcerievans.nz

Acknowledgements

This book was a long time in the making. Thank you to Hanshi Renzie for your decades of insight, patience, care and humour. As a teenager, you opened my eyes to what really mattered in the mental space for performance, and you still do when I go off track. I have lost count of the thousands of hours we have sat together, but I have never lost sight of your original thinking, nor of our partnership in developing the RED–BLUE model: this book is ours in every sense of the word, and your encouragement of me to write it says it all. Thank you for your friendship.

I am extremely grateful to Alex Hedley, Nicola Robinson and the team at HarperCollins ANZ, for your engagement, energy, and expertise in guiding me through the task of writing my first book. Your vision and respectful probing of boundaries was illuminating. To Emma Dowden, I am deeply appreciative of your craft in showing me the way forward, which constantly made me pause and reflect. I have never learned so much!

Working in the mental space is fundamentally a dynamic, two-way process and I am grateful to every individual, coach, team and organisation that I have had the privilege of working with for shaping my thinking. As you all know, my philosophy is that the mental role sits behind the scenes, while your deeds of action take centre stage.

I have been particularly fortunate to enjoy longer-term working relationships with several inspiring groups, including the All Blacks through Gilbert Enoka, the Mercedes F1 Team through Paul Mills, and Arsenal FC through David Priestley:

thank you all personally. To Garry Lund, your timely prompts over many years have been invaluable. Adaptation never stops.

Thank you to all the generous people who have provided kind words for the book about our work together, which, without exception, has been demanding and enjoyable in equal measure. And to Richie, your absorbing foreword draws us into just about the full range of moments this book attempts to address – I cannot thank you enough. You redefined what it meant to take the mental space seriously. Your ability to answer the question, 'What if we don't?' with 'What if we do?' was a turning point.

An important piece of the jigsaw are John Esposito, Martin Fairn and the team at Gazing, who took budding ideas out into the business world of the 1990s and ran with them. Those early years of experimentation and exploration were an unmissable experience – thank you all.

To the invisible backstage cast of teachers, psychiatrists, clinical and academic supervisors, tutors and professional colleagues that have profoundly informed and influenced my understanding of human development – especially the impact of trauma – and therefore my approach to performance: I owe you an enormous amount. Many individuals have gone the extra mile on my behalf – I frequently reflect on you with deep gratitude.

To Dr Les Fehmi, thank you for your generosity in allowing me to include in this book a 'RED–BLUE' adaptation of what you taught me about your innovative Open Focus™ system. Your insight about 'space' remains my favourite account of an 'aha!' moment.

Tēnā Koe Kaihautū Ruru Harepeka Nako Hona, Ngāti Kahu/ Ngā Puhi. Thank you for your spiritual and cultural guidance throughout our professional and personal relationship and your ability to properly place matters within the broader Māori context – ngā mihi nui.

Thank you to Ian Hunt, Phil Brinded and Giles Mountford, not only for your insightful manuscript reviews, but also for your larger roles in supporting me and my work. Ian, your wise ear and professional touch over many years have been invaluable – you are there when I need you. Phil, you bring perspective, care and humanity to the forensic world like no one else – our coffees are a highlight. Giles and the team at *dair**, your impact in respectfully moving me through the book, cover to cover, by revealing the broader personal context has been nothing short of enlightening – your perceptive insights and ability to crystallise complex ideas run deep. In the same vein, thank you to Diederik van Heyningen of Lightworkx – your eyes see things others don't.

My sister Mandy and her husband Gary know only one way: unending encouragement. Mandy, you are the most compassionate person I know. To my late brother, Daryl, you left us too soon. I remember with respect and pride the moments you stood up when we were young. And to my close friends who have had my back throughout, thank you for watching out for me.

My final thanks and deep gratitude belong to Thérèse – your unique combination of boundless backing, grounding, humour and spirit is precious – and each of our children, Oscar, Louis and Izzie – your points of view always make me reflect and I love how you do that, each in your own way. You are all 'in' the book as your individual gems have been incorporated into my approach time and again over the years. You know what they are. And you know what that means to me.

To all who have helped me, I wish you the spirit of a beautiful word from te reo Māori – for when pressure comes calling:

Whakapuāwai. *Blossom, develop, flourish, prosper, thrive.*

Thank you.

CE, 2019

New Zealander Dr Ceri Evans graduated in medicine with distinction from the University of Otago. He gained first-class honours in experimental psychology on a Rhodes Scholarship at the University of Oxford while playing professional football in the English Championship. Awarded the Gaskell Gold medal by the Royal College of Psychiatrists, he then specialised in forensic psychiatry and completed a PhD on traumatic memory. After returning home to Christchurch, he was Clinical Director of the Canterbury Forensic Psychiatric Service and served as an expert witness in major cases. In 2018 he was made a Fellow of the Royal College of Psychiatrists and awarded his football coaching A Licence.

Ceri's reputation generates diverse invitations to work with leading international organisations determined to help their people deliver in demanding situations. His RED–BLUE mind model is used by people serious about performing under pressure, from doctors to lawyers, executive teams to specialist teams, and professionals to amateurs. He is perhaps best known for his work with the New Zealand All Blacks, for whom he has provided specialist consultancy since 2010.

Now in private practice, Ceri can otherwise be found with his head in a book, exercising, or with Thérèse trying to find out what their three children are up to at university.